SEEN BUT NOT HEARD

Strengthening Nonprofit Advocacy

By

Gary D. Bass, David F. Arons, Kay Guinane, and Matthew F. Carter

with Susan Rees

The Aspen Institute
One Dupont Circle, NW
Suite 700
Washington, DC 20036

Published in the United States of America in 2007
by The Aspen Institute

06-016

Nonprofit Sector and Philanthropy Program

Alan J. Abramson, Director

Cinthia H. Schuman, Associate Director

The Aspen Institute's Nonprofit Sector and Philanthropy Program (NSPP) seeks to improve the operation of the nonprofit sector and philanthropy through research, leadership, and communication initiatives focused on critical nonprofit issues. The program's major projects are:

Research:
Developing useful information for those who care about nonprofits and philanthropy.

1. NONPROFIT SECTOR RESEARCH FUND

The Nonprofit Sector Research Fund (NSRF) was established in 1991 to increase understanding of the nonprofit sector and philanthropy. Since its founding, the Fund has awarded over $11.5 million in research grants to 420 projects examining a broad range of issues facing nonprofit organizations, philanthropy, and the people they serve. NSRF is currently focusing its work in three areas:
- Nonprofits and public policy, including the impact of federal budget cuts on nonprofits;
- Social enterprise, including the development of new hybrid organizations that blend nonprofit and for-profit activities; and
- Foundation policy and practice, including the overall impact of the foundation sector on society.

In each area, NSRF identifies priority research topics, supports research and dialogue on these topics, communicates research findings to appropriate audiences, and works with other organizations to facilitate the use of new knowledge to improve nonprofit practices and policies.

2. STATE OF AMERICA'S NONPROFIT SECTOR PROJECT

The State of America's Nonprofit Sector Project, a collaborative initiative with Lester Salamon of Johns Hopkins University, reports every several years on the major developments affecting the overall nonprofit sector and each of its major fields of activity (i.e., health, education, social services, arts, etc.). The project's initial volumes, which were published by Brookings Institution Press, are: *The State of Nonprofit America* and *The Resilient Sector*.

3. Fast-Growth, High Impact Nonprofits

How have some exceptional nonprofit organizations achieved high levels of impact in a relatively brief time frame? The Fast-Growth, High-Impact Nonprofits Research Project is examining the strategy, organization, and leadership that fuel the success of today's leading nonprofits. The project, which is a partnership with Duke University's Center for the Advancement of Social Entrepreneurship (CASE), is being led by Leslie Crutchfield of Ashoka and Heather McLeod Grant, a research fellow with CASE.

Leadership:
Enhancing the capacity of nonprofit and philanthropic leaders.

1. Seminar Series for Mid-America Foundation CEOs

This seminar series provides foundation executives from the middle part of the country the opportunity to engage in off-the-record, in-depth conversations about the complex issues they face.

2. Seminars for Donors

Seminar participants have the opportunity to learn and reflect on specific strategies available to philanthropists.

3. Community Giving Resource

The Community Giving Resource (CGR) provides objective, accessible information to small family foundations and individual donors committed to strengthening low-income communities. Developed by the Neighborhood Funders Group in partnership with the Nonprofit Sector and Philanthropy Program, CGR offers on-line resources, mentoring, and peer-learning circles to inform donors about community issues, including housing, jobs, education, and health.

Communication:

Communicating valuable information about nonprofits to nonprofit leaders and policymakers.

1. ASPEN PHILANTHROPY LETTER

The Nonprofit Sector and Philanthropy Program produces an electronic newsletter that reports on new ideas and other developments in the field of philanthropy. Free subscriptions are available by sending a message to philanthropy@aspeninstitute.org.

2. WEBSITE

NSPP includes information on all its activities on its own website, www.nonprofitresearch.org, and also maintains important and current information on the Aspen Institute website at www.aspeninstitute.org/nspp.

3. SNAPSHOTS NEWSLETTER

NSPP publishes a bimonthly newsletter that presents key findings from its research activities and convenings in an accessible, easy-to-use format. To be added to the mailing list, please send a message to nsrf@aspeninstitute.org.

4. WORKING PAPER SERIES

Research reports from NSPP-supported projects are available in NSPP's Working Paper Series. These papers are available for download or purchase at www.nonprofitresearch.org.

The Nonprofit Sector and Philanthropy Program is currently supported by The Atlantic Philanthropies, Carnegie Corporation of New York, Ford Foundation, Bill and Melinda Gates Foundation, William Randolph Hearst Foundation, Ewing Marion Kauffman Foundation, W.K. Kellogg Foundation, John D. and Catherine T. MacArthur Foundation, Charles Stewart Mott Foundation, Northwest Area Foundation, The David and Lucile Packard Foundation, Skoll Foundation, and Surdna Foundation.

For more information about the Nonprofit Sector and Philanthropy Program, please contact Winnifred Levy, the Program's Communications Manager, at winnifred.levy@aspeninstitute.org, call (202) 736-5814, or consult our website at www.nonprofitresearch.org or www.aspeninstitute.org/nspp.

Table of Contents

Tables / Charts / Figures

8

Acknowledgements

The Strengthening Nonprofit Advocacy Project (SNAP) was a multi-year research project that could not have been undertaken without the generous support of several organizations and foundations, including: Aspen Institute's Nonprofit Sector Research Fund, Atlantic Philanthropies, Nathan Cummings Foundation, Ford Foundation, Robert Wood Johnson Foundation, David and Lucile Packard Foundation, and the Surdna Foundation. It was the leadership provided by Alan Abramson and Cinthia Schuman at the Nonprofit Sector Research Fund that started us on our research odyssey. They noted the need for additional research and had faith that we could do it.

Matching the generous support was an outstanding research team that included staff from OMB Watch, Tufts University, and the Center for Lobbying in the Public Interest (which recently changed its name from Charity Lobbying in the Public Interest). The authors of this book wish to give credit to the various staff who worked on this project. In addition to Gary Bass, Kay Guinane, and Matt Carter, the OMB Watch team included Patrick Lemmon, Heather Hamilton, Ryan Turner, Barbara J. Western, Melissa Brennan, and Kelly Patterson. The Tufts University team included Jeffrey M. Berry, Kent E. Portney, Erin Desmarais, Catherine Ma, Louis Tavaras, and Mo Twine. In addition to David Arons, the Center for Lobbying the Public Interest team included Carolyn Nelson. Thanks to each of you. You will see your hand in this book.

We especially want to thank Jeff Berry, who was part of the SNAP leadership. His knowledge about interest group politics and his research skills were central to this project – and they were highly complementary to our knowledge of the nonprofit sector. His research challenging the notion that moneyed interests or conservative ideologues always win was an inspiration to all of us.

We want to provide a special thank you to the staff at the National Center for Charitable Statistics at Urban Institute for helping us obtain our survey sample. They generously donated their time and skill in explaining about the IRS Form 990 files they have and provided the stratified sample we needed for this project.

Several people helped in the development of the research design and in the data analysis. In particular, we want to thank Jeff Krehely, Elizabeth Rowland, Amy Stackpole, and Heather Gorski. Bob Smucker and Tom Troyer provided helpful insight into the history of nonprofit and foundation tax law. And Bob sat through endless readings of various drafts and patiently provided comments on all versions. (Yes, Bob, we finally finished!)

We had a team of advisers who were extremely helpful in developing the survey instrument and periodically provided input on various aspects of the research. Those advisers are listed in Appendix B. Focus groups were hosted by a number of organizations, including California Association of Nonprofits, Council of Michigan Foundations, Massachusetts League of Community Health Centers, Michigan Nonprofit Association, Minnesota Council of Nonprofits, McConnell Foundation, Nonprofit Resource Center, Tennessee Conference for Social Welfare, and United Ways of Texas.

We also want to thank a number of other readers, including David Cohen, Pablo Eisenberg, Marcia Avner, and Kirsten Grønbjerg. David Cohen provided insightful commentary and input on Chapter 2, helping to make the story about contemporary history of nonprofits and advocacy much stronger. Marcia Avner of the Minnesota Council of Nonprofits and Kirsten Grønbjerg of Indiana University reviewed the entire book, providing exceptionally useful ideas and corrections. Gregory W. Mott did an outstanding job of copy editing and making important suggestions for improvements. We took their suggestions to heart, using most of their ideas. However, as authors, we accept full responsibility for any errors or omissions.

Finally, we want to thank Winnifred Levy of the Aspen Institute's Nonprofit Sector Research Fund for all the communications assistance in putting together this book. There would not be a book without her.

We want to thank each of these advisers, organizations and readers for taking time out of their busy schedules to help us with this project. Hopefully, the research findings make it all worthwhile.

April, 2007

Gary D. Bass, David F. Arons, Kay Guinane, and Matthew F. Carter with Susan Rees

Introduction
Who Should Read This Book and Why

The Strengthening Nonprofit Advocacy Project (SNAP) marks the first time that a representative sample of the charitable portion of the nonprofit sector has been asked to provide data on the nature and extent of advocacy activities. The book should be of interest to everyone concerned with nonprofits – executives, staff members, academics, students, trainers and funders – as well as everyone who *makes* policy and tries to influence it. It is written from the perspective of one who believes it is right, proper and beneficial for nonprofits to engage in the formation of public policy, but at the same time the authors hope it will be informative and interesting to those who take a different view.

This book is being published a little more than a year after lobbyist Jack Abramoff pled guilty to influence peddling charges. The disgraced lobbyist is working with the Justice Department to untangle a web of schemes to buy legislative favors. It has already resulted in nine guilty pleas and one member of Congress being convicted. These guilty pleas include two senior aides to former House Majority Leader Tom DeLay (R-TX) and other high level officials. There will likely be additional fallout from the Abramoff scandal, much of it good. But there is one troubling aspect: The image of lobbying will be further sullied.

In the past, lobbying conjured up cartoons of smoke-filled rooms with behind-the-scene deals being made. In today's cartoon, it is hard to see the smoke-filled room because of all the money blocking the view. The modern image is of Gucci Gulch lobbyists making money hand over fist and buying access to our elected leaders. The lobbyist arranges trips for elected officials where client-based powerful special interests get to interact. They serve in leadership roles for candidate political action committees, raising money for re-election – and in doing so create a debt to the lobbyist that is paid through special legislation, such as earmarked spending or tax breaks. The perception is that the lobbyist serves as a hired gun to promote the corporate self-interest of his or her client, not the interests of the general public. Even worse, the perception is that somehow the words "lobbyist" and "corruption" go together.

While that image may dominate, especially in the post-Abramoff environment, it is not always the reality. An article in a national newspaper about lobbying classes being taught at universities notes:

> "One surprise: Not every student wants to be a high-priced corporate lobbyist, the sort who, though pilloried, has great sway in Washington.
>
> 'I'd like to be able to affect change,' said Bess Kozlow, 29, a former grassroots lobbyist for the American Bankers Association. She wants to lobby for a nonprofit advocacy group such as the Human Rights Campaign, NARAL Pro-Choice America or the National Gay and Lesbian Task Force. 'Being an advocate for issues that are important to me is a way to make the world a better place,' Kozlow said."[1]

This resonates with David Cohen and Bob Smucker, two highly respected and semi-retired leaders in the nonprofit sector. "Today," they wrote in *The Chronicle of Philanthropy*, "many people disdain all lobbyists. But to us, being a public-interest lobbyist is a career you can write home about. Each of us has lobbied in the public interest for more than 40 years. If a wrong can be repaired by lobbying, our juices flow."[2]

Nonprofit advocacy and lobbying is different from similar activities undertaken by the for-profit sector. Nonprofit policy participation is in the public interest, regardless of whether it is in pursuit of conservative, liberal, or non-ideological objectives. Whereas in the for-profit sector private gain usually motivates policy actions, in the nonprofit sector the end goal is a social good.[3] While

---

[1] Christopher Lee, "Lobbying PMGT 230.10," *The Washington Post,* March 29, 2006, sec A, p. 17.

[2] David Cohen and Bob Smucker, "Lobbying Often Benefits the Public Interest," *The Chronicle of Philanthropy*, April 6, 2006, Letters to the Editor, p. 63. Cohen was executive director of Common Cause and co-founder of Advocacy Institute. Smucker was vice president for government relations for Independent Sector and founder of Charity Lobbying in the Public Interest, which is now called Center for Lobbying in the Public Interest.

[3] This is not to imply that advocacy by the for-profit sector is without social value. The main point is that the for-profit sector must act to protect its shareholders, profits, or market base. Even when business acts to protect social interest, there is usually an underlying benefit to the entity or industry.

What We Mean By the Term "Nonprofit"

Even though we use the term "nonprofit" throughout this book, we are only talking about one subset of nonprofits called charities. Charities are organized under section 501(c)(3) of the tax code for religious, charitable, educational, scientific, and other purposes. There are more charities than any other type of nonprofit group, and contributions to charities are deductible for those who itemize on their income taxes. Other types of nonprofit categories include social welfare groups, such as the Sierra Club or the National Rifle Association (501(c)(4) groups); unions, such as AFL-CIO (501(c)(5) groups); trade associations, such as the U.S. Chamber of Commerce (501(c)(6) groups), and 527 political action groups, such as Americans Coming Together, Swift Boat Veterans for Truth, and the Moveon.org Voter Fund. (Appendix F provides a list of tax-exempt categories.) There has been considerable research about policy participation with these other types of nonprofits. While more research may be needed on these types of organizations, there has been very little research about the largest group of nonprofits – charities – and public policy participation. Hence, we focus on charities in this book.

policy participation by all parties – nonprofit and for-profit – is an essential ingredient of democracy, there is something special about nonprofit participation that should be strongly encouraged and supported by our national leaders. As Cohen and Smucker say, "A public-interest lobbyist helps balance the many self-interests that, naturally enough, push policy in ways that benefit specific parts of the population." Maybe it is simply that nonprofits tend to address the common good. For example, when they advocate for "specific parts of the population," it tends to be the disenfranchised or those without voice in the policy world. In any case, this book has a bias in favor of strengthening nonprofit advocacy.

The first chapter provides an overview of the book. If you can read only one part of the book, we would recommend Chapter 1. (As a fallback, the last chapter provides a conclusion that summarizes some of the key elements from the book and provides some recommendations.)

Chapter 2 reviews the history of nonprofit advocacy and social movements in the United States from shortly after the country's founding up to today. The purpose of the chapter is not to present a history lesson, but rather to review of how nonprofit advocacy has changed and how historical antecedents may be influencing participation today. Chapter 3 discusses the genesis of SNAP and describes the research methodology, which included a random survey of 2,735 charities, 17 focus groups of nonprofit executives and board members and foundation staff, and 45 interviews of survey respondents.

Major survey findings are contained in Chapters 4 and presented as an overview of the more detailed chapters that follow. Chapters 5 and 6 discuss the findings in greater detail for those interested in a statistical analysis of issues for 501(c)(3)s of different types. (Note that universities, hospitals, religious congregations and very small nonprofits were purposely excluded from the research sample.) The final chapter provides ideas for using the research as a springboard to strengthen nonprofit advocacy.

SNAP should be of interest not only to practitioners and students whose identity is primarily with the "sector" but those who see themselves as specialists in health, education, environment, social justice, arts, recreation, housing, human services and the other inhabitants of the nonprofit world.

Nonprofit executives, policy directors, board members and students of nonprofit management will find the book helpful in describing what their counterparts are doing by way of advocacy (or what they were doing as of 2000). They will get insight into what motivates participation in public policy and how to overcome objections to their involvement. They will also gain a certain amount of "how to" information, along with guidance on the myths and facts surrounding nonprofit lobbying laws.

National organizations and associations will get insight into how to make the most of their efforts to engage grassroots and state-level nonprofits in the policy process. If they are in a position to inform their members and followers through training or written materials and websites, they will also learn what kinds of advocacy-oriented content will be most appropriate for organizations of different sizes and types and at different stages of their life cycles. The book should help inform the design of new kinds of organizational development tools for nonprofits that will enhance their likelihood of joining the policy process and their ability to be effective.

We hope the book will contribute to academic reading lists and find a place on university library shelves. The nation's 40-plus nonprofit academic centers and more than 250 schools of public policy and many other disciplines that prepare workers for nonprofit careers will benefit in all of the ways mentioned above. In addition, the data may be useful for doctoral dissertations and other research. SNAP data and methodology can be adapted to in-depth study of particular issues or can be used as a baseline for future study.

Philanthropists will learn from the book the crucial role their financial support plays among advocates. They will hear a plea for more and learn about the forms of grant making that are most useful and conducive to policy involvement. Those who do not currently support advocacy we hope will find justification for doing so in the future.

Finally, policymakers will learn, among other things, that nonprofits undertake advocacy mainly as a way to achieve the same goals they seek through their other charitable activities, namely to help improve the quality of life for individuals and communities.

Some who reviewed this book felt that changes in the economy, voter participation strategies, and other policy developments at the local, state and federal level, including citizen interest in national security policy since 2000, when our survey was conducted, may have shifted the findings from our research. The authors believe that there may be fluctuations in nonprofit policy participation, but that the overall trends established by our research are not likely to change. However, we do think it would be a good idea to use our data as a baseline for future surveys every ten years to monitor nonprofit policy participation.

Seen But Not Heard
An Executive Summary of SNAP

OMB Watch, Tufts University, and Center for Lobbying in the Public Interest launched a multi-year research to action project, called the Strengthening Nonprofit Advocacy Project (SNAP), to investigate factors that motivate nonprofit organizations to engage in public policy matters.[4] The SNAP research addressed four major questions:

- What language do nonprofit staff and volunteers use to describe public policy participation?
- What factors influence nonprofits' participation in the public policy process?
- How do nonprofits make decisions about whether and how they participate in public policy?
- What would be helpful and encouraging to nonprofits as they make decisions about public policy issues and decide whether and how they will get involved?

The findings are based on a three-part research process including:
1) A national survey of 1,738 nonprofit organizations – tax-exempt public charities organized under Section 501(c)(3) of the federal tax code – conducted between January and June 2000;[5] 2) Telephone interviews with 45 of the survey respondents (primarily executive directors) – conducted from September 2000 to February 2001; and 3) 17 focus groups with executive directors, board members, and foundation staff held in different parts of the country from February through September 2001.

---

[4] In this book when we use the term "nonprofit organization," we are referring to tax-exempt organizations recognized as 501(c)(3) under the tax code, commonly called charities. If we are talking about a broader set of nonprofit organizations, we refer to them by their tax code designation, such as 501(c)(4) groups.

[5] The SNAP survey did not go to hospitals, universities, religious congregations, private foundations, or 501(c)(3) organizations that do not file the annual Form 990 tax form, such as those with budgets of less than $25,000. It also did not go to any nonprofits that are not public charities, including 501(c)(4) organizations.

On the State of Nonprofit Public Policy Participation

- *Roughly three of four nonprofits say they have engaged at least once in key types of public policy activity* such as direct or grassroots lobbying or testifying at a legislative or administrative hearing. This was considerably higher than predicted. For example, 78 percent of nonprofits report that they have encouraged their members to write, call, fax or e-mail policymakers; 74 percent report that they have lobbied for or against a proposed bill or other policy pronouncement; and 71 percent report that they have testified at legislative or administrative hearings.

- However, *the frequency of policy participation by nonprofits is inconsistent and generally low.* For example, of nonprofits reporting that they lobby, roughly three out of five say they lobby with a low level of frequency. And the majority of these organizations actually report that they lobby at the lowest possible level on the survey. Sixty-three percent of nonprofits report that they either have never encouraged others to write, call, fax, or e-mail policymakers, or have done so infrequently; the same is true with 69 percent of nonprofits regarding lobbying and 77 percent regarding testifying.

- *Nonprofits say that public policy participation is essential to carrying out their mission.* Executive directors in focus groups and interviews repeatedly said that being a policy advocate is a key responsibility of running an organization. Yet when probed, they note that spending time on public policy matters detracts from doing other work that they must do, such as fundraising, running direct service and public education programs, and handling day-to-day crises.

- *Even when nonprofits engage in public policy matters, they do not think of themselves as influencing public policy.* For example, 46 percent of survey respondents who said they "never make any effort to influence government" also identify themselves as "participators," which means they have lobbied, encouraged others to lobby, or have testified before a legislative or administrative body. Generally, health and environmental groups report the most involvement in public policy matters. Arts and recreation organizations report the least involvement.

Language Makes a Difference

- *There is great variation in how nonprofits interpret words that are used to describe public policy participation, particularly the words "lobbying," "advocacy," and "educating."* For example, roughly one-third of nonprofits (34 percent) in our survey report "lobbying" two or more times a month. However, when a different word was substituted on the same question, nearly half of the respondents report either "advocating" or "educating" government officials two or more times a month: 45 percent report "advocating," and 47 percent report "educating."

- *The "L" word* – Nonprofits do not like to use the word "lobbying," even when they are doing it. In focus groups, participants go out of their way to avoid using the word. One executive called it "impact analysis." Another described a lobbying campaign to get a state spending bill passed, but claimed that they do not lobby. Many board members and foundations had a negative attitude toward "lobbying," but felt more comfortable with the idea of "educating" policymakers, even when the activities described were ones that would be considered lobbying. This antipathy toward the word "lobbying" adds to the difficulty of measuring or defining it. One result is that words like "advocacy" and "lobbying" are often used interchangeably for the same activities, even though they may mean very different things.

There are Persistent Barriers that Need Addressing

- Nonprofits report *the top three barriers to policy participation as being limited financial resources, tax law or IRS regulations, and limited staff or volunteer skills.*

- *Three of four (77 percent) respondents that receive government grants feel that government funding is a barrier to their participating in policy matters.* Moreover, as government funding increases as a share of an organization's revenue, so does the perceived barrier to participating in public policy.

- *Many nonprofits that receive government money expressed fear of retribution for engaging in public policy matters.* Stories of

18

organizations losing government grants because of policy positions they took are common and serve to chill nonprofit action. One comment made during a Michigan focus group echoed what many others had said: "Government grants can dilute advocacy." An interview with an executive from a disability group in Pennsylvania clarified: "If you [receive] government funding, then there are subtle ways government can coerce you."

- Although 58 percent of respondents said that receiving foundation grants is not a barrier to policy participation, it proves to be a major barrier for certain types of nonprofits. Those that do not lobby were significantly more likely to see foundation funding as a barrier to policy participation when compared with those that do lobby. *As with government grants, as foundation funding increases as a percentage of the organization's revenue, so does the perceived barrier to participating in public policy.*

- In focus groups, *nonprofits raised concerns that foundations do not support advocacy activities undertaken by nonprofits, and unnecessarily place restrictions on using grant funds for lobbying purposes.* Many nonprofit leaders felt that most foundations do not like to fund advocacy work. Foundation leaders concurred, adding that some encourage advocacy cloaked in language such as "public education." But nonprofit leaders expressed frustration with these approaches and noted that grant award letters often place unnecessary restrictions on their activities.

- *Even when nonprofit leaders receive foundation grants for advocacy, it is often limited and inconsistent.* "Foundations will fund something for a few years... Unfortunately, two or three years are not how change works. They want instant gratification... Foundations think there is an instant solution for social problems," said a representative of a national organization in a focus group.

- Ironically, as *government and foundation revenues increase, nonprofits tend to become more involved in policy matters* despite the perception of a barrier to such activity. This trend is stronger regarding government funding.

- *Staff and budget size are also strong predictors of public policy participation.*

Nonprofits Lack Knowledge about Key Rules and Laws

- *There is a broad understanding of the general laws and regulations governing policy participation.* For example, 94 percent of nonprofits report that they know they cannot use federal funds to lobby, and 91 percent know that they can talk to elected officials about public policy matters.

- Interviews and focus groups revealed that *the general understanding nonprofits have of the federal advocacy and lobbying laws may be described as thin.* Even nonprofit representatives that claimed to know the rules did not know the basic limits on lobbying or even the definition of what constitutes lobbying under IRS rules. The survey showed that only 72 percent knew that they could support or oppose federal legislation, and only 79 percent knew that they could support or oppose federal regulations.

- *Two areas that present potential major problems for nonprofits relate to federal grant rules governing lobbying and voter education activities,* specifically candidate forums. Half of nonprofits incorrectly thought that they could not lobby if part of their budget comes from federal funds. While nonprofits know they may not use government funding for lobbying expenditures, most are unaware or uncertain of their right to lobby with private funds even when their organization receives government funding for other services. Also, 43 percent of nonprofits incorrectly thought they could not sponsor a candidates' forum or debate.

- In focus groups, executive directors noted that others, including elected officials, do not understand the rules that 501(c)(3) organizations must follow. Moreover, *directors in several cities spontaneously described pressures from political candidates for endorsements or campaign contributions,* even though charities are prohibited from such activities. Many directors say that as a result of pressure from candidates, they make personal contributions to help preserve the organization's relationship with current and future policymakers.

Decision Making Authority Has Implications for Policy Participation

- *Most nonprofits (58 percent) identify the executive director as having responsibility for government relations or public policy.* And the executive director is perceived as having the most influence regarding decisions concerning government relations. *Yet organizations where the executive director has responsibility for public policy are less involved* in public policy than organizations that assign the responsibility to others.

- *Organizations most involved in public policy* – whether testifying before a legislative or administrative hearing, lobbying for or against a proposed bill or other policy pronouncement, encouraging members to write, call, fax or e-mail policymakers, or releasing research reports to the media, public or policymakers – *have staff, a board committee or an outside lobbyist assigned the responsibility for public policy.*

Addressing Barriers to Nonprofit Participation is Vital for a Robust Civil Society

- *Many nonprofits need to better understand the importance of public policy participation.* This is especially true for board members who set direction and policy for the organizations. It is essential to help nonprofits understand that public policy participation is as important as other day-to-day program, management and governance activities. There is also a need for foundations and governments to recognize and support the role of nonprofits in making public policy.

- The research points out the *need for various types of capacity-building activities, including training* on lobbying restrictions under government grant rules, lobbying and advocacy restrictions under tax rules, how to be an effective advocate, and building internal organizational capacity. Training and technical assistance materials should be differentiated for the audience since not all nonprofits have the same needs with regard to public policy participation.

- There is a *need to simplify the rules governing lobbying, advocacy, and voter education* in order to strengthen nonprofit public policy participation.

- *Nonprofits perceive political risk by getting involved in public policymaking.* They need help determining whether risks exist and coping with them where they do.

Moving Beyond Barriers to Strengthen Policy Participation: Finding ways to Motivate

- *The number one issue is to find ways to motivate nonprofits to engage in public policy.* Nonprofit leaders are very mission driven and will likely engage in advocacy to help the people and causes they serve. At the same time, there are a host of factors that challenge participation: addressing staff crises, day-to-day program issues, and various other management functions, including fundraising. Nonprofit leaders do not see how engaging in public policy can ultimately help them with their day-to-day functions. Yet our training and technical assistance mostly focuses on understanding the laws and regulations surrounding lobbying and other forms of policy engagement or on how to be an effective advocate. Too often the support services are provided in times of crisis, resulting in a rapid decline in participation when the crisis ends. Invariably, we miss the key issue: focusing on factors that provide motivation for participation.

- *Passion plays a part in motivation.* Nonprofit leaders often act with passion and out of compassion. At the same time, our nonprofit leaders have professionalized and toned down their rhetoric to such a degree that workers in nonprofit organizations and the larger audience are not reached. We need to rely a little more on passion to engage our audiences and to do so not simply at times of crisis.

- *We must make advocacy and lobbying activities part of what is considered ordinary nonprofit activities.* A first step is to finally bury the notion that lobbying is "unclean." By lobbying and engaging in other forms of policy participation, we can improve lives and society. All of us concerned about the nonprofit sector should take steps to portray the policy process, including lobbying, as an honorable activity, one that should not be compromised or apologized for. Second, we must strengthen the support services to nonprofit organizations that help to heighten the comfort level staff and board members have with the policy process. Third, powerful institutions, such as universities and foundations, must signify that advocacy and efforts to strengthen democracy are *expected* nonprofit activities. Universities can do this through teaching nonprofit managers that policy participation can not only advance the mission of the organization, but also enhance the effectiveness of the organization itself. Foundations can do this by providing consistent financial support and encouragement for both building capacity to participate and for engagement in public policy.

Chapter 1
The Challenge Today:
Strengthening Nonprofit Advocacy
An Overview

The story of nonprofit advocacy is central to our American history.[6]
Nonprofits have played a role in many major national debates, providing
research, public education, lobbying and other forms of advocacy to win
public policy changes. So why does it seem that nonprofits today are so
timid when it comes to policy engagement? Or maybe that appearance is
at odds with reality and nonprofits are still the vital force in society that they
were during periods of major policy changes such as the 1960s and 1970s?

We set out to answer these types of questions and others, such as what it
would take to engage nonprofits more in public policy. We were mindful of
the recent history of what might be perceived as government antagonism
toward nonprofit advocacy. The 1966 IRS decision to revoke the Sierra
Club's 501(c)(3) tax exemption because of its advocacy to protect part of
the Grand Canyon from flooding from proposed dams on the Colorado
River sent a powerful message. As Chapter 2 describes, the head of the
Sierra Club noted that the exemption was not revoked because the Sierra
Club did too much lobbying, but rather because it was too effective with
its ads. The Sierra Club thrives today as a 501(c)(4) organization, but the
loss of its status as a charity created great uncertainty about what such
organizations could do without losing tax exemptions.

Following on the heels of the Sierra Club decision were the 1969 changes
in tax law that affected foundations. While there are many differing views
on the implications of these tax changes, there is one common agreement
– the tax changes created an atmosphere of uncertainty for foundations
about support for advocacy that continues today. This foundation antipathy
toward policy participation contributes to an environment in which nonprofit
leaders may not see advocacy as equally important as other organizational
functions such as fundraising or staff development.

---

[6] In this chapter we are mainly referring to the role charities have played in American
public policy development. Without doubt, other types of nonprofits, such as unions, have
had a profound impact on public policy. But our focus is on the role of charities.

While many other events may have discouraged nonprofit executives from policy participation, three major events in the 1980s and 1990s added to the chill. In the early 1980s, the Reagan administration launched a "de-fund the left" initiative through the Office of Management and Budget (OMB) that put nonprofit federal grantees in the middle of the bull's eye. Under an accounting rule called Circular A-122, which governs cost principles regarding use of federal grant funds, the administration proposed that recipients of federal grants could not engage in any public policy matters even with their non-federal funds. While this rule was discontinued after opposition from the nonprofit sector, it left a powerful legacy that has lasted until today, with some nonprofit executives believing that if they receive government grants they cannot engage in any public policy matters.

In 1986, a few years after the Circular A-122 fight, the IRS proposed rules to implement tax changes from the previous decade. The 1976 tax changes were intended to deal with the ambiguities of the Sierra Club revocation by creating a bright line test on allowable lobbying expenditures. In the ten years following the tax changes, many lawyers and organizations, such as Independent Sector, encouraged nonprofits to "elect" the expenditure test (also known as the 501(h) election) since it only counted as lobbying those communications that cost money, and placed a clear threshold on how much could be spent on lobbying. Thus, if the Sierra Club did not spend more than a specific threshold on its ads regarding flooding of the Grand Canyon, then its tax exemption could not be revoked. Unfortunately, the 1986 IRS proposed rules were antagonistic toward lobbying. In 1990, after nearly four years of negotiation with the IRS, constructive, positive final rules were issued but, like Circular A-122, the initial proposal left a chill in the air. Today, less that three percent of charities "elect" to fall under the expenditure test even though the final rules are beneficial to most nonprofits.

The Circular A-122 fight emerged once again in 1995 under the Contract with America, ushered in by the Republican takeover of the House of Representatives. This time, Representatives Ernest Istook (R-OK) David McIntosh (R-Ind.), and Robert Ehrlich (R-MD) proposed legislation that, like Circular A-122, would restrict nonprofits that received federal grants from using their own funds to engage in public policy, but, unlike Circular A-122, it added a bounty hunter provision that encouraged ferreting out abusers. After much organized opposition from the nonprofit community this too was discontinued – but like the other examples it added to the stigma and fear surrounding nonprofit advocacy.

Given this backdrop, maybe it should not be surprising to hear some executive directors who were part of the 17 focus groups in 11 cities or the 45 interviews we conducted under the Strengthening Nonprofit Advocacy Project (SNAP) say that spending time on lobbying detracted from doing the work that they should or must be doing – such activities as fundraising, dealing with staff issues, and day-to-day crises.[7] As the leader of a faith-based group in San Antonio, TX said, "We simply don't do those types of things." She spoke as though advocacy, ranging from talking with policymakers about policy issues to organizing to lobbying, was an "unclean" thing to do.

A nonprofit executive of an organization dealing with substance abuse in Sacramento, CA added: "It is not our mission to engage in public policy. It is inappropriate to lobby." Maybe she did not know the history of substance abuse legislation in this country or that nonprofits have played a leadership role in passage of key laws. Or maybe her reaction is a part of the legacy of the attacks on nonprofit advocacy.

The disenchantment with public policy participation is also strong among board members. Some board members do not fully understand the role charities play with regard to public policy or actually have negative views about them engaging in lobbying – or even advocacy. A board member in Texas told us that lobbying is not a good thing for his organization to do. He echoed what other board members told us, that board members "have a fiduciary responsibility. We would be violating that responsibility by taking a position on a policy issue that might anger a locally elected official." His reasoning was that the organization is heavily dependent on local financial support, and he does not want to upset the relationship with an elected leader which, in turn, might influence decisions to continue funding the organization.

Notwithstanding these voices questioning whether nonprofits should be involved in public policy, most of the nonprofit leaders who were part of the SNAP research recognized that engaging in public policy is essential to successfully implementing organizational mission, and that being a policy advocate is a key responsibility of being an executive director. The head of a Minnesota environmental group emphasized that you can't keep "putting out forest fires every day. You have to change the system ... To impact

---

[7] In this book when we use the term "nonprofit organization," we are referring to tax exempt organizations recognized as 501(c)(3) under the tax code, commonly called charities. If we are talking about a broader set of nonprofit organizations, we refer to them by their tax code designation, such as 501(c)(4) groups.

public policy is very important for nonprofits." A director of a community services organization in Tennessee reflected comments from many other nonprofit leaders: Nonprofits need to "get beyond that negative connotation and realize this is their voice, and without it they're left behind."

Nonprofit leaders throughout the country talked about the importance of engaging in public policy matters. Some, like a Minnesota housing group, focused on trying to influence legislation. "We do legislative work. We put together an agenda and advocate for [it]." Others, including a Pennsylvania disability association, talked about "partnerships" with government. "We carry out a core function of government; therefore we insist on a partnership with government. But that sometimes means we have to pressure government for a place at the table and to act upon our recommendations." Yet others talked about more subtle ways of influencing public policy. An executive director of a small human services organization in Nebraska noted, "I try to sit on as many committees and commissions as possible so I can try to influence public policy."

Leaders of nonprofit human services agencies described a growing divide between advocacy and service delivery, although many emphasized they were trying to bridge the divide. The divide is created by increased service demands unmatched by increased revenues. The pressure is to try to do more to meet the demand, forcing less support for advocacy, especially since nonprofit professionals were trained in service delivery, not advocacy. A leader of an organization that provides family counseling services told us: "This agency has been kind of insulated. It's very focused on therapies… Over the years, the directors of this agency were therapists and they did what they felt comfortable with." The person went on to describe new efforts to get more involved in state advisory panels and engage in various mental health policy initiatives. He also noted that the organization has a way to go before the staff and board realize that advocacy is essential to strengthening service delivery, that it is not an either-or situation but rather both-and.

Getting a handle on the extent of nonprofit public participation was not easy. We found in the survey data from SNAP that the choice of words can greatly influence the response.[8] For example, in our survey we asked

---

[8] Details on the research methodology are in Chapter 3. We conducted a random survey of 2,735 nonprofit 501(c)(3) organizations filing IRS Form 990 in 1998, excluding hospitals, universities, and foundations. We had 1,738 responses, a 64 percent response rate.

a question about the frequency of policy participation, but wanted to test whether the choice of words influences the results. We used the word "lobby" with one-third of the survey population, "advocate" with another third, and "educate" with the final third.[9] Only the verb changed. Thirty percent of respondents said they never lobby, whereas only 12 percent said they never educate policymakers and 15 percent said they never advocate. There is a sense that the word "lobby" is a dirty word. Nonprofit leaders do not like to use that term; they are far more comfortable with "educating" policymakers or talking about "advocacy." They say the public reaction, and the reaction of their boards, is overwhelmingly negative when they use the term "lobby." So our task was to ask our questions in different ways since the same type of activities might be described differently by various people. In fact, one nonprofit executive who described lobbying activities used the phrase "impact analysis" to describe those types of activities.

Moreover, even when nonprofits engage in public policy matters, they do not think of themselves as influencing policy. Forty-six percent of survey respondents who said they "never make any effort to influence government" also identify themselves as "participators," meaning they either lobby, encourage others to lobby, or testify. In fact, in sending out the survey one recipient called to say that "our organization is inappropriate for the study because we're not involved in public affairs." Yet, when asked if they deal with public officials, she said, "Oh yes, we harass our state legislators all the time." This suggests that nonprofits do not view their actions as attempting to influence public policy, even when that is what they do.

Finally, we recognized that one executive's sense of high level policy participation might be considered low level by another nonprofit leader. There is no standard to gauge involvement. In interviews we conducted, a leader of a local nonprofit talked about how deeply her organization was engaged in public policy while another said they were not very involved. With more discussion, it turned out that the high participator mostly put articles in the nonprofit's newsletter about legislation affecting their program. The low participator was organizing members to lobby state legislators on legislation. After hearing each description, we questioned

---

[9]The question was: "For some nonprofits, there is a need to [lobby, advocate, educate] those in government so that policymakers will have a better understanding of the problems facing the community. How often does your organization undertake an effort to [lobby, advocate, educate] government officials at any level?"

the self-assessment by the two leaders and realized that many groups' characterization of their policy engagement may be at odds with others' perception of it.

That is why we complemented our national survey with focus groups and interviews. Additionally, we structured our survey to ask about specific behaviors so that we had common benchmarks to make policy participation comparisons. See Table 1-1 on page 30 for the types of activities we measured. According to the survey, 86 percent of respondents said they have participated in public policy by either lobbying legislators, getting others to take such direct action, or by testifying. At the same time, the frequency of participation for the vast majority is very, very low. For example, 70 percent said they either never lobby or do so infrequently. In fact, three out of five nonprofits that say they do so at a low level.

The real problem is that nonprofit advocacy is limited and intermittent; groups fail to sustain their engagement over time. Executive directors say advocacy is important, an essential part of the job. But the rhetoric is not matched by action. A number of factors seem to contribute to this situation.

The Number One Barrier to Participation: Limited Resources

The number one barrier cited by nonprofits is lack of resources to engage in public policy; in fact, more than eight in ten respondents said that limited financial resources were some type of barrier with roughly half saying it was a significant barrier (see Table 1-2). In virtually every interview and focus group, lack of staff and funding were mentioned by executives as a key barrier to participation. One Florida nonprofit education leader said: "More knowledge of the law would be helpful, but lack of staff is the big problem. Additional funding would be a big help." She went on to explain that more training on the law won't help them if there is no staff person to follow through. An organization providing services to the elderly expressed a common refrain about service demand increasing but funding staying the same. "Our attitude has been if it isn't being spent on services, let's not spend the dollar."

Table 1-1. Nonprofit Policy Participation
Percentage Responding

Types of Policy Participation	All Respondents			Those under the Expenditure Test			Those under the Substantial Part Test		
	Never	Low	High	Never	Low	High	Never	Low	High
Encouraging members to write, call, fax or e-mail policymakers	22.3	40.8	36.8	13.0	42.8	44.1	29.6	39.4	31.1
Lobbying for or against a proposed bill or other policy pronouncement	26.3	42.8	31.0	14.2	47.4	38.4	36.2	38.7	25.0
Testifying at legislative or administrative hearings	29.0	47.9	23.1	15.9	54.7	29.4	39.6	42.2	18.1
Working in a planning or advisory group that includes government officials	18.4	36.5	45.1	10.1	36.2	53.7	25.2	36.7	38.1
Meeting with government officials about the work we are doing	15.0	40.2	44.8	6.4	39.6	54.0	22.1	40.6	37.2
Responding to requests for information from those in government	12.9	46.0	41.0	5.7	46.8	47.5	18.9	45.3	35.9
Discussing obtaining grants or contracts with government officials	29.2	42.6	28.2	27.4	42.3	30.3	30.5	42.9	26.6
Interacting socially with government officials	19.3	55.5	25.2	47.4	44.2	8.3	65.1	23.7	11.1
Releasing research reports to the media, public or policymakers	31.0	47.1	21.8	18.8	52.8	28.4	40.9	42.5	16.6

If a nonprofit organization did any one of the top three activities (shaded Items), we called them a "participator." We asked participants in 17 focus groups which of the activities listed above are considered policy participation. The three shaded activities were universally described as examples of nonprofit policy participation.

There was a significant difference between those organizations under the expenditure test and those under the substantial part test on every activity except discussing grants or contracts with government officials. p < .05 for each.

Q6. A variety of means of communicating and interacting with those in government are listed below. Please use the scale on the right to indicate how frequently, if at all, your organization engages in these activities. (By "your organization" we mean the executive director, other staff, volunteers, or members of the board.) In this scale, "0" means never, "1" is relatively infrequent interaction, and "4" is ongoing interaction.

("Low" above aggregates those marking 1 and 2 on the survey; "High" aggregates those marking 3 and 4 on the survey.)

Note: N= 1,657 to 1,671 depending on the activity

These pressures are compounded by a sense of political anomie, a type of alienation stemming from a perception that politics is being stacked against them. Some leaders talked about "the other side" having far more resources than "we do." This was particularly true for environmental and healthcare groups. "We can [face] being outspent 4-1. But we can't [compete] being outspent 5-1, 6-1, 42-1," a frustrated family planning director described. The spending imbalance was also raised in the context of political campaign contributions. Several executives, such as a leader in Idaho, noted that "we can't contribute money to candidates. But for-profit agencies can fatten [candidate] coffers. We're at a significant disadvantage. We can talk about morality, doing what's right, but we can't compete with PACs or fat pockets."

It was not solely the amount of money available for advocacy, but also the source of the organization's revenue. One of the single greatest sources of funding for nonprofits is government revenue. The SNAP data show that three of four respondents said that the receipt of government funds serves as some type of barrier to engaging in policy matters with ten percent saying it was a major barrier. In fact, the perception is that the level of the barrier increases as the amount of revenue from government increases as a percentage of organizational revenue. The same phenomena exist for nonprofits that receive money from foundations. Those that do *not* lobby are significantly more likely to see foundation funding as a barrier when compared to those that do lobby – and the perception of the barrier grows with more foundation funding within the organization.

Table 1-2. Barriers to Nonprofit Participation
Percentage Responding

	All Respondents			Participators*			Non-Participators		
Type of Barrier	None	Low	High (Major)	None	Low	High (Major)	None	Low	High (Major)
Limited financial resources	18.9	32.8	48.3 (26.2)	16.2	34.2	49.6 (26.4)	41.5	21.4	37.1 (24.5)
Tax law or IRS regulations	32.8	44.5	22.7 (11.8)	30.0	47.2	22.7 (11.4)	55.4	21.6	22.9 (15.3)
Staff/Volunteer skills	35.4	43.2	21.3 (6.2)	33.0	45.8	21.2 (5.2)	55.0	22.5	22.5 (14.4)
Government funds	48.6	34.2	17.3 (9.6)	45.6	37.0	17.3 (9.5)	73.4	10.3	16.2 (9.7)
Board/Staff attitude	45.2	39.1	15.8 (5.1)	44.1	40.4	14.5 (3.7)	53.8	19.7	26.6 (16.5)
Public's attitude	46.3	42.0	11.7 (3.5)	44.7	43.8	11.5 (3.3)	59.5	27.4	13.0 (5.2)
Attorney/Accountant advice	49.3	42.1	8.7 (3.4)	47.4	44.2	8.3 (2.9)	65.1	23.7	11.1 (7.2)
Foundation funds	58.8	35.1	6.1 (2.5)	57.0	37.3	5.7 (2.3)	73.9	16.3	9.8 (4.6)

* "Participators" are organizations that report that they lobby, encourage others to lobby, or testify.

Q15. In the previous section we asked you about your direct involvement in the public policymaking process. Now we would like to know about factors that you feel are barriers to your organization's involvement in the policymaking process and how significant those barriers are. In the scale below, 0 represents no barrier, 1 a low barrier, and 4 represents a major barrier. ("Low" above aggregates those marking 1 and 2 on the survey; "High" aggregates those marking 3 and 4 on the survey.)

Note: N=1,423 to 1,465, depending on the barrier.

Because of the frequently expressed frustration about funding sources, it was surprising to find that as government and foundation revenue increased, it was more likely that an organization would engage in public policy activities. Groups that received no government revenue were significantly less likely to lobby, encourage others to lobby, or testify than those receiving government revenue. The same was true for foundation grants: groups that received no foundation funding were significantly less likely to lobby, encourage others to lobby, or testify than those receiving foundation funds. An explanation for this seeming contradiction is that, while perceived as a barrier, government and foundation funds are necessary to reach a size that enables an organization to lobby.

Government Funding

There are two problems nonprofit executives face when they have government funds. First, there is confusion over rules regarding government grants and participation in public policy matters. Half of survey respondents did not know that the organization can still lobby even if part of the organization's budget comes from federal funds (see Table 1-3). Even more startling, 83 percent of respondents who do not participate in public policy wrongly thought they could not lobby if their organization receives federal funds. While there is a general understanding that nonprofits can get involved in policy debates and that tax law permits some lobbying, there is very little understanding of government grant management rules. This may stem from the Circular A-122 and Istook amendment fights in the 1980s and 1990s, respectively, where federal nonprofit grantees were targets, or it may result from other factors. Whatever the reason, the problem is significant, especially since about one-third of nonprofit revenue comes from government sources.

One rule nonprofit executives know is that organizations cannot use government funds to lobby. More than 90 percent of survey respondents knew this rule. This rule makes it very difficult to lobby or engage in other types of advocacy if the organization is heavily funded by government grants. A number of nonprofit executives reported that many staff members are paid as full-time employees on a government grant, meaning the staff person could not lobby. This suggests the organization is not structured in a way that allows for it to engage in public policy.

Table 1-3. Nonprofit Understanding of Advocacy Rules
(Correct answer indicated by X)

There is a good deal of confusion about whether activities by nonprofits relating to the policymaking process are permissible. Based on your understanding, can your organization:	Yes	No	% Correct
Use government funds to lobby Congress		X	93.6
Talk to elected officials about public policy matters	X		91.1
Endorse a candidate for elected office		X	87.4
Take a policy position without reference to a specific bill under current regulations	X		81.8
Support or oppose federal regulations	X		79.3
Support or oppose federal legislation under current IRS regulations	X		72.5
Sponsor a forum or candidate debate for elected office	X		56.5
Lobby if part of your budget comes from federal funds	X		50.4

Second, nonprofit executives fear retribution from government officials if their organizations take positions on policy matters. One human services director in Texas said they expected their grant from the state to be eliminated or cut because they lobbied a point of view opposite from a legislative staffer who now works in the state agency that provides the grants. The director of a healthcare provider in Massachusetts said, "Literally, you take a position critical [of a policy], the next day the special audit team from the state, they're in all your records.... [I]t's very hard to be an advocate when you're dependent upon state money." A Pennsylvania disability group added: "If you [receive] government funding, then there are subtle ways government can coerce you. When this happens our board begins to tremble."

These feelings are widespread. In Michigan, many supported the comment made by a participant that "government grants can dilute advocacy." The price for advocacy can be significant, although there are no statistics to verify how widespread the problem is. One large voluntary organization claimed in an interview that they "lost 80 percent of their state grants because of lobbying."

Foundation Funding

Nonprofit leaders identified four concerns about foundation funding when it comes to advocacy. First, many feel as though advocacy is ignored or minimized as a funding priority within the foundation community. Local groups think that foundations are funding national groups to undertake

33

advocacy activities. "Foundations are interested in national advocacy but not in supporting it locally...They want to have a national impact," according to the director of a health group in Pennsylvania. Yet in interviews representatives of national groups also say foundations do not support advocacy. National, state and local groups all concur that foundations do not consider advocacy a high priority, but they often think that foundations probably fund someone else to do advocacy.

Even when foundations fund advocacy, it is not the type of ongoing support that is necessary for systemic change. "Foundations will fund something for a few years...Unfortunately, two or three years is not how change works. They want instant gratification.... Foundations think there is an instant solution for social problems." This quote from a leader in a national arms control organization was echoed not only by nonprofit leaders but also by foundation staff who participated in focus groups. While some nonprofit leaders felt that foundation staffers don't understand the need for continued support for advocacy, others thought the problem was more profound. They felt that the problem is that there are many foundation trustees who do not understand the importance of advocacy. Additionally, trustees often want to change funding priorities, making it difficult to provide ongoing support, according to some foundation staff.

Nonprofit leaders also voiced concern that foundations provide support for advocacy when it is too late or in the middle of a crisis. The director of a Minnesota housing program echoed a common refrain: "In the past, [foundations] have denied us [grants]. But now the housing situation here is getting so desperate that they realize that they need to get behind the advocates." This criticism could also be leveled at the entire nonprofit sector since nonprofit leaders also tend to get involved in advocacy efforts when a crisis arises.

Finally, nonprofit leaders felt that foundations unnecessarily restrict advocacy. In both interviews and focus groups, nonprofit executives mentioned lobbying restrictions placed in foundation grant award letters. As a Tennessee human services leader said, "All the major foundations have a clause [in grant letters] that says you cannot do any lobbying with their money, every one of them." Some organizations, such as the Alliance for Justice and the Center for Lobbying in the Public Interest, have emphasized that these foundation restrictions are unnecessary, but they continue to occur. Adding to the negative impact of the restrictions in the award letters, some nonprofit staff thought they were forbidden to lobby if they receive foundation funds.

Two Other Key Barriers to Participation

While the major barrier to policy participation had to do with resources, nonprofits also voiced concerns about other types of barriers, particularly the complexity of tax law regarding advocacy and development of staff and volunteer skills (see Table 1-2). Sixty-eight percent of respondents in our survey said that tax law or IRS regulations were some type of barrier, with 23 percent saying they were a significant barrier. (By comparison, more than twice as many said limited financial resources were a significant barrier.[10]) Sixty-four percent of respondents said that staff skills were some type of barrier, with 21 percent saying they were a significant barrier.

Tax Law and Regulation as a Barrier

The sense of whether tax law is a barrier depends on whether the nonprofit group is already involved in public policy. Among organizations that lobby, encourage others to lobby, or testify, seven in ten view tax law and regulation as a barrier to participation. Among those that do not lobby, encourage others to lobby, or testify, only 45 percent viewed tax law or regulations as a barrier. Those nonprofits that tend to be more involved in public policy matters, such as environmental and healthcare groups, are more likely to view tax law and regulations as a greater barrier than groups less involved in public policy, such as arts and recreation groups.

Regardless of whether nonprofits believe tax law or regulations are a barrier, there is considerable confusion about the restrictions on lobbying. In our survey we asked eight yes/no questions about understanding of the law. More than one-quarter of respondents did not know that they could support or oppose federal legislation under current Internal Revenue Service regulations, and for those who do not lobby, encourage others to lobby, or

---

[10] One reviewer of this publication commented that limited financial resources can always serve as a "smoke screen" or an excuse for not participating. The heart of the matter is motivation, which our research demonstrates, the reviewer noted.

testify, more than two-thirds did not get the answer correct.[11] In follow-up interviews, even for those who got the answer right, they demonstrated a very minimal understanding of the IRS regulations. Some said they could lobby only when a government official asked them for their point of view, which is inaccurate. Very few understood how much lobbying was permissible, generally thinking they could do much less lobbying than what the law and regulations permit. Even in focus groups of high participators, most executives did not know basic information about lobby laws, such as how much lobbying they could do or even what constitutes lobbying by IRS definitions. Under the tax code, lobbying refers to attempts to influence legislation, not regulations. Many nonprofit leaders did not know this distinction.[12] Board members and foundation staff, in particular, do not have a good understanding of lobbying rules.

Under current tax law, lobbying can account for "no substantial part" of the organization's activities unless they "elect" to fall under an expenditure test. The expenditure test provides more concrete standards and definitions on how much lobbying a nonprofit can do since there are specific dollar limits on lobbying. While it only requires filling out a very short IRS form to convert from the substantial part test to the expenditure test, it does require the nonprofit organization to take some action to make the change.[13] It is likely then that an organization that switches to the expenditure test is doing so because its leaders are already aware of the need to lobby and may plan to do so some time in the future.

As might be expected, our survey found those organizations under the expenditure test to be significantly more involved in public policy than those under the substantial part test. The data cannot be interpreted to mean that choosing the expenditure test will mean the organization will suddenly become more involved in public policy. Instead, it appears based

---

[11] On the yes/no questions about understanding of laws and regulations on advocacy restrictions, there was a significant difference in correct answers when comparing those who lobby, encourage others to lobby, or testify with those groups who do not do those activities. Ninety four percent of participators answered six of the eight questions correctly, whereas six percent of non-participators got that many questions right.

[12] Some of the confusion may stem from state disclosure requirements. In some states, nonprofits must disclose information about attempts to influence legislation as well as government regulations. These disclosures have nothing to do with overall limits on lobbying established by the federal tax code.

[13] IRS Form 5768 is available at http://www.irs.gov/pub/irs-pdf/f5768.pdf. A copy is also found in Appendix B.

on interviews that those organizations that selected the expenditure test did so as they became motivated to engage in public policy. Moreover, when comparing participation levels for those under the expenditure test that report lobbying expenditures to the IRS on the annual Form 990 versus those that do not have any lobbying expenditures, we found participation was significantly lower. In other words, it is not simply choosing the expenditure test that makes groups participate more. Nonprofit executives told us that participation was more about motivation or facing programmatic crises than anything else. The selection of the expenditure test usually comes after consultation with experts (e.g., lawyers, accountants) and board discussion about the role of advocacy.

Staff Skills as a Barrier

Roughly one-quarter of both advocacy participators (those who lobby, encourage others to lobby, or testify) and non-participators considered staff or volunteer skills a major barrier to policy participation. In focus groups and interviews, nonprofit leaders included a broad range of topics under building staff advocacy skills. A Pennsylvania statewide disability group talked about how "many nonprofits have huge turnover in staff" and noted that there is little time to train new staff in advocacy skills. In a focus group in Kentucky, participants agreed that new staff simply have to "find their own way" to be effective advocates because there is little time or ability to train them. Addressing staff turnover was a key issue in building staff skills.

When asked about training needs, nonprofit executives placed a heavy emphasis on basic advocacy skills, such as how to lobby, how to write a letter to an elected official, how to influence administrative decisions such as agency rule-makings, and how to build an effective coalition to address policy issues. A New York family services organization noted they have staff skilled in various organizational needs such as development and program services, but "there is nobody who would be good at [advocacy] without more training." At the same time, few nonprofit executives were able to identify available resources, such as trainers, books, or online services, to assist them.

Those who say staff skills are a key reason for inconsistency or lack of policy participation described the importance of coalitions and joining other organizations. A faith-based group in Pennsylvania described being part of a "consortium" that sends them most of their information about federal public policy. The Pennsylvania group provides money to the consortium, and "they do most of the lobbying," as they have the skills. Lots of nonprofit leaders feel it is smarter to pay membership organizations to engage in public policy on their behalf rather than build the requisite staff skills.

For those who were already engaged in advocacy, there was a pressing need to talk about building staff skill for effective and strategic approaches to their advocacy. A New Hampshire library association noted that "we have 600 members and they are very prominent people in their communities," but the organization needed expert advice on how to maximize their clout on policy matters. At focus groups that involved organizations already engaged in public policy, the conversation often turned to how to be more effective. Many talked about the "deck being stacked against them" and cited the need for innovative approaches to engaging in public policy. They talked about how to use limited resources to "compete against others who have more resources," as one Michigan nonprofit leader in the state capital put it. This included more training on how to use the news media, as well as how to operate in a "conservative bastion," as was described by an Orange County, CA nonprofit leader.

A nonprofit environmental group in Vermont described a slightly different approach in which they convene a summit of environmental groups in the state to "plan and to think about how to use our resources." These strategy sessions are aimed at identifying priorities and developing strategies. "We'll never have their [bankers, power companies, Chamber of Commerce] financial resources, but we do have resources. We have people, numbers, and expertise." Those nonprofit leaders already engaged in public policy want to talk about strategies for being more effective advocates, including engaging voters on issues central to the mission of the organization.

Getting Nonprofits More Engaged

Simply reducing barriers does not necessarily mean that nonprofits will suddenly get more involved in public policy. For example, even if nonprofits had more resources that could be used for advocacy, it is doubtful they would do that. Similarly, even if there was a robust education program to train nonprofits about the lobby provisions in tax law, it is doubtful that nonprofits would consistently engage in public policy matters.

The SNAP research shows that the key to consistent nonprofit policy participation is providing strong motivation for engagement. While crisis situations may produce participation, it tends to be short-term and limited. Instead, the data suggest linking the organization's mission and issues to governmental policies is necessary to demonstrate why nonprofits should be involved. Of those who either lobby, encourage others to lobby, or testify – what we call participators – 86 percent said that promoting government policies that support the organization's mission was a high inducement for policy participation. Similarly, more than three-quarters of participators said that raising public awareness about important issues or protecting government programs that serve the organization's constituents or community were also high motivating factors for engaging in public policy.

Nonprofit leaders look to these mission-driven reasons for engaging in public policy. In fact, nonprofit leaders agreed that opportunities for obtaining government funding provided the least incentive for advocacy of the list presented to them. Respondents, whether they were participators or not, consistently put their constituency, issues and mission concerns above their own organizational interests, such as fundraising.

As one healthcare leader in Boston said, "We act to improve the public good." The for-profit community lobbies to make a profit; there is always a self-interest. We lobby to protect the people we serve; there is no self-interest, only a public interest." That sentiment was consistently echoed across the country by large and small nonprofits, by urban and rural groups, and by those who are actively engaged in public policy and those who are not engaged. Regardless of the accuracy, there is a presumption that the public understands that advocacy by the nonprofit sector is far different than advocacy by the business community.

The challenge is finding ways to link policy advocacy to strengthening the organization's mission. In interviews and focus groups, nonprofit executives felt that most training and technical assistance addressed how-to issues and background on tax law. Most did not feel that there was adequate support to show how policy engagement could benefit the mission of the organization overall.

Table 1-4. Factors that Motivate Nonprofit Participation
Percentage Responding

Type of Motivation	All Respondents			Participators*			Non-Participators		
	None	Low	High	None	Low	High	None	Low	High
Promoting government policies that support our mission	8.2	11.1	80.8	3.8	9.9	86.3	45.3	20.5	34.1
Raising public awareness of important issues	8.2	16.2	75.7	3.8	15.4	80.8	44.7	23.0	32.3
Protecting government programs that serve our client, constituents or community	13.4	14.9	71.6	9.2	14.0	76.8	47.8	22.4	29.8
Defending nonprofits' advocacy rights	23.2	39.7	37.1	19.3	41.5	39.2	56.1	24.8	19.1
Opportunities to obtain government funding	35.5	24.6	40.0	32.5	25.9	41.6	60.2	13.7	26.1

* "Participators" are organizations that report they either lobby, encourage others to lobby, or testify.

Q16. Turning from barriers to inducements, what factors motivate your organization to become involved in the public policymaking process?

The scale was 0-4, where 0 represents no influence, 1 low influence, and 4 a high influence. In this table, "Low" aggregates those marking 1 and 2 on the survey; "High" aggregates those marking 3 and 4 on the survey.

Note: N=1,471 to 1,595, depending on the motivating factor.

Other Motivating Factors

Interaction with government officials significantly increases policy participation. The degree to which a nonprofit organization participates in public policy matters is directly related to two factors: its perception that government officials care about its work, and the number of government-initiated contacts that occur. Respondents who believe government officials are interested in what they have to say and are interested in working with them are far more likely to lobby, encourage others to lobby, or testify than groups that think government officials are not really interested in hearing their views.

There is a linear relationship between the number of times people in government approach nonprofit staff and the level of policy participation by that nonprofit organization. Groups that are approached four or more times a month by policymakers are five times as likely to lobby as those who are never approached and nearly twice as likely as those approached once a month or less. That trend is less obvious regarding encouraging others to lobby or what is often called indirect lobbying. In the case of indirect lobbying, there is a large difference in the amount of lobbying between organizations not approached by government policymakers and those that are. The number of government-initiated contacts has less impact, however, on the frequency of indirect lobbying; that is, the frequency of indirect lobbying activity is less determined by whether the number of contacts is one a month or four or more a month

In addition to government contacts, joining an association that represents your organization before government plays a significant role in whether that organization decides to participate in public policy matters, particularly if it is a national association (see Table 1-5). The amount of lobbying, encouraging others to lobby (called indirect lobbying), and testifying is significantly higher for organizations that pay dues to national associations that represent them before government than for groups that have not joined national associations. This is also true for lobbying and indirect lobbying when joining a state association. The relationship between policy participation and joining a local association is not significant, except as it applies to indirect lobbying. This correlation may be surprising since nonprofit leaders said, as previously mentioned, that they joined associations so they did not need to engage in advocacy themselves.

Table 1-5. Correlation Between Frequency of Policy Participation and Membership in Associations

Belongs to:	Lobbying	Frequency of: Indirect Lobbying	Testifying
National Association	.199**	.160**	.150**
State Association	.079**	.109**	-.009
Local Association	.027	.051*	.000

** Correlation is significant at the .01 level (2-tailed) using Pearson Correlation
* Correlation is significant at the .05 level (2-tailed) using Pearson Correlation

Q13. Is your organization a dues-paying member of one or more associations that represent you before government? If yes, check all that apply:

N= 1,659 to 1,693 depending on question

In focus groups and interviews, nonprofit executives complained about getting multiple alerts from national and state organizations to take action. They felt overloaded with the requests and noted that many of the requests are duplicative, with each membership organization putting "their spin on it in order to get credit," as one human services leader in California put it. Yet Table 1-6 shows that members of associations act when asked, no matter how many times they are asked. As the number of asks increases, the number of actions also increases. Moreover, when contacted four or more times per month to contact a policymaker, 45 percent of organizations take four more actions each month and 78 percent take two or more actions per month.

Table 1-6. Requests by Associations to Take Action are Acted Upon

Number of times an association contacts its members each month	Percentage of times an organization acts upon at least one request
Never	0%
Once a month or less	90.0%
2 or 3 times a month	95.3%
4 times a month or more	98.1%

For nonprofit associations that have nonprofit members or communicate with other nonprofits, the above information suggests that if you ask nonprofits to act they will. Yet survey respondents report nearly six out of ten associations (57 percent) contact them once a month or less to communicate with policymakers. Only 12 percent of respondents reported associations contacting them four times a month or more to ask them to communicate with policymakers. This was true regardless of whether the organization was a member of a national, state, or local association.

Other factors that show a strong correlation with increased policy participation are budget size and staff size. As each goes up, the frequency of policy participation increases, although with staff size it begins to flatten out after staff size exceeds 25.

Profile of a Participator

As described above, we defined a "participator" as an organization that has either lobbied or encouraged members to write, call, fax, or e-mail policymakers, or testified at a legislative or administrative hearing. To be classified a participator, the organization only had to do one of the above activities at least once. Thus, the threshold to become a participator is not high.

The SNAP data provide a profile of the types of organizations that are likely to be participators. Table 1-7 provides a summary of the findings.

Table 1-7. Factors Influencing Participation

Likely Participators	Not Likely Participators
Mission: health, environment, social action	Mission: arts, recreation, religious, philanthropic
Sees connection between advocacy and promoting organizational mission and protecting programs serving constituents	Views advocacy as a diversion from implementing organizational mission and believes it impairs service delivery
Someone responsible for government relations	No staff person or volunteer assigned to government relations
Bigger budget	Smaller budget
Multiple funding sources	Single funding source
Foundation and government funding	Other types of funding
Has members	No membership
Joins associations and coalitions that engage in public policy	Does not join associations and coalition that engage in public policy
Seeks professional advice (e.g., legal, accounting) on advocacy	Does not seek professional advice on advocacy
Uses information technology (e.g., Internet)	Does not use technology
Chooses the "expenditure test"	Stays under the "substantial part test"

What Nonprofits Can Do to Strengthen Involvement

There are at least five simple things the SNAP research suggests that nonprofit executives can do to strengthen nonprofit advocacy.

1. Discuss advocacy with board and staff.

Probably the most important thing a nonprofit executive can do is create a supportive climate for advocacy within the organization. There is no magic for how this should happen. But people in focus groups and interviews emphasized that without strong support from the organization's identified leaders, advocacy is unlikely to flourish. The leaders within the organization, particularly the executive director, must demonstrate strong, consistent support for engaging in public policy matters.

The SNAP data show that the executive director has the most influence when making major decisions concerning government relations, followed by the chair of the board and the board itself or a board committee. In focus groups and interviews, participants echoed the survey results, with many describing the importance of discussing advocacy with the board and the staff. Given the antipathy many board members seem to have toward advocacy, involving board members in understanding why advocacy is intrinsically tied to the organization's mission will likely help create a legacy of organizational support for advocacy.

2. Establish internal organizational procedures that make policy decision-making easier.

In addition to creating the right environment for advocacy to flourish, there must be a clear set of decision steps delineated for staff to follow when taking organizational positions. Some organization leaders described very complex decision-making processes, barring the executive director from taking a position until the board meets to discuss the issue. Given that board meetings may occur only several times a year, it could prove difficult to get decisions made on a faster pace. By the time the organization takes action on a policy matter, there may be little or no opportunity to influence the outcome. In focus groups and interviews, several nonprofit executives described similar situations that occurred in their organizations.

To correct this problem, these nonprofit leaders suggested at least two different approaches. If the board feels it must be involved in policy decisions, then it was strongly suggested that a board committee be established. A board committee could have the advantage of being able to meet with greater frequency than the full board, and a committee could develop the needed expertise to make policy decisions on shorter notice. With the ubiquity of the Internet and low-cost conference calling, it was also suggested that such board committees might meet virtually, rather than physically, to expedite decision-making. The SNAP survey supports the importance of having board committees that address public policy issues, since such organizations are significantly more likely to engage in public policy matters and with greater frequency than those without such a board committee.

A second approach, not mutually exclusive from the idea of creating a public policy or governmental affairs board committee, was to delegate more decision-making authority for government relations to the executive director. The SNAP data supports this approach. Organizations in which the executive director had a high degree of influence in governmental relations decision-making, but not responsibility for carrying out day-to-day advocacy tasks (see next item below), were significantly more likely to engage in public policy and with greater frequency.

Finally, staffs need to fully understand the decision-making structure so that they know how to negotiate organizational structure to get a decision about government relations.

3. Assign day-to-day advocacy responsibilities to someone other than the executive director.

Nearly three-quarters of survey respondents (73 percent) indicated that their organization has at least one person who has day-to-day responsibility for public policy activities. As might be expected, assigning public policy responsibility to a person in the organization significantly increases the likelihood that the organization will engage in public policy.

In most cases (58 percent of the time) that person is the executive director. Unfortunately, the executive director is not the best person in the organization to have lead day-to-day responsibility for conducting public policy activities (see Table 1-8). Organizations that assign public policy responsibilities to anyone other than the executive director, including a lobbyist outside the organization, other staff members, board committees, or even volunteers are more likely to engage in lobbying, indirect lobbying, and testifying and with more consistency.

**Table 1-8. Don't Let the Executive Director
Lead Day-to-Day Responsibility for Public Policy**

Who has Lead Policy Responsibility?	Lobbying		Indirect Lobbying		Testifying	
	% of Orgs with High Level	Rank	% of Orgs with High Level	Rank	% of Orgs with High Level	Rank
Lobbyist	58.7	1	56.6	1	42.6	1
Staff	51.5	2	54.8	3	40.0	3
Board Committee	50.8	3	53.1	4	40.7	2
Volunteer	45.9	4	56.1	2	34.6	4
Executive Director	40.6	5	45.6	6	30.6	5
Board Member	38.4	6	47.3	5	27.1	6

This makes sense given that the executive director often has a broad range of duties to perform or oversee, including fundraising, personnel matters, and program functions. To the extent that the executive director also tackles public policy matters, advocacy activities are likely to be moved to the back burner as other functions are addressed. Accordingly, it makes enormous sense to assign day-to-day public policy responsibilities to someone other than the executive director, leaving it to the executive director to set overall direction.

4. Belong to associations that represent you before government.

As mentioned above, joining an association that speaks out on public policy issues is linked to whether an organization engages in public policy itself. Those joining associations engage in more lobbying, indirect lobbying and testifying, and do so with greater frequency than those not joining associations. This factor is particularly strong for those who join national associations, but it is also true for those who join state associations. This suggests that nonprofit executives should structure annual budgets to reserve funds for joining associations that engage in public policy.

5. Get training.

Nonprofit executive directors often express feelings of disengagement from government. Government is too complex, too difficult to follow or influence, they say. Furthermore, many in the nonprofit sector were trained to do the professional work they do, such as helping families or cleaning up the environment or providing cultural services. They are not knowledgeable about the workings of government or effective advocacy techniques. With that in mind, it would be a wise investment to budget for training and technical assistance in any, and all, of the following areas:

- **Why engaging in public policy is important.** This would cover the topic of motivation and how advocacy is central to the organization's mission. It should involve the board and staff.

- **Organizational capacity building.** Organizations that specialize in nonprofit management are becoming more aware of the need to apply their expertise to helping nonprofits create the right type of organization structure (e.g., board role, staff responsibilities) to engage in advocacy. Finding management consultants knowledgeable about advocacy can make a world of difference for the future of the nonprofit organization.

- **How to lobby and advocate effectively.** There are various training academies, graduate school programs, and technical assistance providers that are skilled in advocacy techniques and the workings

46

of government. For example, the Center for Lobbying in the Public Interest, an organization based in Washington, D.C., has established a network of fellows skilled in advocacy training and technical assistance. In addition, there are many exciting activities happening nationwide. In the state of Washington, for example, organizations dealing with children's and low-income issues conduct an advocacy camp where skills on effective advocacy are taught. Increasingly, the academic centers and programs at colleges and universities that focus on the study of nonprofit organizations, voluntarism, or philanthropy are teaching students about the importance of advocacy. Many of these academic centers are beginning to offer certificate programs for nonprofit executives that include advocacy training. Additionally, many graduate public policy and public affairs programs teach courses on lobbying and the policymaking process that can be enormously helpful to nonprofit leaders. Finally, there are numerous useful documents on the Internet that can help provide insights on how to effectively lobby or advocate. For example, there is a one-stop website operated by OMB Watch called NPAction.org that has case studies of nonprofit advocacy campaigns, including what worked and what did not. There are also many other websites, including organizational ones, such as the Alliance for Justice and the Center for Lobbying in the Public Interest, and projects, such as the Nonprofit Good Practice Guide (www.npgoodpractice.org), which is a project of the Philanthropic and Nonprofit Knowledge Management Initiative at the Dorothy A. Johnson Center for Philanthropy and Nonprofit Leadership.

- **Training on public policy processes.** Being an effective advocate also means understanding how policymaking works. Nonprofit leaders may need help in basic civics lessons, including how our three branches of government work, how a bill becomes a law, how government works at the local and state and federal level, and information about basic tools for influencing the public policies. Nonprofit leaders also could use a refresher course in what happens once a law is passed, including how to monitor and comment on regulations.

- **Training on laws and regulations.** There are three high-priority areas for training:

47

- *Government grant rules on lobbying.* Although roughly one-third of nonprofit revenue comes from government, fifty percent of nonprofit respondents do not know they can engage in advocacy if they get government grants. Furthermore, focus groups show that understanding of lobby restrictions under government grant rules is very poor.[14]

- *Tax rules on lobbying.* Nearly 30 percent of nonprofit respondents do not know they can lobby and advocate. Moreover, focus groups reveal that understanding of the laws and regulations is not very good – even among those who are very engaged in public policy.

- *Voter engagement initiatives.* Nonprofits need to better understand the rules concerning electoral activity, particularly since many are being asked for candidate endorsements. Forty-three percent of survey respondents incorrectly thought they could not sponsor a forum or debate featuring a candidate for elective office.

Systemic Change within the Nonprofit Sector

The steps above are intended as steps any executive director can begin taking. Now we turn to systemic changes that must occur to strengthen nonprofit advocacy. We recognize that each of the ideas below is not simple to implement; increasing advocacy activity will require commitment and persistence.

1. **Change the climate concerning advocacy.** There appears to be public confusion over the role of nonprofits in influencing public policy. The news media and others conflate different types of nonprofit organizations, such as 501(c)(3), 501(c)(4) and 527 organizations, as simply one type of nonprofit organization. Yet there are major differences that the public must understand. For example, 501(c)(4) and 527 groups can support or oppose a candidate for elected office, whereas a 501(c)(3) organization cannot. Additionally, there are no limits on the amount of lobbying 501(c)(4) and 527 groups can

---

[14] While there is variation in state regulations, no state permits grantees to use government funds to lobby or engage in electioneering.

undertake, where there are limits placed on 501(c)(3) organizations. It is not simply the public; elected officials and leaders in the nonprofit sector are confused about what different types of nonprofit organizations can and cannot do.

Clarifying the role of 501(c)(3) organizations would greatly help elected officials understand the importance of nonprofit advocacy. It would also serve as a means for thwarting future attacks on nonprofit advocacy, such as those like the Istook amendment or those that occurred during the Reagan administration. Our collective objective should be to establish a public education campaign that has community-based leaders speaking out against any future attacks on advocacy and praising proposals that strengthen nonprofit advocacy.

This assumes, of course, that our leadership in the nonprofit sector – from national organizations to local leaders – begins to talk positively about lobbying and advocacy. One person who reviewed the SNAP data commented that it has taken 20 years to get the term "advocacy" to become more acceptable within the nonprofit sector. Hopefully, we can be faster with the term "lobbying." We must strive toward changing what is perceived as extraordinary – nonprofit policy participation – into the ordinary.[15]

The Challenge:
Turning the Extraordinary into the Ordinary

Ordinary Tasks
Service Delivery
Fundraising
Staff Issues
Responding to Day-to-Day Issues
Administration

Extraordinary Tasks
Lobbying
Testifying
Policy Advocacy

It is essential to help nonprofits understand that public policy participation is as important as other day-to-day organizational activities

---

[15] Shifting nonprofit advocacy from being "extraordinary to ordinary" is a phrase we first heard used by Florence Green, the executive director of the California Association of Nonprofits.

2. **Encourage foundation support of advocacy.** Foundations – from private to community foundations – can be more supportive of nonprofit policy participation in three ways. First, they can seize legal opportunities to fund nonprofit public policy activities and by expressing that understanding in grant letters.[16] The rules are different for private foundations than for community foundations; while both can support advocacy, community foundations have far more leeway to support lobbying activities. Some foundations are stepping up to the advocacy table with consistent support for nonprofit advocacy.[17] It might be possible to showcase these types of foundations to their colleagues as positive examples. Second, foundation trustees and staff need greater information about the importance of nonprofit advocacy.[18] Such information and training should include information on why ongoing, consistent support for advocacy is essential for implementing the foundation's objectives. Third, foundations should invest in advocacy by providing capacity-building support on topics such as how to lobby or build coalitions.

Changes in foundation behavior occur slowly. On a more optimistic note, philanthropic support groups, such as the Northern California Grantmakers Association, have made great strides in encouraging change within philanthropic circles regarding funding of advocacy activities. In 2005, NCG announced a Public Policy Grantmaking Toolkit that explains how funders can support public policy activities, and includes information on legal issues and success stories.[19] NCG hopes this kit will be widely used by foundations and will become a model for other associations to encourage public policy participation.

3. **Strengthen national- and state-level groups that provide advocacy capacity-building services.** The Urban Institute was asked to prepare a map of national nonprofit infrastructure organizations for a special issue of the Nonprofit Quarterly. In doing so, the lead author,

---

[16] Too often foundations insert unnecessary lobbying prohibitions in grant letters. A number of legal experts on nonprofit law have repeatedly indicated that such prohibitions are not required and only serve to limit the activities of nonprofit grantees.

[17] See Arons, David F. ed. 2007. Power in Policy: A Funders Guide to Advocacy and Civic Participation, Fieldstone Alliance, St. Paul, MN.

[18] Some organizations, such as the Alliance for Justice, have foundation education programs to increase support for advocacy

[19] http://www.ncg.org/toolkit/home.html

Linda Lampkin, calculated that such organizations had total revenue in 2002 of $137.4 million. National organizations dealing with public policy training and advocacy only accounted for 5.5 percent of that total. If we are to change the climate around nonprofit advocacy, the groups that promote, protect, and support nonprofit advocacy need much better financial support.

4. **Management consulting and academic centers must build advocacy into required core curriculum**. While graduate public policy and public affairs programs offer courses on the policy process, lobbying, and other advocacy activities, it is not very common for nonprofit management programs to offer such classes. Of the more than 270 universities or colleges that offer nonprofit-related courses and/or degree programs, only about 35 provide courses or units within courses that focus specifically on how to implement nonprofit advocacy strategies.[20] Of those that have advocacy course offerings only a few have advocacy as part of the required curriculum. As more people launch or renew careers in the nonprofit sector by earning degrees and certificates in nonprofit management, advocacy should be elevated to a mandatory part of the curriculum, thereby reaching more nonprofit practitioners and equalizing the importance of advocacy with other functions of management and leadership. Whether it is a workshop on leadership for board members or a strategic planning session with executive directors or a lobby how-to workshop for staff, information about public policy participation should be integrated into the discussion.

5. **Make sure nonprofit lobby laws do not serve as a disincentive to policy participation**. Tufts University Professor Jeffrey Berry, our colleague in conducting the SNAP research, has used the SNAP findings to argue that the "underlying answer to why the 501(c)(3)s' constituencies are at a severe competitive disadvantage in legislative policymaking is that government has decided that nonprofits should be constrained in their lobbying." (Berry 2003, 147-48) Berry concludes his book, *A Voice for Nonprofits*, "If the law were different, there surely

---

[20] We distinguish courses that teach how to do advocacy from more traditional public policy courses that teach how to understand policy and the process but do not teach specific lobbying skills, or organizing tactics, etc. The figure, 270, is reached by adding the number of institutional members of the National Association of Schools of Public Administration and Public Affairs with the approximately 40 institutional members of the Nonprofit Academic Centers Council. There may be some overlapping members – hence this is an approximation.

would be more lobbying" (165). He argues that the limits on nonprofit lobbying are "unjust."

Whether existing law is unjust or not is certainly worthy of public debate. While it is important to compare limitations imposed on nonprofit organizations with those imposed on for-profit entities or professional or business associations, it is also vitally important to assess whether the complex labyrinth of state and federal laws serve as a disincentive to participation. At the federal level, nonprofit organizations must follow the tax code and rules generated by the IRS. They must also comply with the Lobbying Disclosure Act if they lobby the U.S. Congress and selected executive branch officials above specified thresholds. They must also comply with what is commonly called the Byrd Rule if they advocate in the executive or legislative branch for a grant or contract above a specified threshold. They must also comply with OMB Circular A-122 limits on lobbying if they receive federal grants. In each these cases, the definition of lobbying is slightly different. And that is just the federal level. Most states have disclosure requirements for lobbying activities. Their definitions of lobbying are often different from those at the federal level. For example, some states require disclosure of attempts to influence executive branch activities, which the federal tax rules do not consider lobbying.[21]

This short, admittedly facile, description of the complexity of laws is an attempt to highlight the need for thoughtful discussion on how to harmonize state and federal laws on lobby limits and disclosure of policy participation in order to simplify compliance and ensure any requirements do not serve as an additional impediment to participation. The need for harmonizing and simplifying laws and regulations, however, cannot be accomplished devoid of political context. Changing

---

[21] One reviewer of this book wondered whether the confusion in definition of lobbying vitiated the value of our survey questions, thinking that different states may have rules that are different from the federal rules. It is not a problem for our survey research or focus groups. The differing definitions on lobbying at the state level only refer to disclosure requirements at the state level. For 501(c)(3) groups, the operative rules are the federal tax code on what they are permitted to do. This clarity is less true for electioneering communications where state law may differ slightly from federal. But in all cases, 501(c)(3) organizations are not permitted to engage in electioneering. Similarly, there are differences between federal grant rules regarding lobbying and some state rules, particularly for specific programs. But in no case, except where expressly allowed in a program statute, can grantees use government funds to lobby.

the climate around nonprofit advocacy (discussed in #1 above) must serve as a precursor to any serious undertaking that involves changing laws and regulations.

6. **Differentiated public policy training is needed for different roles within nonprofit management and leadership.** For a nonprofit to be an effective and accountable player in the public policy arena, it is important for the executive director, staff, key volunteers, and the board of directors to be knowledgeable and involved decision makers. Each of these jobs requires similar and different skills and abilities with respect to advocacy and public policy. Moreover, such training must be designed to reflect different levels of understanding, ranging from novice to advance. Training offered by management support organizations, academic centers and advocacy training groups should take into account various roles, as well as the differing levels of understanding of public policy participation. Training offered by the various support systems also needs to be targeted to experts, such as lawyers and accountants, providing assistance and advice to nonprofits. Many of these experts are not familiar with the intricacies of nonprofit policy participation.

Conclusion

There are persistent barriers to nonprofit policy participation that must be addressed if there is to be a robust civil society. Nonprofits account for roughly ten percent of economic activity and roughly ten percent of the workforce. Millions of Americans work for nonprofit organizations, contribute to nonprofit organizations, or are involved with nonprofit organizations as volunteers or board members. To the extent nonprofit organizations become more involved in public policy, their actions will be seen by everyday people in every part of the country. Our fondest hope is that a nonprofit sector actively engaged in public policy will rub off on the community, thereby strengthening civic participation.

Even if this ultimate objective is not achieved, we believe stronger participation by the nonprofit sector is healthy for our society. Nonprofit organizations often speak for those who have no voice or less of a voice than powerful special interests, and thereby help to equalize imbalances in power. Nonprofit organizations help to elevate key social and economic issues and put a human face to these problems; they are central to the vitality of the communities in which we live, and in that respect are important representatives in a pluralistic society.

Unfortunately, nonprofit policy participation occurs in fits and starts. It mostly occurs during periods of crisis, but ceases when the crisis abates. Some nonprofits, particularly those involved in providing direct services, view policy participation as beyond their scope, if not an inappropriate activity. Words like "lobbying" are associated with activities that are looked upon with disdain, which leads to a problem: nonprofit advocacy is limited and intermittent.

Even when motivated, many nonprofit leaders are not ready to engage in public policy. They lack the financial resources, organizational infrastructure and staff skills. Our advocacy support systems are very weak, making it that much more difficult for nonprofits to hurdle various barriers. As a result, nonprofit policy participation, when it occurs, appears to be an anomaly. The objective of this research is to lay the groundwork for changing this situation – to make advocacy a part of the everyday routine for most nonprofit organizations.

Ten Ways to Stimulate Nonprofit Participation in Policy Making

1. Training and support services demonstrate how public policy participation can help a nonprofit organization achieve its mission and work more effectively; in other words, let's find ways to motivate nonprofits to participate.

2. Foundations and other funders issue funding initiatives for advocacy activities, increase their use of general operating grants and remove language restricting lobbying from grant letters.

3. Nonprofit executives assign specific staff – other than the executive director – to monitor policy, mobilize members and undertake direct lobbying campaigns.

4. Universities make public policy participation an integral part of the nonprofit management curriculum, augmenting the work of public policy, public affairs and social work programs.

5. Nonprofit associations communicate the urgency of policy developments to their members and constituents and include them in decision-making about policy and strategy.

6. Nonprofit infrastructure organizations make way for policy to permeate their training and publication offerings, including leadership development for executives and board members.

7. Management support organizations teach how policy participation and change can promote organizational effectiveness and efficiencies.

8. Infrastructure and support organizations offer training on government relations including partnering, lobbying skills, substantive policy issues and the legal rights of nonprofits to advocate.

9. Everyone concerned with the sector works to give lobbying a better name by educating the public on what it is and how it is part of our democratic process and serves mission related goals.

10. Policymakers remove legal obstacles for nonprofits to become equal players with for-profits in the policy process and open new channels, such as nonprofit advisory boards, for ongoing communications with charities.

Chapter 2
The Legacy and Challenge of Nonprofit Advocacy

The story of nonprofit advocacy in American history is a key component of our nation's civic life. The United States was founded by the most aggressive acts a people can take against government – mobilization and revolution. Shortly thereafter, associations and social movements flourished to organize people and advocate policies before a young democratic government. Indeed, the story of social achievement flowing from organized advocacy through which nonprofits mobilize citizen participation in the policymaking process is an important part of the American legacy. From civil rights, to education, to clean water and workforce protections, the list of important policy changes that have improved our quality of life is long and something of which to be proud. Yet, at the beginning of the 21st century, many nonprofits exhibit considerable discomfort with the role of advocacy, lobbying and other forms of policy participation. This state of being is troubling considering the importance of the nonprofit sector in society today. In his historical overview of the nonprofit sector, Peter Dobkin Hall notes that other than England, "no other nation has depended as heavily as has the United States on private nonprofit organizations for performing so many public activities."[22]

This chapter includes the following topics. [Note that it is not intended to be a scholarly, historical, or legal treatise. It is rather, a cursory look at events and forces that motivated this inquiry into the status of nonprofits' participation in public policymaking and ways to strengthen it.]

- Historical observations about the role of nonprofit advocacy
- Societal and policy influences on nonprofits' participation in the policymaking process
- Discussion of the "Istook Amendment" as one of the epic struggles over nonprofit advocacy rights.
- The role of the growing field of nonprofit infrastructure as related to policy participation.
- Observations about citizen participation in the democratic process and nonprofits' role as fostering agents.

---

[22] Peter Dobkin Hall, "A Historical Overview of the Private Nonprofit Sector," *The Nonprofit Sector: A Research Handbook*, ed. Walter W. Powell (New Haven, CT: Yale University Press, 1987).

Notwithstanding that nonprofit advocacy has played an important role in our society since the founding of the country, we have seen a decided shift away from public policy activity in the last 30 years or so. This chapter highlights five factors that may be significant in discouraging or limiting nonprofit policy participation and that helped shape our research:

- **The role government grants, contracts, and fees play with regard to nonprofit advocacy.** Since the 1960s there has been a large increase in government assistance to nonprofits.[23] Some have speculated that this partnership has had a deleterious impact on nonprofits' engagement in public policy matters, forcing nonprofits to focus more on service delivery;

- **A spate of legislative and regulatory proposals that would have dramatically limited nonprofit advocacy.** These proposals, most of which were defeated, may have left as their lasting legacy the chilling of nonprofit speech;

- **An emphasis on improved nonprofit management that highlighted various efficiencies from the for-profit sector, but did not convey the importance of public policy involvement.** This has left an impression that fundraising and organizational efficiencies are expected of our nonprofit leaders, but that advocacy is not – and that it is not valued;

- **Nonprofit "infrastructure" similarly places little emphasis on advocacy.** From academic courses preparing nonprofit leaders to the ongoing activities of the national organizations providing nonprofit sector leadership, little priority is given to public policy participation; and

---

[23] Federal outlays for human resources, excluding Social Security, jumped from $17.4 billion in 1960 to $990.1 billion in 2004 (see Historical Tables, Budget of the U.S. Government). While not all of this category of government spending goes to nonprofits and while there are other categories of government spending nonprofits depend on (e.g., housing, economic development, environmental protections), it is an indication of the growth in spending. Alan J. Abramson, Lester M. Salamon, and C. Eugene Steuerle provide a more detailed analysis of the federal budget impact on nonprofits from the 1980s to the mid-1990s in "The Nonprofit Sector and the Federal Budget: Recent History and Future Directions," in *Nonprofits & Government: Collaboration and Conflict*, by Elizabeth T. Boris & C. Eugene Steuerle (eds), 1999, Urban Institute Press.

- **Foundations provide far too little in support of nonprofit public policy participation.** A very low percentage of foundation grants are aimed at building advocacy capacity or for implementing advocacy activities.

These factors contribute to an environment that suggests to nonprofits that service is a higher priority than engaging in public policy.

Beyond Tocqueville: The Roots of Nonprofit Advocacy

Since its earliest days, America's most prolific social product has been associations, which today we call nonprofit organizations. Benjamin Franklin may have been among the first and foremost of early countrymen to promote associations. Franklin helped create a discussion club of fellow tradesmen, known as the Junto. (Isaacson 2003). In November 1727, Franklin persuaded 12 of his friends to form a club dedicated to mutual improvement. That group met every Friday night to discuss the topics of the day. The group lasted for 40 years and eventually became the nucleus of the American Philosophical Society. It morphed from a supper club into a very effective forum for sharing ideas that benefited both its members and the rest of society. In Franklin's club, the rule was that every three months each member had to write or expound on an essay. According to Jefferson, there were small fines for "expressions of positiveness in opinion or direct contradiction" (56). When the club threatened to become too big, rather than expand it beyond its convivial scale, Franklin arranged that each member should go out and start another independent club on the same lines, such as the Vine and the Union.

Out of those meetings, the Junto over the years invented the first subscription library in North America, the most advanced volunteer fire department of the time, the first public hospital in Pennsylvania, an insurance company, a constabulary, improved streetlights, paving and what became the University of Pennsylvania. As Franklin said in the motto for the library he and the Junto founded, "To pour forth benefits for the common good is divine" (Isaacson 2003, 103).

From these early beginnings, there has been controversy surrounding nonprofits' rightful role in making and shaping the rules of society. During the writing of the Constitution, James Madison, in Federalist 10 (1787), warned against the growing power of associations as the creators of special interest influence. He wrote, "The instability, injustice, and confusion introduced into the public councils, have, in truth, been the mortal diseases under which popular governments have everywhere perished; as they continue to be the favorite and fruitful topics from which the adversaries to liberty derive their most specious declamations" (Rossiter 1961, 77).

The Madison perspective, which held that popular political control would lead to great social unrest, did not comport with the rapid growth of early nonprofits like the Junto. The French observer, Alexis de Tocqueville, noted that:

> "Americans of all ages, all conditions, and all dispositions constantly form associations. They have not only commercial and manufacturing companies, in which all take part, but associations of a thousand other kinds, religious, moral, serious, futile, general or restricted, enormous or diminutive. The Americans make associations to give entertainments, to found seminaries, to build inns, to construct churches, to diffuse books, to send missionaries to the antipodes; in this manner they found hospitals, prisons, and schools. If it is proposed to inculcate some truth or to foster some feeling by the encouragement of a great example, they form a society. Wherever at the head of some new undertaking you see the government in France, or a man of rank in England, in the United States you will be sure to find an association." (Tocqueville 1969, 513).

In 1831, Tocqueville, who was then 25, and Gustave de Beaumont, 28, received permission to travel to the United States for the purpose of studying the U.S. prison system. John Huebler, undertaking a graduate student project for the Council of Michigan Foundations and Grand Valley State University, writes about the Tocqueville-Beaumont visit. Huebler cites Cornell Professor Isaac Kramnick's introduction to a recent edition of *Democracy in America* in arguing that Tocqueville and Beaumont actually were looking for an excuse to leave France because they had disagreements with the new government of Louis Philippe and that what they really wanted to do was study U.S. democracy, especially since Tocqueville had his own political ambitions. ("Philanthropy Described in *Democracy in America* by de Tocqueville"[24] (Huebler 2003)).

---

[24] http://www.learningtogive.org/papers/concepts/americatocqueville.htm

Tocqueville and Beaumont spent nine months traveling throughout the United States, spending most of their time in Boston, New York, and Philadelphia. They traveled as far west as Michigan (which was about as far west as anybody got in those days) and went as far south as New Orleans, LA. They had little difficulty arranging meetings with some of the most prominent and influential thinkers of the early 19th century, including presidents, lawyers, bankers and settlers, and they even met with Charles Carroll of Carrollton, MD – the last surviving signer of the Declaration of Independence.

It was through these experiences that Tocqueville wrote *Democracy in America*, a two-volume book on America's social and political institutions, and what some regard as a seminal piece on the emergence of philanthropy in the United States. Tocqueville "…saw this country's network of voluntary associations not so much as service providers but as the 'moral associations' where such values as charity and responsibility to others are taught and where the nation's crusades take root" (O'Connell 1994, 43). As Tocqueville said, "Nothing, in my opinion, is more deserving of our attention than the intellectual and moral associations of America. The political and industrial associations of that country strike us forcibly; but the others elude our observation, or if we discover them, we understand them imperfectly because we have hardly ever seen anything of the kind. It must be acknowledged, however, that they are as necessary to the American people as the former, and perhaps more so. In democratic countries the science of association is the mother of science; the progress of all the rest depends upon the progress it has made."

Tocqueville also saw a mutually beneficial relationship between voluntary associations and political parties. The practice of politics fueled the formation and participation in associations. "So one may think of political associations as great free schools to which all citizens come to be taught the general theory of associations" (Tocqueville 1969, 522). For Tocqueville, civil associations serve to strengthen political association. "As soon as several Americans have conceived a sentiment or an idea that they want to produce before the world, they seek each other out, and when found, they unite. Thenceforth they are no longer isolated individuals, but a power conspicuous from the distance whose actions serve as an example; when it speaks, men listen" (516).

Yet in nearly the same breath, Tocqueville also drew a line between political and voluntary associations, suggesting that limits on the political role of associations are sometimes justified in a civil society, "I certainly do not think that a nation is always in a position to allow its citizens an absolute right of political association, and I even doubt whether there has ever been at any time a nation in which it was wise not to put any limits to the freedom of association" (ibid., 524). As discussed throughout this chapter, the questions of whether and where to draw a legal boundary line between nonprofits' political and policy activities, and service activities are recurring themes still hotly debated today.

While Tocqueville was describing political and voluntary associations, public policy advocacy was already a central driving cause behind the growth and effectiveness of the early nonprofit sector. In the early- to mid-1800s voluntary associations learned to practice democratic decision-making and the civic skills necessary to operate in a democracy. The internal organizational operations of the Grange was one such example. "Because the mimicry of U.S. rules of taxpaying and representative governance was so central to group procedures, members gained knowledge very relevant to what they needed to know as American citizens" (Skocpol 1999, 68).

Nonprofits also began to engage in formal efforts to influence public policy and even lobby. Groups such as the Mechanics Union of Trade Associations led the labor rights movement. Abolitionist causes were led by the Anti-Slavery Society, the Liberator and hundreds of anti-slavery groups (Arons 1999, 11). Temperance and suffrage organizations were also among the voluntary organizations that actively launched grassroots lobbying campaigns – including mass letter-writing to Congress – to win civil and economic rights (Arons 1999; Hall 1987; Schudson 1998; Skocpol 1999). Theda Skocpol (1999, 69) points out that nonprofit lobbying in the late 1800s and early 20th century was not only about the practice of democracy but was also about power. "Voluntary membership federations, in short, have often rivaled political parties in affording organized leverage in civic and legislative affairs to large numbers of Americans. As American women's federations splendidly demonstrated in their campaigns for mothers' pensions and the Sheppard Towner Act in the 1910s, campaigns coordinated by many states at once can have a decisive impact on elected representatives, regardless of party."

By the first part of the 20th century the nonprofit sector, largely because of its organizing, mobilizing, and lobbying, helped change workers rights and child labor laws, freed slaves, created momentum for women's voting rights, and won programs for rural farmers. The groups behind these victories were practicing democracy internally with members and externally with citizens and government. During this period a defining characteristic of nonprofit organizations was advocacy and speaking out to promote a just society. They were successful in part because many of the associations were led by the middle and upper classes, and the organizations were as powerful as they were numerous (Schudson 1998, 108). Although the use of the label "golden age" probably should not be applied to nonprofit advocacy, one may argue that the period covering the late 19th and early 20th centuries was one in which advocacy was a fundamental function and citizens benefited from regular civic engagement through associations. It was also a period where the associations served as one vehicle for mitigating the power of the elite and influential.

The Professionalization of Government

Beginning in the late 1800s, the locus for creating and implementing public policy shifted from nonprofits, including political parties, to the federal government largely due to the civil service reform movement. (Schudson 1998, 155). This process of centralization was especially detrimental to nonprofits outside of Washington that did not have a day-to-day presence.[25] Based in the grassroots, nonprofits were accustomed to gathering petitions and presenting them to government. By the turn of the century, however, "the petition...would in time give way to the lobby." (Schudson 1998, 100). We can only speculate that some nonprofits, particularly those outside state capitals or the nation's capital, lost power or discontinued policy advocacy because of the physical distances between them and where policy was being made.

Some nonprofits, particularly those in urban areas, used the skills of lobbyists to their advantage. Several of the most successful advocacy groups of the early 20th century were the National Consumers League,

---

[25] Nonprofits outside of Washington focused more on improving community life at the local level. For example, the early community welfare organizations in the southwest, the "mutualistas," advocated for better treatment from police and local authorities. See http://www.cr.nps.gov/history/online_books/5views/5views5c.htm.

General Federation of Women's Clubs and the American Association of University Women. Their respective lobbying efforts led to the enactment of mothers' pensions, access to college for women and minimum-wage laws. During this period, Jane Addams founded the first settlement house to help inner-city poor people in Chicago. Her conceptualization of a new settlement house as a place to provide "higher civic and social life," connected the functions of public policy advocacy and charity as complementary services. The organizing and lobbying of Addams and her colleagues Alice Hamilton and Florence Kelley raised the public health, safety, and environmental problems of the inner city to the public policy platform of big city government.[26] The efforts and tactics of Addams and Hull House were replicated by other groups; and for a while, the management model of service with advocacy kept the service-advocacy divide from happening in other parts of the sector.[27] The advocacy of Hull House, the American Association of Labor Legislation, the American Medical Association, the PTA, and other groups to establish child labor laws, old-age and workers' pensions, minimum wage, fair labor standards, and health care, paved the way for the Social Security Act signed into law by President Franklin Delano Roosevelt in 1935.[28]

The Mid-20th Century: Social Movements Rising

Nonprofits began to play prominent, active roles in a broad range of social policies. Nonprofits, for example, worked with government in the construction of the social programs launched under Roosevelt, such as Title XX of the Social Security Act, which pumped millions of dollars into groups such as Catholic Charities and other nonprofits. During the 1950s, nonprofits were the central organizing vehicles for the nuclear-freeze and anti-communist movements, respectively (Hall, 1987). And arguably the most important judicial act of the decade, if not the generation, came in the 1954 *Brown v. Board of Education of Topeka,*

---

[26] This sense of civic engagement and policy involvement was present in other nonprofits. In 1919 the PTA, for example, urged members to attend citizenship and government study classes and throughout the early 1900s lobbied school systems to install basic safety precautions for children in public schools. See http://www.pta.org/aboutpta/history/mile1910.asp.

[27] Addams was also part of the founding of the NAACP, the nation's leading advocacy organization on behalf of African Americans, in 1910, see www.naacp.org. This summary describes the role of charities, not other nonprofits such as unions.

[28] For a chronological history of the Social Security Act see, http://www.ssa.gov/history/history.html.

Kansas, school desegregation decision by the U.S. Supreme Court.[29] This landmark case, led by Thurgood Marshall, then the chief counsel for the National Association for the Advancement of Colored People (NAACP), demonstrated, ten years before the 1960s civil rights legislation was passed, the importance of consistent advocacy by nonprofit leaders to achieve social justice.

By the time of the 1960s, movement builders turned to nonprofits as an outlet to implement ongoing action directed toward social problems. The issues highlighted in the 60s still dominate the nonprofit landscape today. Catalysts for nonprofit advocacy during the sixties and early 70s included John Kenneth Galbraith's *The Affluent Society* (1958) and Michael Harrington's *The Other America* (1962), which launched efforts to address the gap between the richest and the poorest in this country; *Rachel* Carson's *Silent Spring* (1962), which spawned a powerful environmental movement; Ralph Nader's *Unsafe at Any Speed* (1965), which led to a sustained consumer movement; Betty Friedan's *The Feminine Mystique* (1963), which propelled the women's movement; freedom rides and the formation of the Student Nonviolent Coordinating Committee (early 60s), which drew national attention to the civil rights movement; police attacks on Greenwich Village's Stonewall Inn (1969), which led to the first Gay Liberation Front meeting and the start of a gay rights movement; the work funded by foundations such as that Ford Foundation that led to the genesis of the community action program and important social legislation[30]; and the formation of Common Cause by John Gardner in 1970 to be a citizen's lobby to promote political reforms such as those dealing with money and politics.

The hard work of the social movements paid off and in doing so, made clear that advocacy was vitally important to the nonprofit sector. Some of

---

[29] *Brown v. Board of Education*, 347 US 483 (1954), *Brown v. Board of Education*, 349 US 294 (1955).

[30] The Ford Foundation describes philanthropy as a vehicle of social reform at http://www. fordfound.org/elibrary/documents/0173/115.cfm. The Foundation describes its Great Cities, Gray Areas, and Community Development initiatives and how they led to policy changes in the country. "[T]his sequence of programs has been largely responsible for the public's perception of Ford Foundation as an 'up front' social welfare institution, characterized by… a willingness to test the outer edges of advocacy and citizen participation…"

the most important social achievements of the 20th century had nonprofits in the forefront. Notably, they include both social movements driven by local power and nationally led institutional initiatives[31]:

- Migrant labor laws
- Child protection laws
- Social Security Act – old-age pensions*
- School desegregation
- 1964 Civil Rights Act and 1965 Voting Rights Act*
- Medicare and Medicaid*
- Government support for the arts and culture
- Welfare protections
- Housing assistance*
- Clean Water and Clear Air Acts*
- Community reinvestment requirements on lending institutions*
- And many more[32]

There is absolutely no doubt that nonprofit advocacy has made a difference in terms of the quality of life in this country for people of all backgrounds and political persuasions. Given these high points in the history of nonprofit advocacy, it would seem counterintuitive that 30 to 40 years later we need an organized effort to strengthen nonprofit advocacy.

From Agitators to Partners: The Era of Big Government

The social movements and institutional initiatives of the 1960s and 70s left an important footprint on the social fabric of the United States as new rights, new leaders and new institutions were born. This rise of citizen group power also initiated a new relationship with government. In the modern era of nonprofits – from 1960 to today – the advocacy role of nonprofits was the focal point for what has been described as a series of "boundary wars" between nonprofits and government (Van Til 2000, 32). While the government and the nonprofit sector entered into a "paradigm of partnership," the partners also fought numerous heated battles over the

---

[31] * denotes laws and policies established as a result of institutional initiatives by nonprofits in conjunction with the work of policymakers.
[32] When we include the role of unions, the list becomes even larger. For example, minimum wage laws, workplace safety protections, and fair labor standards are just a few that can be listed.

scope of nonprofits' role in the public policy process.[33] During this period nonprofit advocacy reached a zenith in terms of power due to the public passion and involvement in social movements that were successful in building institutions to carry out their values.[34] Following the volatile era of the 60s and early 70s, advocacy took a back seat to the service role as social movements evolved into institutions and the era of partnership with government became more financially and politically complex (Salamon 1987, 1995, 2002).

The Great Society programs (some mentioned earlier) increased the size of federal bureaucracy and allocated billions of dollars in new spending for social services including welfare, housing, health and education (Grønbjerg and Smith 1999, 146-49).[35] As the federal government went to scale with these programs, there was a deliberate effort to engage nonprofits as service providers and as informers of the policymaking process. Ironically, nonprofits got closer to government, but as junior financial partners rather than as advocates. Grants, contracts and fee payments became the vehicles for what Lester Salamon calls "third-party government," to describe the nonprofit-government relationship that began in the sixties and still grows.

While the federal government under the Kennedy and Johnson Administrations wanted, and increasingly sought nonprofit participation and expertise in program design and implementation, local government felt threatened by some of the Great Society programs, including the creation of the community action agencies. Nicholas Lemann's seminal two-part series in *The Atlantic Monthly* (1988, 1989) describes factors that contributed to the difficulty in implementing the War on Poverty, one of which was the role nonprofits were to play. A key element was the creation of community action agencies.

> "The theory of community action was that what poor people
> needed were new neighborhood-based organizations. As it
> were, there were many government efforts to help the poor

---

[33] Salamon (1995) first used this term to describe the relationship between nonprofits and government that makes up the social compact.

[34] For example, the establishment of government offices dealing with equal opportunity and civil rights were the result of nonprofit advocacy.

[35] For an excellent description of the evolution of the contracting relationship between government and nonprofits see Smith and Lipsky (*Nonprofits for Hire* 1993).

– nutrition programs, employment programs, welfare programs – but there was no coordination among them, and no concerted attempt had been made to find out what services the people in the poor neighborhoods most needed. Under community action, the government would set up a kind of planning board in the neighborhood, the board would consult with the poor people there, and, eventually, a mission would emerge. In principle, a Community Action Agency could do anything – it was not an anti-poverty program so much as a mechanism through which new anti-poverty programs would be invented. Also, rather than take on all the traditional functions of a government agency itself, it would be small and would coordinate the work of existing agencies. The only rule was that the solution to the neighborhood's problems could not be imposed from above (that is, from Washington)" (ibid. 1988).

As Lemann notes, the federal funding for community action agencies bypassed the state and local government machinery, going directly to nonprofits. This created a power struggle in which local and state governments were surely to win. As Karen Paget wrote in an *American Prospect* article: "These programs threatened local power structures. Long before Nixon tried to kill them entirely, these programs were partly neutralized by Democrats after fierce opposition from mostly Democratic local elected officials. In a series of amendments in the late 1960s, Community Action Agencies were put under City Hall's control; governors were given 'check-offs' before federal programs such as VISTA could operate locally; and only a few anti-poverty programs, such as Head Start, retained direct federal funding" (1999, May).

Public employee unions also raised concerns about the direct funding of nonprofits by the federal government. The issue was not over whether government wanted a partnership with nonprofits, it had more to do with who had the authority to grant the money; state and local authorities definitely did not like being cut out of the loop, and the public employee unions concurred, especially since state and local government jobs were at stake. Notwithstanding this issue of financial and political control, government found it more agreeable to outsource services to nonprofits and nonprofits liked the role of service provider.

As more and more money flowed to nonprofits from local, state and federal governments, the grant and contract relationship proceeded in a businesslike fashion, as did the advocacy activities of nonprofits. Nonprofits learned to defend the government pipelines of revenue vital to organizational viability. Smith and Lipsky (1993, 179) succinctly describe the government relations paradigm of third-party government: "The emergence of a new relationship between government and nonprofit providers suggests that the United States is developing a corporatist politics of service provision. Public policy is made with close consultation of affected parties; those consulted are expected to, and would have a stake in, the agreed-upon arrangement. Corporatism would make service providers more powerful, but it would also constrain their advocacy." It appeared the risk-taking, social movement mindset of nonprofits was changing as service delivery emerged as a primary mission of organizations and as the dependence on government funding became more complete. Later in this book we will discuss the findings of survey, interview and focus group information on the influence of government funding on nonprofits' participation in the public policy process.

De-clawing the Foundations

Private foundations have been part of the nonprofit landscape since the mid-1800s and were encouraged by government through creation of charitable trusts. The growth in the number and size of grant making foundations in the post-World War II era also gave way to considerable congressional scrutiny, particularly in the 1950s and 1960s. While Marion Fremont-Smith provides a definitive history of foundation regulation, our purpose is to better understand why foundations are skittish about support for advocacy.

As early as 1915, Congress expressed concern about the activities of foundations. It created the Walsh Commission, which reported in 1916 that foundations were being used by industrialists to control social life in this country. It recommended a number of regulations, including a limit on the life of a foundation, but no congressional action occurred. The 1940s saw a number of recommendations from the Treasury Department and Congress to reform foundations, but no legislation passed Congress. The Tax Reform Act of 1950 contained some changes in law, most notably dealing with foundation self-dealing in response to a Senate congressional investigation of Royal Little, the head of Textron who had acquired nearly 70 different companies outside the textile industry in building one of the world's largest and most successful conglomerates. Little was accused of using a foundation to finance several of his business dealings.

There were further congressional investigations into foundation behavior during the 1950s and 1960s. The most significant was a House investigation led by Rep. Wright Patman (D-TX). Patman maintained that most large foundations existed not for charitable purposes but as tax dodges for the wealthy families that established them. He called for strict regulation of foundations, noting the "destructive effect [of foundations] on our tax base."[36] (Philanthropy Roundtable, website)

There were dramatic congressional hearings during the late 1960s highlighting a number of foundation abuses. But the most memorable part of the hearings was the testimony of Ford Foundation President McGeorge Bundy. He was asked to testify about a series of grants made for what Congress was calling political purposes. Among the controversial Ford Foundation grants were ones to:

- Southern Regional Council to help voter registration drives for black voters (1966);
- Congress on Racial Equity for a voter registration drive (1967);
- A highly volatile school desegregation project in New York (that possibly involved an attempt to influence legislation); and
- Members of the late Robert F. Kennedy's staff to help their transition to private life (Fishman and Schwarz 1995, 594; Troyer 2000, 20).

Following the explosive hearing, Congress in 1969 passed the Tax Reform Act, which provided new accountability standards for foundations, including a requirement that foundations pay out six percent of their assets annually (which was changed to five percent in 1976), regulation of foundation administration, enforcement sanctions, an excise tax of four percent on net investment income, and much more, including a working definition of private foundations (which did not exist before). The new law also had limitations on lobbying by foundations and some restrictions on funding lobbying activities; however, there were no restrictions on funding broader advocacy

---

[36] Philanthropy Roundtable, "A Timeline of Congressional Oversight," http://www.philanthropyroundtable.org/magazines/2004/julyaugust/timelinejulyaugust.htm

activities. For all intents and purposes, the Tax Reform Act of 1969 was the start of the modern era of philanthropy.

Foundations were shell-shocked by the new law, and it has had a lasting impact. Karen Paget captures this well as she writes, "Waldemar Nielsen, an eminent observer and critic of foundations, wrote that the experience 'left most of the prominent figures in philanthropy in a state of panic, almost terror.' Indeed, fear of congressional hearings and new restrictions is part of the collective DNA of the foundation community, passed on as a cautionary tale to successive generations of program officers." (1999, May) Peter Frumkin of Harvard's Kennedy School notes that another lasting result of the Tax Reform Act was to make foundations more bureaucratic.

Many foundation presidents, Frumkin argues, were advised by their legal departments to be cautious in review of all grants and all applicants. The result was that the 1970s was the decade in which foundations became much more heavily structured. Smaller foundations for the first time began hiring full-time program officers, and larger foundations hired more staff. Thus, the average amount a foundation spent on administration rose from 9.7 percent of grant outlays in 1969 to 16.3 percent by 1975, a level that has persisted since. (*Lagemann 1999*) The increased staff mostly came from other foundations, which helped to professionalize grant making. But by limiting the pool of those making decisions on grants so narrowly and by abiding by the cautious recommendations of legal advisers, foundations were also limiting the grants to programs that were safe, conventional, and respectable instead of bold and daring – and that meant very little for public policy work by nonprofits.

According to information from the Foundation Center, private foundation giving for public policy and social action ranks near the bottom of types of grants made.[37] While there are limitations imposed on lobbying by foundations, there is no restriction on broader activities regarding the public policy arena. They can speak out on broad policy issues. They can provide grant support to nonprofits engaged in public policy matters. And certain

---

[37] See "Foundation Giving Trends," Chronicle of Philanthropy, March 7, 2002. It is difficult to get precise data on this point because the research categories are very imprecise. According to the 2000 data reported in the Chronicle of Philanthropy, 12.4 percent of grants made were for society and public benefit. The National Committee for Responsive Philanthropy notes in various publications that foundation support for public policy work is very low. However, with funds given as general operating support it is impossible to categorize them.

foundations, particularly community foundations, do not face the same restrictions as private foundations on lobbying.

Even passage of the 1976 Tax Act, which made it clear that it was permissible for charities to lobby and that a range of policy activities are not defined as lobbying, has not been enough of a motivating factor to heal the wounds of 1969.[38] On a more optimistic note, there is some evidence that the trend may be changing, but if it is, it is not yet widespread.[39] Some foundations may be heeding the advice of Thomas A. Troyer, who was an attorney in the Department of Treasury's Tax Policy Office before going into private practice in 1965. Reflecting on his work with the Council on Foundations during the 1969 hearings he wrote, "The limitation on foundation lobbying in 1969 rested on no stated ground not equally applicable to public charities." He added, "The special restrictions on foundation participation in political campaigns and support of voter registration arose from specific examples presented to the Ways and Means Committee in 1969 and, hence, did not in themselves point to similar restrictions on public charities" (Troyer 2000, 27).

The Troyer message may gain additional traction with release of a December 9, 2004, letter from the IRS to Charity Lobbying in the Public Interest (now called Center for Lobbying in the Public Interest) regarding whether foundations may fund lobbying activities.[40] The IRS states, "Yes, private foundations may make grants…to public charities…that lobby, with certain restrictions. The tax rules include explicit safe harbors for general

---

[38] The 1976 Tax Act and 1990 regulations carved out several exceptions under which private foundations may lobby and may fund charities that lobby. See Internal Revenue Code §4945-d2, §4911 and information from Charity Lobbying in the Public Interest (www.clpi.org) and Alliance for Justice (www.afj.org) on the lobbying rules governing private foundations.

[39] In light of increasing pressure on philanthropy to fill gaps in government spending on nonprofit programs, some foundations have determined that it is a sound investment decision to fund groups that lobby. See Ruth Holton and Gary Yates, "How Foundations Can Help in Tough Times," The Chronicle of Philanthropy, December 12, 2002. See also, "Foundations and Public Policy: Illustrations of High Impact Grantmaking," Charity Lobbying in the Public Interest. Additionally, an initiative promoted by the Council on Foundations encourages community foundations to engage more in public policy matters.

[40] See letter from Joseph J. Urban, Manager, Exempt Organizations Technical Guidance & Quality Assurance, Internal Revenue Service, December 9, 2004, to Charity Lobbying in the Public Interest. The letter is available at http://www.clpi.org/doc_pdf/clpiIRS.pdf. Charity Lobbying in the Public Interest has recently changed its name to Center for Lobbying in the Public Interest.

support grants." The IRS adds that as long as grants are not earmarked for lobbying, they "will not be taxable expenditures." The letter also notes that private foundations can make a grant for specific projects that include lobbying as long as no part of the grant is earmarked for lobbying and the size of the grant does not exceed amounts for activities of the project that are not lobbying. The IRS also makes very clear that community foundations can lobby and can provide grants for lobbying within the limits of allowable lobbying by IRS.

Even before the IRS letter, there was a buzz among foundations leaders about re-engaging in public policy. For years, conservative foundations had pursued public policy advocacy through their grant making. Several articles highlighted this fact, including three reports from the National Committee for Responsive Philanthropy that noted conservative foundations were providing general support to selected organizations that were shaping conservative policy agendas.[41] In the first report, Sally Covington examined the funding philosophies and activities of twelve conservative foundations during the years 1992-1994. During that period, these foundations gave away $300 million, targeting $210 million of it to support sixteen national think tanks and advocacy organizations; nine media groups; nine law reform groups; five state and regional think tanks and advocacy groups; three religion reform groups; and two philanthropic institutions and networks. According to Covington, these grantees represented a coherent nationwide network linking conservatives in academia, Congress, the media, law firms, think tanks, and churches. Between them, they created and maintained an unrelenting rightward pressure on colleges and universities, newspapers, magazines, and TV stations, state legislatures, the Congress, the federal judiciary, and on philanthropy itself. They not only influenced public debate; in many instances they defined it.

Today, mainstream philanthropy sees the importance of advocacy. For example, the Northern California Grantmakers' Association had been

---

[41] Sally Covington, "Moving a Public Policy Agenda: The Strategic Philanthropy of Conservative Foundations," *Responsive Philanthropy* (1998). See also Sally Covington, "How Conservative Philanthropies and Think Tanks Transform U.S. Policy," *Covert Action Quarterly*, 63 (1998): 6-16.

Another key report was: Jeff Krehely, Meaghan House and Emily Kernan, "Conservative Foundations and Public Policy," *Responsive Philanthropy* (March 2004).

developing "a toolbox containing the continuum of activities (roles, tactics, strategies, campaigns) available to foundations to affect public policy, including evaluation tools and effective strategies to support long-term changes in public policy."[42] The California Wellness Foundation had been promoting advocacy, noting on its website that "we provide grants for public education and public policy, in the belief that social attitudes and public funding priorities need to acknowledge the key role of prevention in public health."[43] The George Gund Foundation had made it a practice to make general purpose grants to 501(c)(3) organizations to help them to develop public policy capacity including hiring a full-time staff person (Arons 2006). Government budget cuts, heightened interest in accountability within the tax-exempt sector, and the 2004 Presidential election all served as events that have motivated private and community foundations to become, at least temporarily, important players in the civic arena.

Hopefully these types of examples will serve as inspiration to encourage foundations to support advocacy within permissible bounds. Increasingly foundations are wrestling with how to evaluate advocacy grants. In *Foundation News & Commentary,* the Council on Foundations' magazine, Marcia Egbert and Susan Hoechstetter provide eight tips to help foundations "evaluate grantees' work that are consistent with the nature of advocacy"[44] (Egbert and Hoechstetter 2006, 42). These types of articles and activities add to the growing awareness within the philanthropic community that nonprofit advocacy is important. The timing could not be better because the absence of an affirmative voice from philanthropy contributes to the reticence of many nonprofit executives about engaging in public policy matters.

Government Changes the Rules

Underlying nonprofit advocacy is the First Amendment constitutional right of Americans to speak, assemble, and petition government for redress of

---

[42] See http://www.ncg.org/services_policy.html

[43] See http://www.tcwf.org/grants_program/what_we_fund.htm

[44] For a comprehensive paper on the complexities of evaluating advocacy, see Kendall Guthrie, Justin Louie, Tom David, and Catherine Crystal Foster, October, 2005. *The Challenge of Assessing Advocacy: Strategies for a Prospective Approach to Evaluating Policy Change and Advocacy* (San Francisco, CA: Blueprint Research & Design, 2005).

grievances.[45] Throughout the history of the United States, the Supreme Court has reinforced First Amendment rights and recognized groups, including for-profits and nonprofits, as having advocacy rights.[46] One extreme example is in the Supreme Court's decision to permit the National Socialist Party to assemble, display swastikas and promote hatred of Jews in Skokie, Illinois.[47]

In 1919, the federal government first sought to curtail unfettered lobbying by nonprofits. The Department of Treasury included in regulations a provision stating that associations formed to promote propaganda do not fall within the definition of an educational organization for purposes of charity status (Fishman and Schwarz 1995, 501). The courts supported this position in 1930 when Judge Learned Hand ruled that the American Birth Control League failed to qualify for tax-exempt status because it had lobbied to repeal birth control laws.[48]

In 1934 Congress saw reason to condition the First Amendment rights of charitable nonprofits based on the theory that the public subsidizes charities' political views by permitting charitable contributions to be tax deductible.[49] Included in the Revenue Act of 1934 was a sharp restriction on legislative lobbying in effect today that "no substantial part of an organization's activities may constitute carrying on propaganda or otherwise attempting to influence legislation."[50] Although the legislative history is limited, the record indicates that Congress may have intentionally or unintentionally over-restricted charities from engaging in lobbying. The

---

[45] The First Amendment states: "Congress shall make no law respecting an establishment of religion, or prohibiting the free exercise thereof; or abridging the freedom of speech, or of the press; or the right of the people peaceably to assemble, and to petition the Government for a redress of grievances."

[46] In *NAACP v. Alabama*, 357 US 449, 460 (1958), the Supreme Court recognized that "[e]ffective advocacy of both public and private points of view, particularly controversial ones, is undeniably enhanced by group association."

[47] *National Socialist Party v. Skokie*, 432 US 43 (1977).

[48] Judge Hand's decision in *Slee v. Commissioner*, 42 F.2d 184 (2d Cir.1930) undoubtedly supported Congress' decision in 1934 to codify limits on charity lobbying. For an excellent description of the history, see Fishman and Schwarz, 1995.

[49] In essence, the amount that it costs the federal government in revenue forgone by permitting taxpayers to lower their adjusted gross income through deducting the amount of their contributions to charities is considered by the federal government to be a subsidy – a special benefit. Since charities in turn may use individual contributions to influence the legislative process, the public is thereby supporting the political views of special interests.

[50] See Revenue Act of 1934, or Internal Revenue Code § 501(c)(3).

Senate sponsor of the provision, Senator David Reed (R-PA), felt that the provision went beyond the intent of Congress: "There is no reason in the world why a contribution made to the National Economy League should be deductible as if it were a charitable contribution if it is a selfish one made to advance the personal interests of the giver of the money. That is what the committee was trying to reach; but we found great difficulty in phrasing the amendment. I [did] not reproach the draftsmen. I think we gave them an impossible task; but this amendment goes much further than the committee intended to go."[51]

The legislative history seems to indicate that Reed would have preferred that a distinction be made between what he considered true charities such as the Society for the Prevention of Cruelty to Children as opposed to the National Economy League, a political advocacy group. For the true charities, he would not have placed any restrictions on lobbying. It is unclear whether the rest of the Finance Committee agreed with Reed's view or whether the members simply intended to restrict all lobbying by charities (Kindell and Reilly 1998, 265). Either way, the 1934 restriction on lobbying sent a clear message to charities that they had better not engage in too much lobbying if they want to maintain their right to receive tax deductible contributions as well as their overall tax-exempt status.[52] The unspoken but direct message was: stick to services and leave policymaking to government. The law also conditioned free speech by limiting citizens' rights (through nonprofits) to petition government. This subsidization argument placed the interests of the taxpayer above those of the citizen in a hierarchy of American democracy.

As if the death penalty consequence for engaging in too much lobbying was not enough, neither Congress nor the Internal Revenue Service ever defined the terms "carrying on propaganda," "attempts to influence legislation," or what determined "substantiality." Between 1934 and 1990, three federal court cases attempted to settle the question and define

---

[51] 78 Cong. Rec. 5,861 (1934). Quoted in Kindell and Reilly, "Lobbying Issues," IRS. p. 264.
[52] Charities cannot be treated as 501(c) (4) organizations if the 501(c)(3) statuses are lost as a result of substantial lobbying. See IRS Pub 557 at http://www.irs.gov/publications/p557/ch03.html#d0e7391.

how much lobbying was substantial.[53] They each came to a different conclusion, thereby contributing to current myths about what constitutes substantial lobbying. For example, some charities deliberately limit lobbying expenditures to no more than five percent of their budget as a rule of thumb believing that the IRS will judge any amount below to be insubstantial. There is no indication that the IRS uses or has used five percent as any sort of guideline for determining substantial lobbying.

In fact, in June 1966, the IRS hand-delivered a notice of revocation of the Sierra Club's status as a tax-deductible group. As Michael Cohen notes in *The History of the Sierra Club*, the Sierra Club appealed administratively, arguing that the cumulative lobbying efforts each year comprised less than five percent of the organization's budget (Cohen, 1988). Michael McCloskey, the executive director of the Sierra Club at that time and an expert on these issues, recently commented, "The IRS argued, in turn, that our offense was not that we lobbied too much but too blatantly. In other words, we were too loud and effective and not subtle; we had been running a series of full-paged ads in major newspapers for about six months, on both the Grand Canyon issue and the Redwood National Park issue."[54] In 1968, when the Sierra Club unsuccessfully finally exhausted all administrative remedies, the organization decided not to file a lawsuit to challenge the findings. Instead they activated the Sierra Club Foundation, a tax-exempt 501(c)(3) organization that had already been established, and decided that the Sierra Club itself would become a 501(c)(4)

---

[53] The first attempt to define substantial was in *Seasongood v. Commissioner*, 227 F.2d 907 (6th Cir.1955). *Seasongood* held that if a charity spent less than five percent of time and effort on lobbying it was insubstantial. Almost fifty years later, charities have been found to use 5% as a rule of thumb although it is not law. The second case was *Haswell v. United States*, 500 F.2d 1133 (Ct. Cl. 1974), cert. denied, 419 U.S. 1107 (1975). The Circuit Court used a "fact and circumstances" test that included the amount a charity spent on lobbying as well as the nature of the activities in determining whether substantial lobbying had occurred. In *Christian Echoes National Ministry, Inc. v. United States*, 470 F.2d 849 (10th Cir. 1972); cert. denied, 414 U.S. 864 (1973), the Court takes a slightly different tact in determining criteria for "substantial" lobbying. An "organization was engaged in attempting to influence legislation, even if legislation was not pending" (Kindell and Reilly 1997, 273). A 1975 IRS General Counsel Memorandum (36148) further illustrated the potential difficulty for determining substantial lobbying: "The percentage of the budget dedicated to a given activity is only one type of evidence of substantiality. Others are the amount of volunteer time devoted to the activity, the amount of publicity the organization assigns to the activity, and the continuous or intermittent nature of the organization's attention to it" (Kindell and Reilly 1997, 279). See also Fishman and Schwarz (1995, 501-4).
[54] Communication via email with J. Michael McCloskey, October 14, 2004.

organization and would lobby without limit, but no longer receive deductible contributions. (IRS rules prevent an organization that loses its 501(c)(3) status from converting to a 501(c)(4) organization).

The Sierra Club became a widely cited example of the ambiguities built into the "substantial part test." Due to rising criticism of the vague "substantial part test" and the earlier passage of regulations in 1962 permitting a business expense deduction for direct lobbying expenses (a boon for corporations), charities argued that greater fairness should be extended to them in the form of latitude for lobbying. In 1976, Congress enacted an expenditure test rule to serve as an alternative (not a replacement) to the substantial part test.[55] (See Box 1 for a full description of the lobbying rules.) Charities have to affirmatively opt into the expenditure test by taking what is known as the 501(h) election – named after the section of Internal Revenue Code that permits charities to follow the newer law. (See Appendix A for a copy of IRS Form 5768 that charities must file to come under the expenditure test.)

The new law was intended to encourage charities to be informers to legislators in the policymaking process. The legislative history shows a remarkable change in the attitude of Congress toward the lobbying role of charitable groups. Senator Edmund Muskie (D-Maine), the sponsor of the 1976 legislation, stated for the record, "It makes no sense to decide that these [charitable, educational, etc.] organizations operate in the public interest and grant them tax-exempt status and then silence them when they attempt to speak to those who must decide public policy" (Hopkins 1992, 184). Senator Robert Dole (R-KS.), a co-sponsor, agreed, "Charities can and should be important sources of information on legislative issues." Unfortunately, hopes for a more favorable regulatory climate for nonprofit lobbying were dashed, if not shelved, when the IRS failed to implement regulations in a timely manner.[56]

---

[55] The expenditure test enacted by the Revenue Act of 1976 does not apply to religious congregations or to their integrated auxiliaries, or conventions or associations of churches that, at their own request, remain under the substantial part test. The law also does not apply to charities that do not file an annual tax return because their budget is less than $25,000.
[56] Senator Edmund Muskie (D-ME) first introduced legislation providing an expenditure test for lobbying in 1972. Shortly thereafter, Reps. Al Ullman (D-OR), Wilbur Mills (D-AR) and Herman Schneebeli (R-PA) did the same in the House. The Nixon Administration and Governor George Wallace of Alabama raised concerns during hearings, and Ullman and Schneebeli introduced revised legislation in 1973. Due to further objections, Rep. Barber Conable (R-NY) introduced a consensus bill (H.R. 13500, 94th Cong.) and included it into the Tax Reform Act of 1976 that was signed into law on October 4, 1976, by President Ford (PL 94-455). During the floor debate on the Senate side, Senator Robert Dole was supportive of the legislation.

(The proposed rules are discussed later in this chapter.) So for the next 14 years until 1990, charities still faced hazy and potentially risky lobbying rules – a problem compounded by the fact that there were now two vague laws on the books.

Box 1
Expenditure Test (in brief)

The expenditure test defines lobbying as an attempt to influence specific legislation and puts such activities into two categories: direct and grassroots. A charity choosing to use the expenditure test may spend up to 20 percent of exempt purpose expenditures on lobbying and up to $1 million per year depending on the size of its budget.[57] A charity may spend one-fourth of its overall allowable lobbying budget on grassroots lobbying, whereas they may spend the total allowable lobbying amount on direct lobbying. The difference between the two forms of lobbying is as follows: Direct lobbying is when a charity communicates its support or opposition to specific legislation directly to a legislator or if it asks its bona fide members to communicate such a position on legislation. Grassroots lobbying is when a charity urges the public to take action by communicating the organization's position on specific legislation. Key differences between the substantial part test and the expenditures test include:

- For an action to count as lobbying under the expenditure test, an expenditure must take place. Under the substantial part test there does not necessarily have to be an expenditure. So if no costs are associated with a volunteer lobby activity, it would not be reported under the expenditure test, but would be counted under the substantial part test.
- The penalty for exceeding the expenditure limit includes excise taxes, or fines on the amount of the excess. A charity must grossly exceed their limits for four consecutive years to warrant revocation of tax-exempt status. The penalty for violating the

---

[57] To calculate exempt purpose expenditures: "Add up all of the organization's annual expenditures for its charitable or tax-exempt purposes, including program related expenditures. Subtract investment management expenditures for outside consultants or staff persons who spend a majority of their time fundraising; unrelated business income and expenses associated with generating unrelated business income; and any expenses related to making capital improvements to raise the value of the organization's property" (Arons 2002).

substantial part test (for even a single offense) is revocation of tax-exempt status, which means its right to receive tax-deductible contributions.

- Charities must affirmatively choose to follow the expenditure test rules. They may do so by completing a short form from the IRS (Form 5768 available at http://www.irs.gov/pub/irs-pdf/f5768.pdf and in Appendix A) that indicates they will adhere to the expenditure test rules. Charities are otherwise automatically under the substantial part rule.

- Generally speaking, the expenditure test offers three benefits: safety, clarity and latitude for most charities. The expenditure test regulations, Internal Revenue Code §53.4911 contain numerous examples explaining how the rules are applied.[58] No such guidance exists for the substantial part test.

Depoliticizing Nonprofits:
Separating Lobbying and Electioneering

Throughout the first half of the 20th century, the history of federal regulation of nonprofit advocacy seemed to group influencing legislation as part of broader political activities – there was no clear distinction in the law between lobbying and other forms of advocacy – including partisan electoral activities. However, in 1954 Senator Lyndon Johnson (D-TX) sponsored an amendment to the Revenue Act, which became law that year, stating that 501(c)(3) organizations, "may not participate in, or intervene in (including the publishing or distributing of statements), any political campaign on behalf of any candidate for public office" (Kindell and Reilly 1998, 401 quoting 100 Cong. Rec. 9,604 (1954)).[59] In 1969, Congress tightened the ban on electioneering by private foundations by adding fines as penalties in addition to loss of tax-exempt status if an institution were found to be in

---

[58] At the time of this writing, legislation is pending in Congress that would simplify and expand the rules of the expenditure test to remove the expenditure limit distinction between direct and grassroots lobbying. The effect would be that charities could spend up to four times as much on grassroots lobbying as they are presently permitted. See CARE Act of 2003, 108th Congress.

[59] "The conventional wisdom is that Senator Johnson was out to curb the activities of a Texas foundation that had provided indirect financial support to his opponent in a senatorial election campaign." (Fishman and Schwarz 1995, 502).

79

violation of the law.[60] The legislative history indicates that the congressional hearings leading to the new law were acrimonious at times, and some members of Congress felt like foundations had supported their opponents during the election season.[61] In 1987, Congress strengthened the prohibition on partisan political activities by charities by including opposition to a candidate or party among the prohibited activities. In addition, the Internal Revenue Code was amended to ensure that if a charity lost its tax-exempt status due to partisan political activity it could not reconstitute itself as a 501(c)(4).[62]

There are at least a couple ways to examine the effect of the ban on partisan electioneering by charities and foundations. On one hand, the ban could be viewed as an example of political retribution by Congress, and therefore as one more government attack on nonprofit advocacy. On the other hand, these restrictions shield charities and private foundations from the taint of politics, which may correlate with levels of public and donor trust. We have not tested this hypothesis, but over the last 25 years at least there have been no organized efforts that we are aware of to overturn the ban on electioneering by 501(c)(3)s.

However, two other recent developments may cause public confusion over the role of nonprofits in electoral activities. First is the prominent role 527 organizations played in the 2004 elections. These groups are nonprofit organizations named after the section of the tax code that authorizes their tax exemption; they engage in partisan electoral activities, and include independent groups, political parties and campaigns. Many are affiliated with advocacy groups trying to influence federal elections through voter mobilization efforts and so-called issue ads that tout or criticize a candidate's record. In 2004, they included groups such as Americans Coming Together, which supported John Kerry for president, and Swift Boat Vets and POWs for Truth, which supported George Bush for president.

Part of the purpose of the passage of the Bipartisan Campaign Reform Act in 2002, commonly called the McCain-Feingold campaign finance reform

---

[60] Electioneering is roughly defined as participating in activities designed to influence the outcome of an election for office.

[61] See Kindell and Reilly's description of the 1969 House Ways and Means Hearings on Foundations, p. 401.

[62] See Kindell and Reilly's description in "Election Year Issues," IRS, p.402.

law, was to greatly reduce the role of soft money contributions in federal elections. However, as a result of the new law, soft money contributions to political parties were banned, so large contributors simply gave money to independent 527 groups to carry on the activities previously done by political parties. The role of 527 groups became a flashpoint in 2004, with the Federal Election Commission (FEC) debating whether to constrain independent 527 activities by subjecting them to the same limits and rules as political parties and campaigns.

There was considerable concern that the FEC proposal – which would establish a new threshold for when an organization becomes a regulated political committee subject to fundraising and spending rules under the Federal Election Campaign Act – would affect groups under 501(c)(3) and 501(c)(4) of the tax code. Part of the concern was that the Supreme Court decision upholding the constitutionality of the McCain-Feingold law said the Constitution does not require that regulation of federal elections be limited to statements that expressly endorse or oppose a federal candidate (express advocacy).[63] This could open the door to a new standard that may go beyond express advocacy and extend various types of nonprofit "issue advocacy" to federal campaign finance regulation.

In the end, the FEC rule did not implicate 501(c) groups. But the FEC rule is subject to continuing legal challenges. This could open the door to impact 501(c) organizations. Moreover, legislation was introduced in the 109th Congress by the sponsors of the campaign finance reform law – in the Senate, John McCain (R-AZ) and Russell Feingold (D-WI); in the House, Christopher Shays (R-CT) and Martin Meehan (D-MA). Similar legislation has been introduced in the 110th Congress. Although the sponsors say their intent is not to cover 501(c) organizations, each bill will have to be examined closely for its implications for 501(c) organizations.

This confusion adds to the reluctance of 501(c)(3) organizations to engage in any advocacy activities that might be construed as partisan and subject them to rules governing political committees (e.g., contribution limits and reporting donors to the FEC that would be publicly disclosed in addition to regular reporting of other matters to the IRS). Additionally, most members of the public are not knowledgeable enough to distinguish among 501(c)(3),

---

[63] *McConnell v. Federal Election Commission* 540 US 93 (2003). Docket Number: 02-1674. Abstract. Decided: December 10, 2003.

501(c)(4), and 527 organizations. They may recognize all as nonprofits, but the nuanced distinctions between them and the various permissions they have regarding lobbying versus electioneering is lost.

The second recent development around nonprofits and politics is an ongoing effort in the Congress to allow churches to endorse candidates and fund partisan electioneering activities.[64] As mentioned above, all organizations exempt under section 501(c)(3), including religious organizations, are absolutely prohibited from directly or indirectly participating in, or intervening in, any political campaign on behalf of, or in opposition to, any candidate for elective public office. Clergy, members of congregations, and others can endorse candidates on their own behalf, volunteer for campaigns, or even run for public office, so long as they do not use the resources of a 501(c)(3) organization to do so. Current laws allow unlimited 501(c)(3) time and money to address issues, including comment on public issues from the pulpit, in newsletters, etc.; engage in public education campaigns; publish pamphlets, research, newsletters and analysis; litigate; comment on proposed regulations; participate in agency and commission proceedings and nonpartisan voter education, registration and get out the vote activities.

The current fight over the right to endorse candidates from the pulpit is not new. There have been complaints ranging from charges against Jerry Falwell that he has used his ministry to support Republicans to African-American churches endorsing Democrats. There were many news stories about the role churches and other religious institutions played in the national elections. If Congress proceeds to permit electioneering by churches there will likely be an impact on charities overall. It certainly will add to the public confusion over what nonprofits can and cannot do with regard to electioneering.

Modern Day Governmental Actions Affecting Nonprofit Advocacy

Government actions from 1980 through 2004 have had a profound impact on nonprofit advocacy. In 1983, the Supreme Court ruled 9-0 that denial of

---

[64] *Houses of Worship Political Protection Act*, 109th Congress, H.R. 235. Introduced January 4, 2005 by Representative Walter Jones (R-NC).

tax-exemption by the IRS for substantial lobbying was not unconstitutional.[65] The case reaffirmed the policy that the lobbying rights of charities may be conditioned because they receive a public subsidy through the tax deductibility of individual contributions. The ruling was significant in part because of how overwhelming the decision was that constitutional rights were not violated in the effort to protect taxpayer interest.

Over the next 20 years, there were six major governmental actions that have had significant impact on nonprofit advocacy. The first was a 1983 effort to prohibit nonprofits receiving federal grants from engaging in any type of policy-related work including commenting on government regulations. That effort – a modification of OMB Circular A-122, an accounting rule – was halted due to the work of a diverse coalition of nonprofits and defense contractors. The second was an effort to prohibit nonprofits that engage in advocacy from participating in the Combined Federal Campaign, which is a workplace giving campaign that collects money for charities from federal workers. That effort also was ultimately defeated.

The third came when the IRS proposed regulations to implement the 1976 tax law that created the lobby expenditure test. The proposal was largely inconsistent with the intent of the tax law and would have had a ten-year retroactive implementation date that would have put many nonprofits out of compliance with the law and forced them to pay significant fines and possibly lose their tax-exempt status. Those rules were vastly modified to be consistent with the tax law, but it took enormous effort on the part of the sector and several years of uncertainty.

The fourth dealt with fallout from a Supreme Court decision in *Rust v. Sullivan*, where the Court concluded that government has the right to condition certain speech of nonprofits when it provides money to them as

---

[65] *Regan v. Taxation with Representation of Wash.* 461 U.S. 540 (1983)
461 U.S. 540, reaffirmed that a 501(c)(3) and 501(c)(4) civic league or social welfare organization may be affiliated, but the 501(c)(3) may not fund the 501(c)(4)'s lobbying activities. The permissibility of having an affiliated 501(c)(4) with no lobby expenditure limits provided strong rationale for particularly liberal members of the Supreme Court to vote that the substantial part test presented an unconstitutional violation of free speech. In concurrence with the majority, Justice Harry Blackmun stated: "Because lobbying is protected by the First Amendment, §501(c)(3) therefore denies a significant benefit to organizations choosing to exercise their constitutional rights. The constitutional defect that would inhere in §501(c)(3) alone is avoided by §501(c)(4)."

long as there is a choice of funding options. These "program integrity" rules have led to various restrictions regarding arts and legal services programs.

The fifth episode, called the Istook Amendment, was a repeat of the 1983 effort to modify OMB Circular A-122 to prohibit nonprofit federal grantees from engaging in any policy work. This time, however, it was done through legislative proposals that were ultimately stopped by a broad coalition of nonprofits. But that experience has left in its wake a host of smaller legislative and regulatory proposals to silence nonprofit advocacy. Most of them have been quashed.

The sixth major issue affected whether volunteers in AmeriCorps could engage in advocacy. The debate centered around whether federally funded volunteers working under a Clinton Era program were allowed to organize, protest and engage in policy advocacy as part of their service. Although regulations state that certain public policy or civic activities carried out by the volunteers working in nonprofit Americorps grantee organizations are prohibited, they have not prevented these organizations from fostering important civic engagement.

OMB Circular A-122

In January 1983, the Reagan Administration proposed far-reaching modification to rules affecting nonprofit grantees based on recommendations from the Heritage Foundation for its "defunding the left" initiative.[66] The proposal made unallowable for federal reimbursement all costs of "political advocacy," which was broadly defined as "attempting to influence a government decision" of any type (e.g., legislative, administrative, judicial) at any level of government. It also departed radically from standard cost allocation principles. No federal funds could pay the allowable costs of any staff, equipment, or facility involved in the slightest amount of political advocacy, even if the advocacy costs were paid with non-federal funds. For example, a group that received federal funds for services that also wanted to lobby using private funds would have to have a separate copier purchased and maintained for the government service program and it could not be used for advocacy.

---

[66] OMB Circular A-122, "Cost Principles for Nonprofit Organizations," *Federal Register* 48, 3348-50 (January 24, 1983).

In July 1980, the Carter administration's Office of Management and Budget, after years of discussion, finalized its Circular A-122, Cost Principles for Nonprofit Organizations.[67] The circular identifies various costs as unallowable for federal payment and reimbursement to nonprofit organizations operating federal grants, contracts, and cooperative agreements. The circular establishes the cost allocation principle: federal funds can pay their full, fair share of all direct and indirect costs incurred in carrying out federal grants so long as the costs are allowable, reasonable, and allocable. The Circular did not make lobbying either allowable or unallowable; it did, however, require that lobbying be treated as a direct cost.

Conservatives had argued that grant funds are fungible: nonprofit grantees bury lobbying expenses among indirect costs or use federal funds to free up private funds that, in turn, can be used for lobbying. Either way, they argued, federal taxpayers are subsidizing lobbying by nonprofits. In 1981, in a document prepared by the Heritage Foundation for the Reagan transition team, the conservative think tank proposed dramatic changes to address this problem.[68] They proposed three key ideas, all of which were incorporated in a proposed revision of OMB Circular A-122:

- "Impose some sort of lobbying and advocacy restriction on any organization receiving federal funds" even if paid for with non-federal funds;
- "Specify the type of such 'informational' activity that can be done with federal grants"; and
- "Limit the circumstances under which grants and contracts can go to groups organized primarily for lobbying and advocacy."

An unpublished April 1982 OMB proposal largely tracked federal law that indicated federal funds cannot be used for lobbying purposes, and defined lobbying as dealing with legislative matters as prescribed in the tax

---

[67] OMB Circular A-122, "Cost Principles for Nonprofit Organizations", *Federal Register* 45, 46022-34 (July 8, 1980).

[68] Charles L. Heatherly ed., *Mandate for Leadership: Policy Management in a Conservative Administration* (Washington, D.C.: The Heritage Foundation, 1981), 1091-91.

code.[69] Conservatives were unhappy with this proposal and pressured the OMB General Counsel Michael Horowitz to follow the recommendations from the Heritage Foundation. By January 1983, OMB published a proposal that made all costs of "political advocacy" unallowable for federal reimbursement.[70] Political advocacy was defined very broadly as "attempting to influence a government decision" of any type at any level of government. It also departed radically from standard cost allocation principles by proposing that no federal funds could pay the allowable costs of any staff, equipment or facility if that person or item were used for any political advocacy, even if advocacy costs were paid with non-federal funds. This wall of separation would have meant, for example, the need for two offices if the office were used for political advocacy and federal grant activity.

The proposal created a firestorm of protest from a coalition of charities, business organizations, and even defense contractors.[71] The role of contractors cannot be emphasized enough. John G. Roberts, Jr., then White House associate counsel, wrote a memo on February 3, 1983[72], a little more than a week after the OMB proposal was published, to White House Counsel Fred Fielding, noting that he had been advised that "the logic of the proposed rules would affect traditional lobbying activities of government contractors." Roberts then adds: "The proposals paint with a much broader brush than is necessary to address the activities of government grantees that have been perceived as most objectionable. It is possible to 'defund the left' without alienating TRW and Boeing, but the proposals, if enacted, could do both."

Shortly after the Roberts memo, Lyn Nofziger, a political adviser to Reagan, wrote a February 17, 1983, memo to Fielding, Attorney General

---

[69] The unpublished proposal was: "Lobbying expenses. The cost of influencing the introduction, amendment, enactment, defeat, or repeal of any act, bill or resolution by a legislative body is unallowable."

[70] OMB Circular A-122, "Cost Principles for Nonprofit Organizations", *Federal Register* 48, 3348-50 (January 24, 1983).

[71] The last two groups were worried that the proposal would migrate to cost principles for contracts and affect them. Upon release of the OMB proposal, the White House announced that the main contracting agencies – the Department of Defense, the General Services Administration, and the National Aeronautics and Space Administration – would simultaneously propose changes to their contracting regulations. (OMB 84-4, January 20, 1983)

[72] http://www.ombwatch.org/npadv/Roberts/Roberts1.pdf.

Ed Meese, White House Chief of Staff Jim Baker, and Assistant to the President for Political Affairs Ed Rollins, warning of the far-reaching effects of the proposed revision. Nofziger detailed concerns over the vagueness and burdensome nature of the proposals. "What this is going to do is force companies to keep detailed records on the political activities of their employees. If this is constitutional, and I doubt very much that it is, instead of getting government off people's backs, as we promised to do for lo these many years, you are adding an intolerable burden onto the backs of many, many people." In a handwritten postscript, Nofziger noted that "the opposition is growing not only among the lobbyists but also among the Republicans on the Hill." Nofziger added rumors that House Minority Leader "Bob Michel is upset" and that "Jack Brooks [the Democratic chair of an oversight committee] is thinking about hearings."[73]

The White House responded to Nofziger that the proposal would be revised. But the Reagan Administration argued that the rule change was needed because nonprofits were using federal funds to lobby. As Nofziger predicted, Chairman Jack Brooks (D-TX) used the House Committee on Government Operations in March 1983 for a hearing on the Circular A-122 proposal. At the hearing, Brooks asked OMB Deputy Director Joseph Wright for examples of nonprofits misusing federal funds to lobby. Wright claimed that there were examples of family planning clinics using federal funds for lobbying and that a recent General Accounting Office study documented this problem.

The GAO study actually found, however, that no federal funds were used for lobbying. "Most of the Title X recipients reviewed for lobbying were involved in some types of lobbying activities. Generally, these activities were not paid for with appropriated funds or charged to the Title X programs and were therefore not subject to federal lobbying restrictions."[74] GAO investigators did find several grantees using federal funds for activities related to lobbying that were not prohibited at the time. For example, some Title X grantees were paying dues to organizations that do lobby Congress. GAO recommended that there was a need for clarification of the rules regarding these types of situations, which is not what the Circular A-122 proposal by OMB addressed.

---

[73] http://www.ombwatch.org/npadv/Roberts/Roberts3.pdf.
[74] U.S. General Accounting Office, *Restrictions on Abortions and Lobbying Activities in Family Planning Programs Need Clarification*, HRD-82-106, September 24, 1982.

Wright offered a second example citing another GAO report involving a military contractor, Lockheed, which used federal funds to lobby.[75] Upon questioning by Brooks, Wright acknowledged that this example had nothing to do with allegations that nonprofits use federal funds to lobby. In general, OMB provided no evidence during the hearing or afterward that nonprofits were using federal funds for lobbying.

Groups such as Independent Sector, OMB Watch, which was created during the Circular A-122 public comment periods, and the Alliance for Justice led nonprofits across the country to raise concerns about the proposal and subsequent modifications from OMB. In early 1995, more than ten years later, Horowitz, the architect of the Circular A-122 changes, said, "I broke my pick on this issue," meaning that the issue cost him political capital. James Baker, the White House Chief of Staff, grabbed him in the halls of the White House complex and said, "The leader of the free world has come to me and said that all he has been hearing about is this business of A-122."[76] Horowitz knew when the President of the United States was focusing on OMB Circular A-122 issues that things had gotten out of hand.

In the end, the final rules, published 15 months after first proposed and after several iterations, were vastly different from the initial proposal in that they only applied to "lobbying" (defined as legislative matters) and permitted charities to use non-federal funds to lobby. Yet they left enormous confusion for most charities.[77] Even after the final rules were published, it was not uncommon to hear charities say that they thought there was some federal law or rule that restricted their participation in public policy matters.[78] The Circular A-122 proposal continues to be the backbone for conservative plans to silence the advocacy voice of nonprofits – and it has contributed enormously to the chill in nonprofit advocacy today.

---

[75] GAO Report No. AFMD-82-123, September 29, 1982.

[76] Jeff Shear, "The Ax Files," *National Journal* (April 15, 1995): 924-27.

[77] The final rules were published in the *Federal Register* on April 27, 1984 (pp. 18260-77) with minor corrections published on May 8, 1984 (pp. 19588). Equivalent rules for commercial organizations and military contractors were also published on April 27, 1984 (pp. 18278-79) in the *Federal Register*.

[78] Over the years there were specific attacks on advocacy and lobbying in various agencies, most notably in the National Endowment for the Arts. However, Julie Van Camp in "Freedom of Expression at the National Endowment for the Humanities: The Prohibition on Lobbying and Advocacy" notes that the same concerns were happening at NEH. These types of agency actions may have further chilled advocacy by those receiving federal grants.

Limiting Eligibility in the Combined Federal Campaign

A few weeks after OMB published its proposed Circular A-122 changes, President Reagan issued Executive Order 12404, which limited participation in the Combined Federal Campaign (CFC) to nonprofits not engaged in advocacy. The CFC permits charitable organizations to solicit contributions from federal employees at their workplaces and allows employees to have contributions to organizations deducted from their paychecks. The Reagan changes restricted participation in the CFC to "voluntary, charitable, health and welfare agencies that provide or support direct health and welfare services to individuals or their families," and specifically excluded groups that "seek to influence the outcomes of elections or the determination of public policy through political activity, lobbying, or litigation on behalf of parties other than themselves."[79]

Nonprofit groups that would have been excluded from the CFC sued, and a federal district court barred enforcement of the executive order. The Office of Personnel Management (OPM), which oversees the CFC, issued regulations in April 1984 that dropped the restrictions and permitted any organization "organized, qualified and recognized by the Internal Revenue Service, under 26 U.S.C. 501(c)(3)" to participate.

Opening the CFC to any charity, including advocacy groups, hit a snag. On July 2, 1985, the Supreme Court, in response to a suit filed by the NAACP Legal Defense and Educational Fund, the Sierra Club Legal Defense Fund, the Puerto Rican Legal Defense and Education Fund, the Federally Employed Women Legal Defense and Education Fund, the Indian Law Resource Center, the Lawyers' Committee for Civil Rights Under Law, and the Natural Resources Defense Council, upheld the Reagan Executive Order. The Court concluded "that the Government's reasons for excluding respondents from the CFC appear, at least facially, to satisfy the reasonableness standard."[80] Thus, the exclusion of advocacy, legal defense and other non-health-and-welfare groups was constitutional, as long as it was done even-handedly, without discrimination against any particular political viewpoint. In 1986, OPM began to revise its regulations to be consistent with the executive order.

---

[79] *Federal Register* 48, 6685. Issued on February 10, 1983. This was a revision to Reagan's earlier Executive Order 12353 issued on March 23, 1982 at 47 FR 12785.
[80] *Cornelius v. NAACP Legal Defense and Education Fund*, 473 US 788 (July 2, 1985).

Rep. Steny Hoyer (D-MD) intervened out of great concern that the CFC would exclude charities that do advocacy and charities that do not provide human services. He and Senator Mark Hatfield (R-OR) added an amendment to the Continuing Resolution for fiscal year 1986 declaring that the Office of Personnel Management could not issue the regulations in final form and implement them. Congress directed OPM to either disregard the content of the 1982 and 1983 executive orders or reissue the regulations used in the CFC campaigns in 1984 and 1985, thereby negating the Supreme Court's decision. OPM reissued the 1984 regulations and administered the 1986 and 1987 CFC under the interim rules, which made the CFC open to any charity.

However, many national charities, including those involved in the lawsuit making its way to the Supreme Court, were worried about how OPM would administer future CFC campaigns. They urged Hoyer and other congressional advocates to permanently fix the CFC eligibility issue. Congress did so through a provision tied to the Treasury, Postal Service, and General Government Appropriations Act for fiscal year 1988 (P.L. 100-202). As Rick Cohen, the president of the National Committee for Responsive Philanthropy, notes, however, this effort to limit participation in the CFC did not end.[81]

Several times after the permanent fix, Rep. John Mica (R-FL) and other conservatives tried to limit eligibility.[82] Many of the smaller federated charities, including Earth Share and organizing groups like the Center for Community Change, helped build a large coalition of mainly Washington, D.C.-based associations to fight the Mica proposals. Although backed by Rep. Newt Gingrich (R-GA), the proposals were turned aside. According to Cohen, these legislative efforts died "as the conservatives realized that their attempt to eliminate groups in favor of reproductive rights from the CFC would also have ejected the right-to-life advocates."

While attempts to limit eligibility based on type of organization and whether the group engages in advocacy has not resurfaced regarding the CFC, it has in other matters, particularly around discussions of a charity tax credit.

---

[81] Cohen, Rick, "The ACLU and the Combined Federal Campaign," *The Nonprofit Quarterly* 11, 3 (Fall 2004). Also available at http://www.nonprofitquarterly.org/ section/541.html.

[82] "History of the CFC," National Committee for Responsive Philanthropy" http://www.ncrp. org/afap/cfc.htm.

In 1996, Representatives James Talent (R-MO) and J.C. Watts (R-OK) introduced the American Community Renewal Act which provided for a tax credit for charitable organizations that serve the poor, but shunned those that engage in advocacy. It failed to pass. In 1998, Reps. Mark Souder (R-IN) and Bobby Scott (D-VA) offered an amendment to the Community Services Block Grant reauthorization that would allow states to use a portion of their CSBG funds to set up and administer a charitable tax credit. Any 501(c)(3) organization that primarily provided direct services to poor people would qualify. This would mean that the organization would have to spend 75 percent of its budget on services to poor people, which the bill said excluded lobbying, legal services to the poor, and other items such as fundraising and management costs. This also failed.

These legislative and regulatory attempts to use advocacy as a criteria for exclusion in programs have had profound negative implications. They have created an atmosphere that conveys the idea that advocacy is not a legitimate charitable activity; they foster a false impression that service and advocacy do not go hand in hand. The result is added uncertainty on the part of nonprofit executives about engaging in advocacy activities.

IRS Implementation of the 1976 Lobby Law

Following on the heels of the CFC and A-122 issues, the Internal Revenue Service in 1986 proposed rules to implement the 1976 tax code provisions that created the lobbying expenditure limits (Sections 4911 and 501(h)), which is discussed earlier in this chapter.[83] Many charities had been leery of opting to use the expenditure test because the IRS never issued rules to implement the law. While organizations, such as Independent Sector, and legal experts, such as Thomas Troyer of the Caplin & Drysdale Law Firm, argued that the expenditure test was better than the ambiguous substantial part test, very few charities chose to use it.

The proposed IRS rules seemed to vindicate those who never opted for the expenditure test. The proposed rules would have been retroactive to 1976 and would have reclassified as "grassroots lobbying" many traditional charitable activities, including fundraising and nonpartisan public education. As described previously, grassroots lobbying has a lower lobbying ceiling

---

[83] Internal Revenue Service, "Lobbying by Public Charities," *Federal Register*, 40211-32 (November 5, 1986).

than direct lobbying – only one-quarter of the overall lobbying ceiling.[84] Because of the ten-year retroactivity, many charities would have already exceeded lobby limits and would owe back taxes or lose tax-exempt status.

In 1976, the Treasury Department noted, "The present law with respect to lobbying by public charities is unsatisfactory. It often deprives legislatures of the views of organizations having substantial expertise and, at times, results in the presentation of only one side of a dispute." Yet the 1986 proposal would have greatly expanded what counts as lobbying, making it more difficult for charities to provide legislative bodies with their expertise.[85] For example, all costs of fundraising or advertising would be counted as grassroots lobbying if any part of the message "reflects a view" on legislation.

Nonpartisan research on policy matters, no matter how factual or balanced, would be considered grassroots lobbying if "selectively disseminated" to people who *may* "share a common view" on legislation. Gathering or analyzing information about policy matters would be lobbying if it is used "in connection with" lobbying or if somehow presented "in any manner" that favors persons interested solely in one side of an issue. Communications with elected officials, even when not about pending legislation, could be counted as lobbying. Moreover, many activities that are not intended to influence legislation would have been considered grassroots lobbying under the proposed rules.

The rules would have inhibited foundations because they would have been penalized for giving grants to charities exceeding the lobbying limits. This would have included foundation grants, whether for general purposes or specific projects, that exceeded an organization's non-lobbying budget for the previous year (or the current year, if smaller) unless the organization made a legally "enforceable commitment" not to use the "excess" funds for lobbying, as defined by the IRS.

---

[84] See description earlier in this chapter as well as Chapter 5 for an explanation of the lobby expenditure ceilings under the expenditure test.
[85] For a complete description of the proposal, see OMB Watch, *New IRS Rules: The End of Nonprofit Advocacy*, 1986.

While the OMB Circular A-122 issue was driven by a conservative ideological agenda to "defund the left," the IRS proposal was not. Nevertheless, it had many of the same characteristics. It expanded the definition of lobbying to include many public policy activities not previously considered lobbying, and it threatened the cost allocation rules by making all the costs of an activity allocated to lobbying even if only a portion of the cost was associated with lobbying. So even if the reason for the proposal was not ideological, its impact was the same.

Once again, a coalition of charities formed to oppose another government proposal that would have limited charity advocacy rights, this time the IRS proposal. The coalition was reinforced by a team of sophisticated lawyers knowledgeable about tax law, including Thomas Troyer, Gail Harman, Michael Trister, and Thomas Asher. It also included conservative and liberal leaders who were willing to work together to oppose the regulations. This union of conservatives and liberals proved very powerful.

David Cohen, the co-director of the Advocacy Institute and a liberal, remembers lobbying hand-in-hand with conservatives. He found a friendly ear with former Senator Alfonse D'Amato, a Republican from New York. D'Amato was concerned about what the proposed regulations would do to nonprofits in his state, particularly those in Long Island working on drug abuse issues.[86] While the IRS proposal was a regulation, not legislation pending before Congress, a joint conservative-liberal lobby effort helped to elevate the issue for elected leaders in Congress. This put additional pressure on the IRS as members of Congress raised concerns about the proposed regulation.

It took nearly four years from the time of the proposed rules for the IRS to issue final rules.[87] According to Bob Smucker, a leader in advocating changes to the rules, "the regulations were worth the wait.... [They were] faithful to the 1976 law... which greatly extended the lobbying rights of nonprofits" (Smucker 1999, 51). However, many charities may have been left with a sense that they were prohibited from lobbying during the four years the rules were being finalized. This, coupled with the controversy

---

[86] Personal communication with David Cohen via email, January 11, 2005.
[87] Final rules were issued in the *Federal Register* on August 31, 1990.

surrounding the Circular A-122 , added up to a chilling impact on nonprofit advocacy. And even though the IRS final rules may have been beneficial, they did not result in a flurry of charities opting to use the expenditure test.[88]

Rust v. Sullivan: Federal Grants that Condition Speech

In 1988, the Secretary of the Department of Health and Human Services (HHS) issued new regulations to prohibit certain federally funded projects from engaging in counseling "concerning, referrals for, and activities advocating abortion as a method of family planning, and require such projects to maintain an objective integrity and independence from the prohibited abortion activities by the use of separate facilities, personnel, and accounting records."[89]

The regulations provided three restrictions on the use of Title X grants. First, the regulations specified that a "Title X project may not provide counseling concerning the use of abortion as a method of family planning or provide referral for abortion as a method of family planning."[90] Second, they prohibited a Title X project from engaging in activities that "encourage, promote or advocate abortion as a method of family planning."[91] The types of prohibited activities include lobbying for legislation that would increase the availability of abortion as a method of family planning, developing or disseminating materials advocating abortion as a method of family planning, providing speakers to promote abortion as a method of family planning, using legal action to make abortion available in any way as a method of family planning, and paying dues to any group that advocates abortion as a method of family planning as a substantial part of its activities. Third, the regulations required that Title X projects be organized so that they are "physically and financially separate" from prohibited abortion activities.[92]

---

[88] We do not mean to imply that had the IRS proposed fair rules similar to what was ultimately published that more nonprofits would lobby or be engaged in advocacy. The real issue is not whether nonprofits elect to fall under the expenditure test. It is that the culture did not encourage nonprofits to engage in public policy. Some would argue that it is the nonprofit sector's own fault that it did not seize on the legal rights afforded it to engage in lobbying. But even those who make that point would probably agree that the proposed IRS rules caused additional harm to those contemplating engaging in advocacy.

[89] *Federal Register* 53, 2923-2924.

[90] 42 CFR 59.8(a)(1) (1989).

[91] Ibid., 59.10(a).

[92] Ibid., 59.9.

These program integrity rules were quite strict. According to HHS, "A Title X project must have an objective integrity and independence from prohibited activities. Mere bookkeeping separation of Title X funds from other monies is not sufficient."

A number of Title X grantees and doctors who oversaw Title X funds sued before the regulations were implemented. In a 5-4 decision, the Supreme Court ruled on May 23, 1991, in *Rust v. Sullivan* that the HHS regulations were constitutional.[93] According to the Court, "The Government can, without violating the Constitution, selectively fund a program to encourage certain activities it believes to be in the public interest, without at the same time fund an alternative program which seeks to deal with the problem in another way. In so doing, the Government has not discriminated on the basis of viewpoint; it has merely chosen to fund one activity to the exclusion of another." Prior to this, the Court never before had upheld a regulation that conditioned the eligibility for government funds on the participant's willingness to surrender First Amendment rights. It is possible that the highly emotional abortion context in which this case came about limits the reach of the Court's holding in other areas. But it is certain that the *Rust* decision has had programmatic implications.

Because the program integrity part of the regulations derives from an ambiguous part of the Public Health Service Act that says no federal funds appropriated under Title X for family planning services "shall be used in programs where abortion is a method of family planning," the Supreme Court provided great deference to the Secretary of HHS. This means the Court may not have fully explored the implications of a grantee having to physically separate (e.g., two buildings) permissible and impermissible activities.

The Court ruling leans on the *Regan v. Taxation with Representation* case for its decision that it is not unconstitutional to subsidize certain program activities and not others, namely advocacy activities on behalf of family planning policies. The *Rust* decision contributed to the service-advocacy divide by strengthening the statutory firewalls between activities that Congress considers political and activities considered to be services in the interest of taxpayers.

---

[93] *Rust v. Sullivan*, 500 U.S. 173 (1991).

The Supreme Court's decision was used by Congress and the Legal Services Corporation (LSC) in 1996 to restrict legal services grantees from representing clients to change laws governing welfare, or to declare such laws unconstitutional.[94] Effectively, *Rust* became a mechanism to limit the purview of legal services to service and not lobbying. A series of more recent court decisions may begin to erode the decision in *Rust* and follow standard cost allocation procedures instead of requiring physical and financial separation (see footnote 88).

The Rise and Fallout of the Istook Amendment

On August 4, 1995 conservatives in the House of Representatives passed a rider to an appropriations bill sponsored by Representatives Ernest Istook (R-OK), David McIntosh (R-IN), and Robert Ehrlich (R-MD) that was a rehash of the OMB Circular A-122 fight to "defund the left," but went further. The Istook Amendment, as it was called, would have expanded the existing prohibition on using federal funds for lobbying to include "political advocacy" activities, which were broadly defined. For example, it would have included attempts to influence the executive and judicial branches of government. It would also have barred charities from receiving federal grants if they spent five percent or more of their private funds for "political advocacy" activities. And it would have barred associating with other entities that use 15 percent or more of their money for advocacy activities. The amendment proposed new enforcement procedures, including licensing private citizens as nonprofit "bounty hunters" to find groups in violation of the various provisions of the bill. Anyone could have brought a lawsuit against a grantee for up to ten years after the violation. Organizations found out of compliance with the bill could have been fined $5,000 to $10,000 plus

---

[94] See *Legal Services Corporation v. Velazquez*, et.al., 121 U.S. 1043 (2001). In 1996, Congress imposed restrictions on the advocacy of legal services corporation funded attorneys and placed restrictions on the use of private funds for class-action suits and other advocacy. The restrictions were challenged and the LSC issued new regulations mandating that for private funds to be used for advocacy activities separate facilities would have to be used. These regulations and restrictions on the use of private philanthropy are being challenged in court. A 2001 U.S. Supreme Court decision in *Velazquez* struck down a federal law that had barred LSC-funded lawyers from challenging welfare reform laws. On December 20, 2004, the U.S. District Court for the Eastern District of New York ruled in *Dobbins v. Legal Services Corporation* (Memorandum and Order, No 97-CV-182, online at http://www.brennancenter.org/ programs/pov/dobbins/dobbins_decision.pdf) that certain prohibitions on private money were unconstitutional.

three times the value of the grant. The bounty hunter could have collected up to 25 percent of the recovery. The Istook Amendment also only applied to federal grantees, not to contractors. In fact, an amendment offered by a Democrat in the House of Representatives to apply the Istook Amendment to contractors was defeated, further demonstrating that this was an attack on nonprofit federal grantees.

This amendment, and subsequent legislative proposals from Istook and McIntosh, launched an unprecedented response from charities across the country.[95] Thousands of charities, linked together by the Let America Speak coalition, worked to stop the Istook Amendment at the federal level. The short but intense lobbying to defeat several iterations of the legislation for a moment in time made nonprofits cherish basic advocacy rights.[96] However, any euphoria that came from defeating the Istook Amendment was tempered by continuing fear of government retribution for advocacy, as well as apathy by many organizations.

Politically, there is ample evidence that the Istook Amendment was carefully thought out by Istook, McIntosh and the Republican leadership, including House Speaker Newt Gingrich and Majority Leader Dick Armey (R-TX). Several different but thematically related motivations on the part of the supporters came together in this attack on nonprofit advocacy. It was believed by opponents that McIntosh wanted to exact retribution for nonprofit advocacy against policies he promoted during the first Bush Administration as chief staff person to the Council on Competitiveness chaired by Vice President Dan Quayle. It was also believed that a member

---

[95] See the Let America Speak Web site for the archives of all iterations of the Istook Amendment, including analyses used by the coalition. www.ombwatch.org/las. See also "Handcuffing America's Charities," OMB Watch, 1995.

[96] In fact, the Istook amendment was never defeated on the floor of the House of Representatives. The one time it passed in the House, it was stopped in the Senate. Other attempts were through House-Senate conferences and the Senate stopped it each time. In one last ditch effort, House leaders tried to put the rider into a must-pass omnibus appropriations bill during conference. The bill was needed to keep government running and the Senate conferees rejected the Istook amendment as too controversial. Conservatives, especially newly elected ones, were quite willing to shut down the government if the Istook amendment was not added. When the conference report reached the House floor without the Istook amendment, there were shouts of "Free Ernie" heard in the chamber, referring to the legislation. (Istook's first name is Ernie.) Conservatives were gearing up to vote against the bill, threatening to shut down government. Ultimately, however, reason prevailed and the spending bill was approved without the Istook amendment.

of Armey's staff, Virginia Thomas, wife of Supreme Court Justice Clarence Thomas, helped direct the Istook attack to seek retribution against groups that led advocacy efforts against the appointment of her husband.[97] Another possible source of motivation for the Istook Amendment came from Ernest Istook himself and others who simply wanted to silence nonprofit groups who were opposed to major elements to the House GOP's Contract with America.[98] House Speaker Newt Gingrich originally was not directly involved in coordinating the Istook attack, but he became personally supportive when members of the liberal group the Association of Community Organizations for Reform Now (ACORN) shouted at him during a public speaking event.[99] It turned out that ACORN was also a federal grantee, although it did not use federal funds for its protests.

There may have been many reasons why conservatives were such strong advocates for the Istook amendment. In addition to the personal reasons why some representatives may have been emotionally attracted to the legislation, there were also philosophical reasons. The Heritage Foundation voiced those reasons in 1981, focusing on a "defund the left" agenda. Virginia Thomas was reported being at a meeting held at the Heritage Foundation after the Republicans took control of the House to discuss the ideas that led to the Istook Amendment. Conservatives had been waiting for years to renew the issues raised during the Circular A-122 fight. Now, with Republican control of Congress, here was their chance. Moreover, conservatives have always believed that government grants perpetuate what they call the welfare state. Forcing nonprofits to either choose to take government grants or be an advocate only helps the ideological objective of downsizing government. Under this thinking, with the Istook Amendment nonprofits would no longer be able to lobby for more government money and Congress would be better situated to shrink government.

---

[97] An article in the Wall Street Journal on May 17, 1995, by Christopher Georges said according to Armey spokesperson Ed Gillespie, "A staff member in Mr. Armey's office, Virginia Thomas, the wife of Supreme Court Justice Clarence Thomas, is coordinating the effort."

[98] The Contract with America sought to fundamentally change welfare, human services and other social policies, along with the way government operated. The Contract set specific legislative goals for the House to achieve in passing the slate of bills. It was the focal point for contention between Republicans and Democrats during the 104th Congress and the differences over policy, particularly government spending resulted in a series of government shutdowns in 1995 and 1996. See townhall.com and http://www.townhall.com/documents/contract.html for more information about the Contract.

[99] Christopher Georges, "Republicans Take Aim at Left-Leaning Groups That Get Federal Grants for Assistance Programs," *Wall Street Journal*, May 17, 1995.

During the 104th Congress, Istook served on the House Appropriations Committee, giving him an opportunity to add a rider to must-pass spending bills. Fortunately for the nonprofit sector, Rep. David Skaggs (D-CO) also served on the Appropriations Committee. When Istook moved to put the amendment on a spending bill that covers general government operations, Skaggs noticed it and took action. His staff analyzed the impact of the legislation; he personally reached out to nonprofit leaders at organizations like OMB Watch to urge action; and he provided a forceful and eloquent voice on why the legislation was inappropriate.

While Skaggs challenged Istook, McIntosh had another venue to address the issue as chairman of the House Subcommittee on National Economic Growth, Natural Resources and Regulatory Affairs, which had oversight of government grants and contracts. This assignment gave him an almost perfect forum for accusing nonprofits of violating the law by using federal grant money for lobbying. He said the use of federal grant money for lobbying was "one of Washington's best-kept dirty little secrets: welfare for lobbyists" (Stehle 1995). This was an important shift in messaging. The "defund the left" language did not have traction, but conservatives thought "welfare for lobbyists" would.

The best messages could not disguise the attack on nonprofits. The Democrats offered an amendment to expand the Istook Amendment to also cover government contractors, not just nonprofit grantees. The Republican majority defeated it, spurring criticism from people like Skaggs that Republicans were trying to silence the YMCA but not Lockheed. There was some humor in speculating who members of Congress feared more – the business lobbyist or the nonprofit lobbyist.

Tactics used by the McIntosh committee staff were also extreme. For example, in one committee "investigatory" hearing on Istook-related legislation, committee staff sent a letter to some of the people "invited" requesting detailed information about each organization's activities. At least for OMB Watch, the request was followed by two strident, if not intimidating, calls from committee staff demanding the detailed information. The hearing itself also had its own controversy. On the press table was forged letterhead of the Alliance for Justice (a co-chair of the Let America Speak Coalition in opposition to the Istook Amendment) making it seem as if one of its members, the American Arts Alliance, was a federal grantee (which it was not) that lobbied with federal funds and was therefore in violation of the law.

Skaggs, who was a witness at the hearing, changed his planned testimony and asked about the forged letterhead. After initially dodging questions from Skaggs, pressure began building, particularly from reporters at the hearing, and McIntosh acknowledged that the forged letterhead was done by his staff. These actions resulted in an ethics probe.

On the Senate side, Alan Simpson (R-WY) launched his own investigation of the lobbying by the American Association of Retired Persons (AARP). He argued that 501(c)(4) organizations should not be allowed to receive federal grant money because they do not face the same lobby limits as 501(c)(3) charities. Simpson, however, was suspicious of the Istook amendment when it was being debated as part of the appropriations process. In the end, Senator Carl Levin (D-MI) joined Simpson in pushing for a provision that would prohibit 501(c)(4) organizations that lobby from receiving federal grant funds. But the provision allowed a 501(c)(4) to be affiliated with a 501(c)(3) that could receive the money. This provision took the steam out of the Istook amendment and eventually became law.

Republican intellectuals helped fuel the effort to push the Istook amendment. Michael Horowitz, a staff person at the Office of Management and Budget during the A-122 fight and at the conservative think tank, the Hudson Institute, during the Istook fight, said about nonprofit federal grantees: "They're hooked on the money. It's welfare for middle-class people who think they're doing God's work." Heritage Foundation scholars argued that the receipt of federal grant money by nonprofits constituted a situation similar to the subsidization theory discussed earlier. As one opinion piece noted, "More than 200 years ago, Thomas Jefferson wrote: 'To compel a man to furnish funds for the propagation of ideas he disbelieves and abhors is sinful and tyrannical.' To suggest that Jefferson and Madison and their colleagues would have condoned using taxpayer dollars to fuel special interest-lobbying is preposterous."[100]

Grover Norquist, head of Americans for Tax Reform and a top consultant to Speaker Gingrich was very direct about the intentions of conservatives: "We will hunt [these liberal groups] down one by one and extinguish their funding sources. With control over Congress and in the White House, it's all over. We will go back and sue people who broke the law, who were ripping off taxpayers

---

[100] See Georges, WSJ, and Whitmann, Marshall and Charles P. Griffin. "There's No 'Gag Rule' on Nonprofits," *The Washington Post,* September 1, 1995.

to do political work. If Planned Parenthood is lobbying, taxpayers need to be reimbursed" (Shear 1995, 925). Conservatives like Norquist inserted language into the 1996 Republican Platform supporting the Istook amendment, making clear that the party supported the "defund the left" effort. They called the proposal in the GOP platform the "Let America Know" initiative, saying it would let the public know about "Washington's dirty little secret."

To the ultimate detriment of the House GOP, these high-minded arguments did not square with the law restricting nonprofit federal grantees from using government funds for lobbying.[101] The law makes clear that nonprofits cannot use federal funds to lobby and various government investigations have revealed no systemic pattern of violations. Of course, the Heritage Foundation, Istook, McIntosh and other supporters said nonprofits were skirting the law because money is fungible, meaning that government grants were freeing up private dollars for lobbying.

The fatal mistake by the House GOP leadership that ultimately lost their fight against nonprofits was miscalculating the potential breadth of their proposal. Their "defund the left" proposal squarely hit a broad cross-section of the nonprofit sector, especially since nearly one-third of nonprofit revenue comes from government. It was the mainstreaming of the issue by the Let America Speak coalition and the advocacy by America's bread-and-butter charities that ultimately made the Istook Amendment seem Draconian. Let America Speak coalition members, such as Mothers Against Drunk Driving, the YMCA, and the Arc (formerly the Association of Retarded Citizens), fought back by pointing out the potential damage that could be caused by the Istook Amendment. In one press release blasting the National Beer Wholesalers Association for their support of the Istook legislation, MADD said the "Istook-McIntosh-Ehrlich 'Nonprofit Gag Order' Would Cripple MADD's Lifesaving Advocacy Work and Establish a Big New Federal Bureaucracy to Harass Charities" (MADD, 1995). By humanizing the issue and making it local, charities won the day at the federal level.

---

[101] OMB Circular A-122 prohibits the use of federal funding for lobbying. In addition, the Byrd Amendment, §319, Dept of Interior Fiscal Year Appropriations Act, P.L. 101-121; 103 Stat.701; 31 U.S.C. §1352. "precludes federal funds that are awarded recipients of federal contracts, grants, loans, or cooperative agreements from being used to pay persons to influence or to attempt to influence agency or legislative decision makers in connection with the awarding of any contract, grant, loan, or cooperative agreement." (See Hopkins 1992, 366).

The action of charities across the country was noticed. Newspaper editorials and opinion pieces sprung up everywhere. The topic was central to several conferences and meetings that involved business leaders, policymakers, and nonprofit volunteers. Knowledge of the Istook Amendment reached a very high level. One of the authors of this book met with President Clinton along with a small number of environmental leaders. During the meeting, the President was asked about the Istook Amendment. He said he knew about it and thought it was horrible legislation. He smiled and told the group not to worry, that, "As long as I'm President, it will not happen."

One of the surprises of the Istook Amendment fight was the support of certain private foundations. Some foundations, supported with a legal opinion that direct lobbying on the Istook fight was self-defense and, hence, permitted, signed letters and made calls to Congress. They explained the devastating impact the legislation would have on nonprofits across the country. Recognizing the potential impact of the Istook Amendment and other attacks on nonprofit advocacy, several foundations made timely general purpose grants to key organizations so they could ramp up overall public policy capacity to address the challenges to advocacy. These actions, particularly the investment in nonprofit sector infrastructure groups, paid off during and after the Istook Amendment fights. Seasoned from the federal level and now fully staffed, the co-chairs of the Let America Speak Coalition (Alliance for Justice, Independent Sector and OMB Watch), as well as the rest of the coalition were ready when the attacks on advocacy moved to the states.[102]

There were Istook-like proposals in Georgia, Illinois, and other states. But probably the most significant fallout of the Istook Amendment was coupling nonprofit advocacy restrictions to a conservative agenda to promote "paycheck protection" legislation that affected union members. In 1998, a section of the Campaign Reform and Election Integrity Act, introduced by Representative Bill Thomas (R-CA), had a provision that required nonprofit organizations to annually ask for consent from their members to use their funds for "political activity." Like the Istook amendment, the Thomas provision defined political activity very broadly and included engaging

---

[102] For a description of tactics used by the Let America Speak Coalition to defeat the Istook Amendment see Gary D. Bass, "A Case Study of Nonprofit Advocacy in the U.S." OMB Watch, 1996.

in public policy matters, such as commenting on federal regulations or educating the public about federal laws and regulations. After a flood of letters and calls, Thomas ultimately dropped the provision.

It did not end there. In California, a ballot measure, Proposition 226, would have required charities to get written permission from donors participating in government workplace giving campaigns if they wanted to spend those funds lobbying on ballot initiatives. The "paycheck protection" measure was offered as a way to limit union activism through contributions from workplace donors. But the measure also chilled nonprofit advocacy since many nonprofits received contributions through the workplace fund and would have had to check with contributors to get permission to support or oppose ballot initiatives.[103] Support or opposition to ballot measures is considered lobbying under the tax code and is therefore permissible activity for charities. A ballot measure that was already highly charged – business versus unions – became even more charged with most of the nonprofit sector (with the notable exception of the United Way of America) opposing the measure. Labor and nonprofits saw the provision as a direct attack while proponents sought to disconnect a financial pipeline to liberal advocacy groups through a measure that had a thin veneer of accountability. The proposition was defeated after another all-out lobbying effort led by the California Association of Nonprofits with support from leaders from Let America Speak such as OMB Watch and the National Committee for Responsive Philanthropy.

A similar measure was later introduced and defeated in Oregon. Designed to prohibit union dues from being used for political purposes, it might have significantly restricted the advocacy rights of certain nonprofits – those that receive contributions through charitable giving campaigns from public employees that are implemented through state payroll deduction plans (Let America Speak 1998).[104]

While many believe the Istook Amendment and its subsequent variations created a newfound interest in charity lobbying, it may also have exacerbated the chilling impact that the Circular A-122, the CFC eligibility

---

[103] "Impartial Government Analyses Indicate Charities Affected by Proposition 226," National Committee for Responsive Philanthropy and the Let America Speak Coalition, 1998, http://www.ombwatch.org/las/1998/prop226report.html.
[104] Language like Proposition 226 has again qualified to be on the California ballot in a 2005 special election.

issue, and IRS proposals already started. It may be that charities simply are afraid that they are violating some law or regulation that prohibits engaging in public policy matters because the high visibility that these proposals received at the time.

Since the Istook fight of the mid-1990s, direct attacks on nonprofit advocacy have been sporadic but generate significant attention and fear when they arise. In 1999, anti-advocacy language was included in an appropriations bill for the Veterans Department, Department of Housing and Urban Development, and the Environmental Protection Agency. Legislation supported by Senator Christopher Bond (R-MO) would have imposed new burdens on federal grantees by requiring that they keep separate bank accounts, one for lobbying and litigation, and another for grant funded programs. The provision would have placed onerous new recordkeeping requirements on charities already prohibited from using federal funds for lobbying under OMB Circular A-122. The Bond legislation would also have created a five-year ban on receipt of federal grants if a charity was found to have lobbied or litigated against the federal government with grant money.[105] Pressure from the nonprofit community persuaded Bond to remove the provisions, but the fact that the issue was reminiscent of the Istook battle undoubtedly scared plenty of groups.

In 2003, several challenges to nonprofit advocacy were thwarted. Language included in a bill to reauthorize the Individuals with Disabilities Education Act (IDEA) would have limited the advocacy rights of organizations that involve parents training disabled children. Specifically, the legislation would have made federally funded nonprofit parent centers ineligible for funding if they engaged in "federal relations." Reminiscent of "substantial" in the IRS rules, "federal relations" was not defined, so almost any form of technical advice could be included. One example that might have qualified is a case where "a parent center organization also runs a day care program and provides comments to a federal agency on proposed rules relating to accreditation of staff" (OMB Watch 2003). This provision was very similar to the all-encompassing efforts of the Istook amendment in 1995.

The nonprofit sector moved quickly in lobbying for the removal of the restrictive language. In a 48-hour period, more than 3,400 e-mail messages

---

[105] The effort to oppose the Bond legislation was led by OMB Watch through its fast acting email list reaching thousands of nonprofits.

flooded the House of Representatives Subcommittee on Education Reform, which was considering the bill. Rep. Michael Castle (R -DE), the chair of the subcommittee and author of the bill, received numerous calls from nonprofits in his home state of Delaware. Despite this impressive show of force, occasional swats and slashes at the fundamental advocacy role of nonprofits have continued as the nonprofit sector grows in numbers and in power.

At the end of 2005, the House Republican Study Committee, comprised of approximately 100 conservatives, successfully got the chair of the Financial Services Committee, Michael Oxley (R-OH), to add a nonprofit gag provision to a bill that would have created a new Affordable Housing Fund. The bill passed the House and was awaiting Senate action as this publication was completed.[106] The bill would have required Fannie Mae to create an Affordable Housing Fund from its profits. In the early years of the fund, priority would be given to the Gulf Coast to respond to the devastation resulting from Hurricanes Katrina and Rita.

The bill would disqualify nonprofits from applying for grants under the affordable housing program if they, or an affiliated organization, engaged in any one of the following activities during the 12 months prior to applying for the funds or throughout the duration of grant period:

- Voter registration, voter identification, get-out-the-vote, or other nonpartisan voter participation efforts;
- Public promotion, support, criticism, or opposition of a candidate for federal office, which could be interpreted to include criticism of elected officials who may be seeking reelection;
- Production of broadcasts that refer to federal candidates within 60 days of a general election or 30 days of primary; or
- Lobbying, except for 501(c)(3) organizations lobbying within permissible limits.

Two or more entities would be considered to be "affiliated" if they:

- Had overlapping board members, offices, executives, or staff;
- Share any office space, staff members, supplies, resources, or marketing materials, including Internet and other forms of public communication; or

---

[106] See Federal Housing Finance Reform Act (H.R. 1461).

- Received or gave more than 20 percent of their budgets to one another.

The amendment would also allow future regulations to create even more ways to demonstrate that two organizations are "affiliated." This definition is much broader than the way the word is used in other federal laws. For example, under the federal tax code two groups are only considered to be affiliated if one of them can control the decisions of the other.[107]

Conservatives felt very strongly about this provision. As Rep. Tom Feeney (R-FL) said, "I'd rather burn the money than give it to an advocacy group."[108] The nonprofit sector mobilized very quickly but the Republican leadership would not allow a motion to strip the gag provision. As a result, the overall bill almost failed to pass. Clearly the nonprofit sector (or at least certain leadership organizations within the sector) improved significantly in its ability to spot advocacy challenges and demonstrate stamina and resolve in defending ground. However, the underlying problem remains: that the will, desire and perhaps risk tolerance for advocacy has been eroded by these attacks.[109]

---

[107] See OMB Watch's analysis of the affiliation language at http://www.ombwatch.org/pdfs/10.19.statements/Affiliation_language.pdf. Additional information is available at http://www.ombwatch.org/article/articleview/3133/1/265?TopicID=1.

[108] Dawn Kopecki, "US House GOP Conservatives Dismiss Compromise On GSE Bill", *Dow Jones Newswires*, June 29, 2005.

[109] There have been additional governmental actions that have concerned many nonprofit leaders. In 2003, the IRS began targeted audits of nonprofits that elected the lobbying expenditure ceiling even though the Service had repeatedly said that electing would not increase chances of being audited. After a flurry of trade press stories and meetings with the IRS, the IRS dropped the targeted audits.

In the fall of 2004, just before the national elections, the IRS notified the NAACP that it was conducting an examination into whether a speech by Chairman Julian Bond that criticized policies of President Bush constituted prohibited campaign intervention. This action created great concern for nonprofit leaders, especially when legal experts noted that the speech did not appear to be more than speaking out on broad public policies. As this book goes to press, the issue continues to linger.

As this book goes to press, the IRS announced a new Political Activity Compliance Initiative, a program of increased and expedited enforcement of the prohibition on intervention in elections by 501(c)(3) organizations. Publicity around the program could lead to a flood of retaliatory and harassment complaints this year unless the IRS develops standards to screen out such abuse of its procedures.

AmeriCorps and Volunteer Advocacy

Another episode began in 1990, years before the Istook amendment, when President George H.W. Bush signed into law the National and Community Service Act that generated grants to schools to support service-learning and created the Points of Light Foundation. In 1993, President Clinton stepped up the federal government's involvement in fostering volunteerism by becoming the chief advocate for the new National and Community Service Trust Act that created the Corporation for National Service, which is home to the historic Vista program and newer programs including AmeriCorps and Learn and Serve.

Following the enactment of the law, the new corporation included in its regulations restrictions on lobbying on a broad set of advocacy activities by AmeriCorps-funded volunteers. Already, there were laws and regulations on the books that prohibit the use of federal funds for lobbying (e.g., OMB Circular A-122), but the corporation felt it was necessary to go further, drawing the ire of groups including Independent Sector and the Alliance for Justice. According to Bob Smucker, former chief lobbyist for Independent Sector, "We felt like the regulations did not need to go further than current law. When we found that they were much more restrictive, we were very disappointed and expressed our dismay directly to administration staff."

The advocacy restrictions in the AmeriCorps regulations indeed go well beyond the restrictions on lobbying contained in the federal grant cost principles. Among the prohibited advocacy activities are: attempting to influence legislation (covered by A-122); organizing or engaging in protests, petitions, boycotts, or strikes (not previously covered); assisting, promoting or deterring union organizing (not previously covered); engaging in partisan political activities, or other activities designed to influence the outcome of an election to any public office (covered by IRS restrictions on partisan political activity).[110] The restriction on organizing, protests and related activities stated above was particularly outrageous. The terms were not defined and could be applied to nongovernmental situations. For example, what if a nonprofit using AmeriCorps-funded volunteers, wanted to ask citizens to sign petitions urging the president of the Sara Lee Corporation to change the company's policies on importing coffee? When the federal limitations on nonprofit lobbying were created to protect taxpayers, they were intended to limit the extent of legislative participation and ban partisan political

---

[110] 45 CFR Chapter XXV, § 2520.30.

107

activity. Nothing was said about restricting other types of civic activity, and potentially non-government directed advocacy.

The AmeriCorps advocacy restrictions, still in place today, are a political hot potato if brought up as an issue. During the mid-1990s, the Republican-led Congress sought to gut funding for AmeriCorps because it was viewed as a pet project of the Clinton Administration. In particular, Sen. Charles Grassley (R-IA) was highly critical of the costs per volunteer. Eventually, Grassley and other critics became supporters as the program found its legs and produced results, helping groups like Teach for America and City Year generate countless hours of service and provide opportunities for young people to develop professionally.

The second Bush Administration's significant endorsement of volunteer service and expansion of the Corporation by adding the USA Freedom Corps – a reaction to the September 11, 2001, terrorist attacks – put to rest any question about whether the program will continue.[111] Organizations that rely upon AmeriCorps volunteers to provide services still do not like the advocacy restrictions, but they seem to have found ways to teach civic action and provide opportunities for social change that do not flagrantly violate the regulations (Schmitz, interview 2002). Below the surface, however, a tension still exists. According to one executive director of an AmeriCorps grantee organization, "What's ironic about the whole thing is that under the new AmeriCorps grant guidelines there is funding for citizenship training. How can you on the one hand encourage citizenship training while you restrict petitions and protests?"

Nonprofit Support Structures Grow
But Do Not Include Advocacy

Over the past 30 years with the expansion of government and business, much of the nonprofit sector professionalized from a collection of social movements to a sophisticated growth industry. Key factors in modernization of the nonprofit sector into a social and economic giant include:

---

[111] The future of AmeriCorps may not be as certain as the budget deficit continues to climb. As this book goes to press, there has been discussion about cutting funding for the program.

- The enormous inflow of government funding from fees-for-service, grants and contracts
- Growth in the number of associations
- Exponential growth of private and community foundations
- Emergence of a sub-field of nonprofit infrastructure support and education organizations
- Evolution of a significant body of literature on nonprofit management
- Influence of corporate America into nonprofit management practice
- Increase in the utilization of information technology

To the detriment of people and causes served by nonprofits, the trend to professionalize that began in the 1980s and continued through the end of the century did not inherently include or consider the historic advocacy role nonprofits play. Nonprofits in all fields, mainly through their state and national associations, hired consultants, attended professional development training, diversified funding streams, became more entrepreneurial and put significant time and money into organizational, managerial, and governance development. Nonprofit management gurus emerged, some from the business sector, including Peter Drucker, and others from the nonprofit sector, including Peter Brinkerhoff, John Carver, Francis Hesselbein, and Peter Senge. Their books, seminars, and ideas have permeated management thinking and practice in the nonprofit sector, helping organizations to develop systematic ways of building organizations, programs and communities.[112] A goal of this era of nonprofit management (1980-2000) was to create greater efficiency and scale, and to strengthen overall sector capacity.[113]

---

[112] The Carver series published by Jossey-Bass is one of the most complete sets of books on management and governance, yet it is sparse in its consideration of public policy participation as a leadership or governance function. The Drucker Self-Assessment Tools provide generic materials that can be used for program design and capacity-building of any area within a nonprofit including public policy. While we have not investigated whether these tools are used for public policy we have not heard of them used this way.
[113] In the late 1990s, the concept of social entrepreneurship came to the forefront of nonprofit management thinking. It is an umbrella term, but as used by the National Center for Social Entrepreneurship, it is about strategies for helping nonprofits to become more business-like and to use market strategies to achieve mission-related goals. The emphasis on social entrepreneurship during the 1990s was definitely to encourage nonprofits to develop fee-based revenue streams and to create small business.

However, the new literature and approaches used to help nonprofits were largely adapted from for-profit business models, not from the perspective that nonprofits are also fundamentally institutions of social change and civic empowerment. Integration of public policy participation, advocacy, and lobbying were not identified or nurtured as core competencies of nonprofit management and leadership, and therefore were not stressed equally with other management functions, including fundraising, financing, program strategy, and board development. An illustration of the absence of advocacy in nonprofit literature is the emphasis of the nonprofit management series published by Jossey-Bass (a division of Wiley publishing), the nation's leader in publishing for nonprofits. Out of more than 140 how-to books on managing and leading a nonprofit only three are focused exclusively on public policy engagement.[114] What kind of signal does this send to new and developing nonprofit leaders when they do not see that public policy engagement is something that is inherently connected to their mission or organization's viability?

Lack of Advocacy Education: A Problem of Supply and Demand

During this period, there was an explosion in the number of university-based programs that teach nonprofit management. Growing from a small number of programs at the beginning of the 1980s, there are more than 40 nonprofit academic centers today (Mirabella 2001). There are even more programs where nonprofit related courses from other disciplines are included. For example, out of the more than 250 schools of public policy and public administration that are members of the National Association of Schools of Public Affairs and Administration, more than 100 offer nonprofit courses.[115] Public administration, public health, social work, public policy, law and arts management programs often have units or whole courses that prepare future nonprofit managers. Both at the undergraduate and graduate levels, these programs provide a variety of curricula intended to prepare nonprofit managers for most aspects of running a charitable

---

[114] Rinku Sen and Kim Klein, *Stir it Up: Lessons in Community Organizing and Advocacy*, 2003.; Russell Linden, *Working Across Boundaries: Making Collaboration Work in Government and Nonprofit Organizations*, 2002; Walter Pidgeon, *Legislative Labyrinth: A Map for Not-for-Profits*, 2001. All published by Jossey-Bass. Other publications mention or have chapters on government affairs, but none that we can find specifically help integrate public policy participation into the everyday management and leadership practices of nonprofits.

[115] National Association of Schools of Public Affairs and Administration, www.naspaa.org

nonprofit, yet relatively few include courses or course units that build tactical skills in public policy participation, including community organizing and lobbying. According to a survey of university-based nonprofit academic centers by Baumgarten and Cortes (2002, 6-10), less than half of nonprofit management degree programs that responded to their survey offer a stand-alone course that teaches students how to participate in the public policy process. Nine out of ten do not offer even a module on advocacy skills within other courses. Even lower levels of advocacy-related curriculum offerings were found in other disciplines including public policy and business administration.[116]

While many nonprofit management programs are willing to fit advocacy into their curricula, it is clear that most are not yet willing to include advocacy as one of the basic requirements for graduation, leaving it to rank below financial management and various fundraising-type courses. This is especially ironic given that more funding comes into the nonprofit sector from government than any other source and it usually takes consistent government relations and advocacy to secure grants and contracts. Having an academic field devoted to teaching nonprofit management is one of the milestones of the increasing maturity of the nonprofit sector.[117] These programs are a pipeline for people beginning their careers, changing career paths later in life and for acquiring additional skills while in their current position with nonprofits. Unfortunately, according to a study funded by the Kellogg Foundation, advocacy ranks in the middle of the pack on the list of subjects desired by most students of nonprofit management.[118] Given the importance of the academic community to future leadership of nonprofits, it is troubling that public policy engagement is viewed so low on the priority

---

[116] The Baumgarten-Cortes study had a small sample size and a somewhat low rate of return on their survey. However, the participating institutions provide a useful sketch of the treatment of advocacy and "influencing policy strategies" within the field of nonprofit management education. We also acknowledge that public policy and social work schools might teach about the legislative process, social movements, policy research and generally how to frame policy questions, but we distinguish these types of units from skills-based learning of how to develop a grassroots network, how to design and implement media advocacy, for example.

[117] The evolution of the National Academic Centers Council (NACC) and American Humanics are evidence of the maturation of nonprofit sector as an academic field.

[118] Survey of Nonprofit Management Students, R. Sam Larson and Mark Wilson, Part 3 of 3, Building Bridges Cluster Evaluation, March 2001, http://centerpointinstitute.org/bridges/PapersReports/StudentSurvey3.htm#Table%203.

list. The weakness in nonprofit management education pertaining to advocacy derives from the insufficient number of colleges and universities supplying required coursework in nonprofit advocacy skills on the supply side, and what may be low student interest on the demand side.

There are a few emerging courses and programs that can provide models and resources for colleges and universities that want to begin teaching in the nonprofit public policy arena. Johns Hopkins, University of San Francisco, Georgetown University, and the New School University all have nonprofit advocacy courses.[119] The University of Minnesota-Duluth launched an entire master's program in advocacy and political leadership focusing on nonprofits in 2004 that has produced new graduates who are prepared and motivated to make advocacy a core part of nonprofit work.[120] While promising programs in themselves, few in the nonprofit sector know about them or have career incentives to seek them out. If emerging nonprofit managers don't realize the relevance of public policy and the need for their participation, then schools will be less likely to offer courses and they won't recognize the important and historic role of advocacy as a leadership function.

Nonprofit academic education is only one part of a larger group of organizations that make up what is commonly known as the field of nonprofit infrastructure (Abramson and McCarthy, 2002). Some of the national organizations that comprise this group include the Independent Sector, the Council on Foundations, and the National Committee for Responsive Philanthropy and the Foundation Center. There are also an increasingly large number of nonprofit management support organizations that operate mainly at the local level providing workshops, consulting, and networking opportunities. Many of them are associated with a national umbrella organization called the Alliance for Nonprofit Management. At the state level there are now close to 40 nonprofit associations affiliated through the National Council of Nonprofit Associations.

---

[119] There are also certificate programs for nonprofit professionals, such as one at the Center for Public and Nonprofit Leadership at Georgetown University, that include advocacy training. One of the authors of this book is teaching a course at the Georgetown University's Public Policy Institute on nonprofit advocacy.
[120] University of Minnesota Duluth Program is located at http://www.d.umn.edu/~maplwww/

Over the past 25 years the nonprofit infrastructure subfield has grown significantly, although this trend appears to be either flat or reversing. Similar to the nonprofit academic field, this group of leadership and technical assistance organizations has not consistently promoted advocacy as a core operating activity for nonprofits. A special issue of the *Nonprofit Quarterly* that was devoted to a description of national nonprofit infrastructure groups is striking in that it shows a paucity of groups and resources devoted to public policy advocacy.[121] Those infrastructure groups that have a defined focus, such as addressing information needs of nonprofit boards of directors, often do not focus on the important role advocacy should play. For example, BoardSource (formerly the National Center for Nonprofit Boards), founded in 1988, has grown into the leading provider of information on nonprofit boards of directors. They provide numerous workshops and have more than 70 publications in their catalog – yet they only have two publications for board members on lobbying and advocacy, and nowhere does it say explicitly that participation in the public policy process is a function of board governance (Sparks, 1997; BoardSource, 2004).[122] Moreover, as Urban Institute's Linda Lampkin prepared materials for the *Nonprofit Quarterly* special issue, she calculated that only 5.5 percent of nonprofit infrastructure spending goes to organizations dealing with public policy training and advocacy. This inattention to public policy is even more surprising because, as Abramson and McCarthy note, public policy issues affecting the nonprofit sector play a critical role in why a nonprofit infrastructure is needed in the first place.

This is not to say the nonprofit infrastructure groups have ignored public policy concerns. To the contrary, they have been successful in mobilizing nonprofits to lobby and participate in important legislation when there has been a direct threat or opportunity facing the entire sector; but they do not seek ways to use periods of heightened participation in public policy matters as a moment to further integrate advocacy into nonprofits' business models.[123]

---

[121] *Nonprofit Quarterly*, Special Infrastructure Issue, 2004, http://www.nonprofitquarterly. org/section/496.html

[122] In reviewing the Boardsource Web site, there is no place that we can find that defines public policy participation as a core function of a board.

[123] Although it is too early to assess, several projects have been launched aimed to provide advocacy building models including the Building Capacity for Public Policy project of the National Council of Nonprofit Associations and Independent Sector; and the Advocacy for Social Change course offered by Georgetown University's Executive Nonprofit Management Certificate Program. Our assessment of the field, however, is that while there are many workshops that teach specific skills or knowledge, e.g., what the law says about lobbying, few help nonprofits integrate advocacy into other services from an organizational development perspective.

There is no message promoting policy engagement, only technical information about how to remain within the legal boundaries.[124] Previous research, including findings in this book indicates that the culture within an organization is important to the will and capacity for public policy engagement. The lack of attention to public policy as an essential role of the nonprofit organization – as a management responsibility, as a trustee responsibility, and as a core function – has undoubtedly undermined the willingness of nonprofits to be civically engaged. Findings later in this book will discuss how we can turn this around.

There is no standard bearing message to the nonprofit sector from a wide range of leadership organizations that improving public policy is a core function of 21st century nonprofit management. Rather, there is mostly technical information about how to remain within the legal boundaries. Over the past 20 years the Council on Foundations (COF), the leading trade association for private and community foundations in the United States, very successfully launched or inspired the creation of new organizations, programs, practices and partnerships designed to support and enhance the profession of philanthropy. The Forum on Regional Associations of Grantmakers is one such endeavor that provides support services to state and local clusters of foundations. COF has taken steps to educate foundations about the legal opportunities for public policy grant making and provided foundation staff with lobbying experience through the annual "Foundations on the Hill" day in Washington, D.C. However, COF has yet to put its full muscle behind the message that foundations should encourage and fund organizations and projects designed to influence public policy as a strategy for reaching philanthropic goals. Full muscle would mean far more programming devoted to encouraging the funding of advocacy and civic engagement than panel sessions at conferences or one-hour modules within a larger professional development curricula. COF's community foundations program is beginning to take steps toward the vision of connecting the role of public policy to community leadership through its network of volunteers.

Much more work needs to be done on the private foundation side as legal knowledge of the rules is but one of several factors that influence advocacy

---

[124] We are not critical of BoardSource. Rather, we are using this as an example of a broader situation among the infrastructure groups. We could provide the same example with many nonprofit management support organizations.

grant making, but there are some foundations to reflect on this topic. Recent grant making by the George Gund Foundation and the Minneapolis Foundation shows that funding charities to hire a public policy staff person can result in successful lobbying that leads to far more in government funding for people and projects than the original cost of the grant (CLPI 2003). In addition, the California Wellness Foundation (2002) has gone on the record saying, "One of the most effective ways to leverage foundation dollars is by funding public policy efforts." And as mentioned earlier in this chapter, the Northern California Grantmakers Association has launched a very comprehensive Public Policy Grantmaking Toolkit.[125]

Civic Engagement and Nonprofit Advocacy

To take the next step forward toward an understanding of how nonprofit advocacy might be strengthened, it is valuable to examine nonprofits' role as vehicles for civic engagement by individuals in American democracy. Robert Putnam, in his highly acclaimed book *Bowling Alone*, ignited a debate over the state of civic engagement. Putnam used a wide variety of sources including voting records, but in particular drew from the original membership records of voluntary associations in local communities throughout the past 50 years, to capture a sense of trends in the volume, depth and character of civic activity. He found that levels of civic participation declined over the second half of the 20th century and a number of factors including watching television are partly responsible. Putnam (2000, 354) also finds that increased involvement in associations does not necessarily mean a more tolerant society.

From the perspective of one interested in strengthening nonprofit advocacy, Putnam's findings were initially troubling. Will nonprofits be able to involve and mobilize citizens to influence policymakers on a mass basis in the future? Will membership in nonprofits continue to decline, leaving professional staffs with position papers and no constituents? Today, a large percentage of Americans are associated with nonprofits either as staff, volunteers, or donors, but the meaning of those associations may be changing. As implied in the earlier part of this chapter, nonprofit donations and memberships have greatly increased. As donors, however, it does not necessarily mean that citizens are truly engaged. It may simply mean that these donors are concerned enough to write a check, possibly expecting that the organization staff will provide the needed advocacy.

---

[125] See http://www.ncg.org/toolkit/home.html

Theda Skocpol describes this trend in several publications. "No longer do civic entrepreneurs think of constructing vast federations and recruiting interactive citizen-members. When a new cause (or tactic) arises, activists envisage opening a national office and managing association-building as well as national projects from the center. Members, if any, are likely to be seen not as fellow citizens but as consumers with policy preferences. In short, all sorts of new organization-building techniques encourage contemporary citizen's groups – just like trade and professional associations – to concentrate their efforts in efficiently managed headquarters located close to the federal government and the national media. Even a group aiming to speak for large numbers of Americans does not absolutely need members." (Skocpol 1999, 492; Crenson and Ginsberg, 2002)

However, this has a profound effect on the nature of nonprofit advocacy. National and state groups become more skilled at the policy papers, but operate without a strong base. On certain policy initiatives, the technical expertise is precisely what policymakers need. However, when tackling a broader agenda that requires shaping public opinion and shifting positions of legislators, only a few organizations with large voting constituencies (or promises of campaign contributions) carry much clout.

This shifting role of nonprofits as representing constituencies versus mobilizing constituencies mirrors a national debate that has existed since the founding of the country. It raises the question of whether the nonprofits as conduits for civic engagement are drifting too much toward representation of people and causes as in a representative democracy versus organizing and empowering citizens for participatory democracy. At a conceptual level there seems to be a struggle between Jacksonian- and Madisonian-style democracies. The Jacksonian age – the time when Tocqueville and Beaumont visited the United States – ushered in participatory democracy marked by high voter turnout and robust debate on urgent issues of the day. Some argue that this era died with the industrial age of the 20th century where "public opinion" was subject to manipulation by slick politicians and new forms of mass media and marketing, thereby trivializing citizen participation. Madison, on the other hand, argued in Federalist 10 that representative government would protect the country from the "spectacles of turbulence and contention" characteristic of pure democracies. He had great disdain for public input because it could be manipulated.[126] Other scholars have pointed out that throughout history there has been a natural check and balance system that enables nonprofits to provide what amounts to civic recycling services. "Madison is striking because what in the beginning is an evil turns out ultimately to be a remedy: factions are both an evil and an antidote to the ills of pluralist government" (Graziano 2001, 133).[127] It also seems consistent to conclude that nonprofits as agents of civic engagement are responsible for being their own antidote to extremism on the representation-participation continuum. They must be wary not to be too removed from the people and, at the other end, ensure that they can afford to advocate on behalf of people by ensuring financial solvency and effectiveness in the professional insider game of politics.

This analytical frame helps us seek understanding of the factors that organizations more concerned with representation, or participation, must take into account in trying to build their power bases. Research by Berns, Schlozman and Verba (1995, 2002) finds that education, workforce participation and job position are key indicators of organizational affiliation. Education is particularly important. As educational level increases, so does the likelihood of individual civic participation as part of a nonprofit.[128] Nonprofits interested in mobilizing volunteers for advocacy may be interested to learn that time is not a deterring factor in whether someone will participate (Berns, Schlozman and Verba 2002, 260). To the contrary, the "power of the ask" – the degree to which a nonprofit asks the citizen/donor to participate – in large measure determines whether and how often they will contribute time and money to all activities including advocacy.[129]

---

[126] Madison wrote: "Had every Athenian citizen been a Socrates, every Athenian assembly would still have been a mob." The Founders were terrified of a badly educated populace that could be duped by tyrannical leaders, and of a system that could allow too much power to fall into one person's hands. That is why they constructed a system that filtered the whims of the masses through an elected body and dispersed power by dividing the government into three branches.

[127] Luigi Graziano's *Lobbying Pluralism and Democracy* (Palgrave, New York, 2001) is an interesting opportunity to read about the framers' views of the beginnings of nonprofit advocacy through the lens of a European not unlike Toqueville. This work is enhanced by a forward by David Cohen, co-founder of the Advocacy Institute, framing the issues.

[128] Berns, Schlozman and Verba, *Private Roots of Public Action,* 2001, 220-23. Putnam goes further to say that education is the strongest predictor of "social participation," assuming he also means participation in nonprofits. p. 418

[129] *Giving and Volunteering*, 2001, Independent Sector key findings, p.2., www. independentsector.org.

To some extent, the rise of the Internet as a tool for organizing, accessing information, joining groups, and making donations has bridged the representation–participation divide. The Internet has made individual civic participation incredibly easy and an activity that one may do according to one's own schedule and with complete anonymity if one wishes. Customized Web-based advocacy portals have created opportunities for a virtual participator democracy that enables groups that were at one time advocates without members, to develop loyal followers.

Those interested in further exploration of the factors that influence nonprofit advocacy across the types of nonprofit advocacy organizations should consult the work of Elizabeth Boris and Elizabeth Reid of the Urban Institute. They completed an in-depth seminar series on the topic of nonprofit advocacy that explored many factors including organizational behavior, finances and the law. Boris and Reid have also written extensively on the topic.[130]

As the historic roles of nonprofits in fostering civic engagement are blurring and the techniques of advocacy have become more accessible, certain causes have helped reverse the downward trend in individual civic engagement by engaging many well-educated, well-intended, and well-moneyed donors. Tufts University Professor Jeffrey Berry's research finds that there is a class of "post-material" issues that resonate with the citizen/taxpayer/consumer on both sides of the political aisle, including conservation, patient rights, and consumer protections (Berry, 1999). Collectively they have highlighted new issues to citizens who might not otherwise have joined or donated to nonprofits for purposes of expressing their political views.

The September 11, 2001, terrorist attacks on U.S. soil were tragic events with deep and lasting consequences in all aspects of American society and around the world. In the year after the attacks, trust in government for the first time in a generation shot up substantially.[131] Americans rallied behind

---

[130] See Elizabeth Boris and Jeff Krehely, "Civic Participation and Advocacy," in *The State of Nonprofit America*, ed. Lester M. Salamon (Washington, DC: Brookings Institution Press, 2002); and Elizabeth Reid, "Nonprofit Advocacy and Political Participation," in *Nonprofits & Government: Collaboration and Conflict*, eds. Elizabeth T. Boris and Eugene Steurle (Washington, DC: Urban Institute Press 1999). See also http://www.urban.org/advocacyresearch/.

[131] Robert Putnam, "Bowling Together," *The American Prospect* (February 2, 2002).

the President and the federal government as they prepared for homeland security and for war against the Al Qaeda terrorists. Subsequent events, including new laws pertaining to civil liberties, the war in Iraq, shifts in the economy and the Presidential election of 2004, all may have affected the seemingly upward trend in civic participation at the individual level. Our data set does not account for nonprofits' civic participation following the attacks or the increase in the budget crunch facing nonprofits since that time, so it is beyond the scope of this book to evaluate the levels of civic participation at either the individual or organizational level post-September 11, 2001.[132] However, civic events that seem to have served as motivators for advocacy should be explored including globalization and citizen advocacy for and against the war in Iraq. These events should be studied on an individual level and on an organizational level.

Conclusion

Nonprofits are at the heart of civic engagement and policymaking in American democracy. Throughout history, advocacy in the public interest has yielded a quality of life and freedoms that are the envy of many other countries around the globe. Nonprofit participation in the public policy process was historically the signature function of a rapidly growing sector as observed by early social researchers including James Madison and Alexis de Toqueville. Today's diminished advocacy and policy role of mainstream charitable nonprofits undermines more than 200 years worth of advocacy for people and causes and has implications for quality of life in the future.

This chapter should make clear that no single event has been central to reducing the role nonprofits play in public policy. Indeed, this chapter presents a quick historical overview of events that taken together present a complex web of factors that have resulted in a set of challenges that make the participation barrier difficult to hurdle. Having some understanding of antecedent conditions may help to interpret the research finding presented in later chapters.

---

[132] Harry C. Boyte, who co-directs the Center for Democracy and Citizenship at the University of Minnesota's Humphrey Institute, is a leading expert on citizenship issues. He joined others in releasing a memo on May 6, 2004, with a hopeful message that the "work of citizenship reflects America's ideals for an open and democratic society, a more perfect union of liberty and justice in which all play a role." (Memo from Harry C. Boyte, Nan Skelton, Carmen Sirianni, and David Cohen, with input from others)

For us, five factors stand out from the discussion in this chapter. First, the growing dependence nonprofits have on government funding has had a profound impact on policy participation. On the one hand, there is evidence that this dependence might provide a strong impetus for more advocacy, particularly when it comes to more money for the key programs that the organization cares about or to changes in the way these programs are regulated. Moreover, with funding, nonprofits have a seat at the table. On the other hand, why bite the hand that feeds you?

Second, attacks on nonprofit advocacy by conservatives over the past 25 years have had a chilling impact on policy participation. Even though most policy proposals to limit nonprofit policy participation and attacks on nonprofit advocacy have failed, there has been an unspoken message that it is safer to simply not engage in public policy.

Third, and possibly as a result of the first two points, management training and support to nonprofit executives and to boards of directors do not emphasize the importance of engaging in public policy. Missing in all of today's support systems are mechanisms for building public policy into the basic business model of typical mainstream charities.

Fourth, the nonprofit "infrastructure" groups – that is the organizations that help to represent nonprofits – are very thin when it comes to engaging in advocacy or promotion of public policy participation within the sector.

Finally, the role of foundations is a key part of the story concerning nonprofit policy participation. The fact that they are gun-shy rubs off on the grantees. Additionally, few foundations provide ongoing support for either building the capacity to engage in public policy matters or for actually getting involved in public policy issues.

The end result is that there is a divide between service delivery and advocacy instead of a symbiotic relationship. Service delivery groups and others with a single mission find they simply do not have time or resources to engage in public policy. It is our belief, however, that they can ill-afford not to become involved; far too much is at stake for them to sit on the sidelines.

The factors described in this chapter suggest that simply providing training on lobby rules in the tax code is not going to be enough to motivate nonprofits to engage in public policy matters. Instead, this chapter begins to suggest the need for providing a reason to engage, to think outside of the single issue or purpose of the organization, to find new ways of changing the culture of the organization. Changing the culture will require a major commitment by staff, board of directors, and donors, but it is likely to be an essential element in strengthening policy participation.

Even for those nonprofits that are engaged, many have entered the political arena as purveyors of policy rather than as facilitators of citizens' voices. This raises questions about the best strategies for policy engagement. Many of these questions will not be answered by this book.

The Istook battle of the mid-1990s reminded the nonprofit sector how fundamentally important advocacy is to the survival of programs and to maintaining a critical space in the political process. One might think that because the face-off with Congress was so intense, so basic and was won with unprecedented collective action, nonprofits would have seized the opportunity to be more vocal about why public policy participation is inherent to good service. Not so. Instead, the nonprofit sector might have won the battle but the inconsistency in participation on policy matters today suggests that the lessons of the past have not yet been learned – and that a concerted effort will be needed to boost participation.

Chapter 3
The Need for the SNAP Research
and How It Was Designed

The genesis of SNAP came during a period of heightened alert regarding attacks on nonprofit advocacy rights.[133] As described in the previous chapter, from 1995 to 1998, a number of legislative proposals were introduced to restrict the lobbying and administrative advocacy rights of nonprofit federal grantees. Even though enactment of the leading proposals – often called "Istook amendments" after the lead congressional sponsor, Representative Ernest Istook (R-OK) never occurred, nonprofit leaders worried about the lasting impact on the sector.

In the wake of the Istook amendments, several nonprofit leadership organizations caucused to discuss several issues to strengthen nonprofit advocacy, including ways of getting more nonprofits involved, developing an early warning system to track state and federal proposals affecting nonprofit advocacy, and responding to what many feared would be a chilling impact from the Istook proposals. One of the authors of this publication, Gary D. Bass, had been involved in an earlier controversy during the Reagan Administration, dealing with Circular A-122, which mirrored the Istook amendments (see Chapter 2). Like the Istook amendments, the proposed modifications to Circular A-122, in their most restrictive form, were never implemented. Yet more than five years after the final rules were published, a common question arose at meetings around the country: Aren't there some federal rules that prohibit us from engaging in advocacy?

Many of the nonprofit leaders worried that the Istook amendments would have a similar impact on nonprofit policy participation, dissuading groups from engaging in advocacy. Some wondered whether nonprofits even understood the laws and regulations governing lobbying. To answer these and other questions about nonprofit advocacy, a number of organizations began surveying nonprofits. A 1997 member survey by Independent Sector was followed by a 1998 survey of New York nonprofits conducted by the Council of Community Services of New York State. These two surveys found that, although national nonprofits have at least a basic understanding

---

[133] As a reminder, when we use the term "nonprofit" we are talking about charities organized under 501(c)(3) of the tax code. If we mean other types of nonprofits, we refer to the specific type of nonprofit.

of federal laws governing lobbying, state and local nonprofits generally do not (Independent Sector 1997; Council of Community Services of New York, et. al., 1998). The New York survey reported that 92 percent of respondents had neither opted to use the IRS expenditure test nor registered to lobby in Albany, the state capital. "Eighty-one percent of respondents reported they did not understand whether the lobbying provisions of subsection 501(h) [that created the expenditure limits] applied to their organization."

The New York survey, however, did not ask whether these nonprofits described themselves as engaging in either lobbying or advocacy activities. This left a number of unanswered questions. If they do engage in lobbying activities, it may be that they do not know that they must register in Albany, or they may not understand the benefits of choosing to come under the IRS expenditure test. Another possibility is that their public policy activities may not qualify as lobbying under the IRS or state definition, meaning that there is no need to register or report to the IRS. The more likely scenario that many of the national nonprofit leadership groups feared was that only relatively few nonprofits were really engaged in public policy activities.

During that same period, very few nonprofits nationwide – less than three percent – reported any type of lobbying on annual tax forms submitted to the IRS. In fact, approximately one percent of nonprofits opted to use the expenditure provisions of the 1976 law governing nonprofit lobbying.[134] The changes made by the 1976 law were intended to encourage policy participation by establishing reasonable expenditure limits for lobbying and creating clear definitions of such activities; but the vast majority of nonprofits remain under the older "no substantial part" legal regime, which states that "no substantial part" of a charity's activities may be attempts to influence legislation. This is surprising since the "substantial part" test is vague and has more detailed reporting requirements than the expenditure test and carries more severe sanctions for violations.

---

[134] As of April, 1997, approximately 471,000 charities were eligible to make the election under section 501(h) of the Internal Revenue Code. Only 6,630 of these organizations had filed Form 5768 (the form for choosing to "elect"), roughly 1.4 percent. (Data source: Internal Revenue Service, Exempt Plans/Exempt Organizations Field Systems Branch, 1998.) Section 501(h) allows charities to "elect" to adhere to the lobbying regulations that resulted from the 1976 law, which set an expenditure limit on lobbying activities. For organizations that do not "elect," they fall under a less clear "substantial part" test. To elect, charities must complete a one-page tax form (Form 5768).

Nonprofit leaders also were concerned that the IRS data was serving as a proxy for nonprofit activity, especially since the data only reflected certain types of activities undertaken by nonprofits. Several surveys, such as those conducted by OMB Watch and the National Council of Nonprofit Associations highlighted that nonprofits may be more involved in advocacy than the IRS data would suggest (OMB Watch, 1997; National Council on Nonprofit Associations, 1997). For example, 90 percent of the 600 respondents in an OMB Watch survey supported the goal of encouraging greater public policy participation by nonprofits including groups that do not list advocacy as one of their primary missions (OMB Watch 1997, 27).[135] A 1997 Independent Sector membership survey also noted that most of its members engage in lobbying or advocacy activities.

These surveys may also have been measuring different activities, since words such as lobbying, advocacy, and public policy participation were often used interchangeably, sometimes meaning the same activity and sometimes meaning very different activities. The 1998 New York survey actually tested nonprofit response to the term "advocacy" versus "lobbying" and found that nonprofits prefer "advocacy." But the survey did not define these terms or find ways to describe how advocacy is different from lobbying. In general, existing research did not tell us whether nonprofits use these terms to mean the same thing or whether they ascribe differences between the terms.

Overall, these surveys created a picture of uncertainty:

- How engaged are nonprofits in public policy?
- What do they call these activities – lobbying, advocacy, public education, or other terms?
- What activities do they include under various labels?
- Are the laws and regulations, such as the option to use the expenditure test, confusing and off-putting?
- Is there a chilling impact resulting from the various attacks on

---

[135] OMB Watch, *Building Blocks for the Future: Findings and Recommendations for Strengthening Public Policy Communications and Collaboration in the Nonprofit Sector*, May 1997. See also, Council of Community Services of New York, Inc. (in collaboration with Nonprofit Coordinating Committee of New York), *Advocacy and Lobbying: What Charitable Nonprofits Know and Do In New York State*, January 15, 1998. National Council of Nonprofit Associations, *A Greater Voice: Nonprofit Organizations, Communications Technology and Advocacy*, 1997.

nonprofit advocacy that leaves many nonprofits uncertain whether they can engage in public policy matters?

On July 20, 1998, Cinthia Schuman of Aspen Institute's Nonprofit Sector Research Fund convened a lunch meeting to discuss whether research was needed to help address some of the uncertainties about nonprofit advocacy. During the meeting, participants noted there was little research on nonprofit advocacy and the little that had been done had many shortcomings. For example, participants pointed out that the existing surveys, such as the ones by Independent Sector, OMB Watch, the National Council of Nonprofit Associations, the Council of Community Services of New York and some other state nonprofit associations, were helpful in suggesting issues that needed to be studied more carefully. At the same time, the surveys did not use random samples, sample pools were very small, the survey questions were not tested, and the results could not be generalized to the sector as a whole.

Participants also noted that the research did not identify factors that motivate or deter policy participation. Instead, most research in this area addressed types of lobbying techniques, or explored legal research relating to the law governing nonprofit lobbying.[136]

Despite the significant gap in research, existing nonprofit membership surveys indicated that members need and want additional education about laws governing lobbying (InterAction, 1996; Independent Sector, 1997).[137] These surveys, as well as anecdotal evidence, suggested that nonprofits were fearful of being targeted for IRS audits or, worse, losing their tax exemption if they lobby. By the end of the meeting, there was widespread agreement that more research was needed on nonprofit advocacy.

Walking away from the meeting, Gary Bass of OMB Watch and Bob Smucker of Charity Lobbying in the Public Interest (then a project of

---

[136] See, for example, the following bibliographies: Foundation Center collection on nonprofit lobbying; Beth L. Leech, "Federal Funding and Interest Group Lobbying Behavior," Department of Political Science, Texas A&M University (1997); Anthony J. Nownes and Patricia Freeman, "Interest Group Activity in the States," University of Tennessee, published in the Journal of Politics, Vol. 60, No. 1, February 1998; Miriam Galston, "Lobbying and the Public Interest: Rethinking the Internal Revenue Code's Treatment of Legislative Activities," Texas Law Review, 1993.

[137] Independent Sector survey of its members, 1997; InterAction survey of CEOs of its members, 1996.

Independent Sector and now an independent organization called Center for Lobbying in the Public Interest) began talking about what to do. They felt the confluence of public policy devolution, budget-cutting, privatization of government services, competition for delivery of services, and continuing legislative threats to the advocacy role of nonprofits created a need for thorough, practical research that would identify barriers to nonprofit participation and lead to strategies for overcoming them. The two operated from an assumption that a strong, vital civil society required active policy participation of the nonprofit sector. Accordingly, they agreed to launch a small research project to identify factors that encourage and discourage policy participation by nonprofits, and further agreed that it would be important to bring together experienced academicians and practitioners to investigate the issues involved.

As a first step, the two contacted David Arons, who at the time was a graduate student at Tufts University and was in search of a topic for a master's thesis. Arons worked for Smucker at Independent Sector and was a veteran of the Istook amendment fights, so he knew the subject and cared greatly about it. Arons agreed to focus his attention on a literature review of research related to nonprofit advocacy.[138] Arons' academic adviser at Tufts University, Jeffrey Berry, also became involved, as did Tuft's Lincoln Filene Center for Citizenship and Public Affairs,[139] where Arons was working part-time. Berry had been doing research about the role of citizen groups and citizen participation and was just completing a book on the subject.[140] Arons' initial research revealed that most of the studies on lobbying behavior of nonprofits were based on lobbying expenditures reported on annual tax forms (IRS Form 990).[141] The limitations of such research are numerous. First, the quality of the data collected by the IRS needed significant improvement. As the Urban Institute found when digitizing the

---

[138] David F. Arons, "Holding Back Our Democracy: Nonprofit Participation in the Public Policy Process" (thesis, Tufts University, May 1999).
[139] The Lincoln Filene Center is now called the University College of Citizenship and Public Service.
[140] Jeffrey M. Berry, *The New Liberalism: The Rising Power of Citizen Groups* (Washington, D.C.: Brookings Institution, 1999). Previous books included: *The Rebirth of Urban Democracy* (with Kent E. Portney and Ken Thomson) (Washington, D.C.: Brookings Institution, 1993); *The Interest Group Society* (Boston: Little, Brown, 1984); 2nd ed. 1989; 3rd ed. (New York, NY: Longman,1997); and Berry, Jeffrey M., *Lobbying for the People: The Political Behavior of Public Interest Groups* (Princeton, NJ: Princeton University Press, 1977)
[141] See footnote 138.

Form 990 data, there were many errors. For example, on the lobbying sections of the reporting form, the expenditures might not add up or total lobbying amount might be smaller than the amount listed for direct lobbying. Second, there has always been concern about under-reporting of lobbying activity, particularly because of the complexity of the reporting requirements. Finally, the data only addressed certain types of policy activities by the charities. Many other activities, such as advocating support or opposition to regulations or testifying before a legislative committee, are forms of policy participation not covered by the IRS definitions of lobbying activities and therefore are not reported.

Research on citizen advocacy groups, such as Berry's, lumped together charities (those exempt under 501(c)(3) of the tax code), social welfare groups (501(c)(4)s), unions (501(c)(5)s), and trade associations (501(c)(6)s) (Berry 1999; Shaiko 1999; Vogel 1995). The broader universe of nonprofits, featuring those groups that are not avowedly political, received little attention from scholars. For those interested in focusing on this broader universe, the literature on citizen advocacy groups and political participation does not provide useful insight for charities because of their unique tax status. Yet the comparative role of nonprofits is especially relevant to the current debate over the alleged decline of civic engagement in the United States (Skocpol and Fiorina, 1999; Putnam 2000). It is also important to distinguish charities from other types of nonprofits because they make up, by far, most of the American nonprofit sector.

Despite the limitations of research about charity policy participation, there were several very helpful studies on nonprofit advocacy. Several authors, mostly political scientists, described the types of public policy activities nonprofits engage in (Leech 1998; Nownes and Freeman 1998; Berry 1977). Most of the discussions focused on actions that make nonprofits effective in the advocacy arena, such as lobbying, testifying, and use of media advocacy. One study by Susan Rees attempted to better understand the factors that make nonprofits effective in congressional actions (Rees 1998). She picked several topics, such as budget and healthcare, and asked congressional staff to identify groups that are most effective on these issues. She then did case studies of those groups ranked as most effective, helping to identify their internal decision-making and style of operation.

Lester Salamon's 1983 survey data on charities provided a context for testing several theories for nonprofit advocacy (1998). In an earlier book, he looked at the influence of government funding as a motivating, deterring and complicating factor in nonprofits' decisions to engage in public policy, what he called the public policy "partnership" (1995). Others, such as University of Washington's Steve Smith also used this data to focus on the interaction between government grants and contracts and the policy participation of nonprofits (Smith and Lipsky 1993; Smith 1999).

Additional factors, such as the impact of the tax code provisions on lobbying and voter education, as well as the rules regarding federal grants management, were being studied or discussed to better understand the impact on charity participation. Many nonprofit leaders were looking to materials prepared by luminaries such as Bruce Hopkins (1992) or to practicing lawyers specializing in nonprofit law such as Gail Harmon, Thomas Troyer, Robert Boisture, and Gregory Colvin to provide an understanding of how the tax code provisions affect charity lobbying on bills, ballots and other legislative initiatives. Miriam Galston wrote a law review article raising a number of questions about the impact of the tax code's limitations on nonprofits, including electoral activities (Galston 1993). Even earlier, OMB Watch published a piece about the impact changes in federal grant rules would have on nonprofit advocacy (Bass, Ferguson and Plocher 1985). Betsy Reid also developed one of the better summaries around the issues affecting nonprofit policy (Reid 1999).

Some research addressed organizational structure as well as attitudes influencing decisions about participation in the public policymaking process (Galaskiewicz and Bielefeld 1998). Factors included the size of the organization, whether it is a membership organization, and its age. Judith Saidel (1998) analyzed the relationship between formal and informal governance structures and the public policy roles of nonprofits. In general, however, there was very little research about internal organizational factors that influence policy participation.

As Arons worked on the literature review, he and Bass wrote a proposal to conduct a small research project and submitted it to the Nonprofit Sector Research Fund at the Aspen Institute in October of 1998. It was agreed that OMB Watch would house the project and that the Lincoln Filene Center (in the person of Arons)[142] and Tufts University (in the person of Berry) would

---

[142] When Arons moved to Charity Lobbying in the Public Interest (CLPI) after graduating, CLPI became a key partner in this research.

be partners. The research, through a survey of nonprofits, interviews and discussion groups, was intended to address three broad questions:

- What are the internal processes of nonprofit organizations in deciding whether they will engage in the public policy process?
- What is the impact of law and legal advisers on nonprofits' decision-making processes?
- What additional knowledge and resources would be helpful to nonprofits as they consider participation in policymaking?

While the proposal was being considered, the research team talked with a number of nonprofit leaders and researchers. Through these initial discussions it became increasingly clear that the research was needed to:

- Understand how to motivate more public policy participation by nonprofits in the United States.
- Inform organizations working with nonprofit leaders about the factors that influence and deter public policy participation and how to help organizations hurdle persistent barriers to policy engagement.
- Investigate current perceptions of nonprofits' lobbying, advocacy and public policy role.
- Provide a comprehensive body of national research on the state of nonprofit advocacy and public policy participation.

We recognized that to achieve these objectives we would need to broaden the research design. Accordingly, we submitted a number of proposals to other foundations and recast our initial three questions into four broader questions:

1) What words and phrases do nonprofits use to describe public policy activities?
2) What internal and external factors motivate and deter nonprofit participation in the public policy process?
3) How do the staffs of nonprofits and their volunteer leadership make decisions about the course of their public policy participation?
4) What resources are needed to strengthen nonprofit advocacy and public policy participation?

From the start, SNAP was designed as a research-to-action project whose objective is to translate research findings into ways of helping to get nonprofits more engaged in public policy matters. As a result, from the first day we sought input from researchers and practitioners about the research design, the questions to be asked, ways of disseminating results, and ideas for using the data to help strengthen nonprofit policy participation.

We invited 25 people to serve as informal advisers and convened a set of meetings of researchers and practitioners to help us develop themes and questions for the survey, interviews and focus groups. On May 10, 1999, we sent the 25 advisers a draft survey to get their input. On March 31, 2000, we convened scholars and people representing national organizations to reflect on the project's design, suggest methodology changes and go through a planning process to determine key themes and questions that should be addressed. We conducted a similar meeting with practitioners representing grassroots organizations and state-level organizations on April 10, 2000, although this meeting also put more emphasis on how to use the research results. The list of the advisers and participants are in Appendix B.

Table 3-1. Major SNAP Milestones

Major Activity	Date
Meeting at Aspen Institute's Nonprofit Sector Research Fund triggers idea	July 1998
First Foundation Grant Approved	Spring 1999
Planning the SNAP initiative & proposal writing	Remainder of 1999
Survey sample obtained from National Center for Charitable Statistics	1999
Survey development and pretest	Summer 1999
First mailing of survey to 2,738 charities	January 15, 2000
Postcard reminder to return survey	January 22, 2000
Second letter reminder to return survey	February 15, 2000
Third letter reminder to return survey (certified mail)	March 15, 2000
Meeting of Researchers & National Organizations for advice	March 31, 2000
Meeting of Practitioners for advice	April 10, 2000
All surveys returned	June 15, 2000
Data entry and clean-up	Summer/Fall 2000
Telephone interviews of 45 survey respondents	September, 2000 – February, 2001
17 focus groups in 11 cities	February – September, 2001
Data analysis	2002 – 2003
Preliminary Analysis Released	May 2002

The remainder of this chapter describes the research design followed by a discussion of the action steps taken under SNAP.

The Research Design

The research portion of SNAP had three phases. Phase One was a national survey of a random sample of charities. (See Appendix C for the questionnaire and the responses.) We surveyed organizations that were tax-exempt under 501(c)(3) of the federal tax code (charities) that file annual tax returns (IRS Form 990). Some charities, such as religious organizations and those with annual revenues of less than $25,000, do not file Form 990 and thus were not covered by our survey. Additionally, we excluded universities, hospitals, and private foundations. More about our methodology for the survey is described below.

Phase Two involved interviewing 45 of the survey respondents. (See Appendix D for the interview protocol.) Phase Three included 13 focus groups with nonprofit leaders conducted in diverse areas of the country. (See Appendix E for the focus group protocols.)

Phase I – The Survey

The research team has written a detailed description of the survey methodology, published by the Aspen Institute.[143] The book, *Surveying Nonprofits: A Methods Handbook*, was not part of the original plan, but as we moved through the stages of the survey, we realized there was not much written to guide us or other researchers. Since we received an unusually high return rate on the survey (64 percent), we thought it might be helpful to thoroughly document our steps to help other researchers.

The *Handbook* covers selecting which types of nonprofits to survey; drawing a stratified random sample; constructing a questionnaire; utilizing the Urban Institute's 990 data set and the logistics of executing a large-scale survey. It is highly detailed and intended to be a substantial guide to survey work with nonprofits. In this section, we summarize the key points, but we encourage readers to use the *Handbook* for a better understanding of the methodology.

---

[143] Jeffrey M. Berry, David F. Arons, Gary D. Bass, Matthew F. Carter, and Kent E. Portney, *Surveying Nonprofits: A Methods Handbook* (Aspen Institute, 2003).

The Sample

According to the *New Nonprofit Almanac and Desk Reference*, data from the IRS Form 990 indicated there were 734,000 nonprofit organizations in the United States in 1998, of which nearly 221,000 were 501(c)(3) organizations (i.e., charities) (Weitzman et al 2002, 5). As Kirsten Grønbjerg notes, charities with revenue of less than $5,000 are not required to apply for recognition of exempt status with the IRS and those with revenue of less than $25,000 are not required to file an annual tax return, so the true number of nonprofits is difficult to gauge (Grønbjerg 2002, 1746).

In selecting the Form 990, we understood that we would not capture the full range of charities in the country. For example, we knew we would not be surveying organizations with revenues of less than $25,000 or religious congregations, since both types of organizations are not required to file the annual tax return to the IRS. Some organizations with budgets less than $25,000 voluntarily file Form 990, but the number is very small. Faith-based service organizations and associations of religious groups are, however, included in the sample since they must file Form 990. We also planned to have focus groups with both types of organizations – religious congregations and small entities. We also excluded private grant making foundations since they are prohibited from grassroots lobbying and direct lobbying except in self-defense.[144] However, we did include organizations that represent private foundations and other types of philanthropic grant making institutions, such as community foundations, since they are permitted to lobby.

We also decided to exclude colleges, universities, hospitals, and hospital systems for several reasons. First, we felt these organizations, as larger institutions, were not similar to average charities. We wanted our research findings to focus on smaller, community-based groups. We were also concerned that because these are usually larger organizations, it was unlikely that the executive director or other senior level employee would complete the survey or that the survey would be completed at all. Finally, we assumed that many of these institutions already are engaged in public

---

[144] Grassroots lobbying is defined by the IRS as encouraging the general public to attempt to influence legislation. For a lobbying communication to count as grassroots lobbying, it must refer to specific legislation, reflect a view on it, and encourage recipients to contact legislators (Smucker 1999, 56; Harmon 1995; Amidei 2000, Appendix). Private foundations file the IRS Form 990PF, which we did not use in our research.

Table 3-2

Nonprofits Excluded From the Sample

- Hospitals

- Colleges and universities

- Private grant making foundations

- Religious congregations since most do not file IRS Form 990

- Other organizations that do not file the IRS Form 990, such as those with budgets of less than $25,000

- Organizations that are not charities, such as 501(c)(4)s (social welfare) and 501(c)(6)s (trade associations)

policy matters and might skew the results (Boris and Mosher-Williams, 1998, 502). Although we excluded universities and hospitals, we did include other types of education and healthcare charities in the sample.

Our sample only included 501(c)(3) tax-exempt organizations. This is an important limitation since it is believed that there is an increasing number of charities that have affiliated "social welfare" groups (501(c)(4), defined as civic leagues, social welfare organizations that operate primarily to further the common good and general welfare of the people in the community such as by bringing about civic betterment and social improvements. We hope other researchers pick up from where we have left off by looking at behavior of social welfare groups and the linkage between them and charities. Some initial work has been done in this area (Krehely and Golladay 2002). Our research also did not include other types of nonprofits that often lobby actively such as trade associations (501(c)(6)) or unions (501(c)(5)) as political scientists have devoted ample attention to these groups (Berry 1997; Schlozman and Tierney 1986; Walker 1991).

Since the focus of our research was not centered on very small charities or religious congregations, we felt the Form 990 served our purpose of defining the study population. Moreover, it was much quicker and cheaper to use the Form 990 as the pool for our sample than to create a representative sample of all charities. Form 990 filers, however, may be inappropriate if small nonprofits need to be included or if they are to be a key component of the research. Grønbjerg (2001, 2002) provides a useful approach for addressing smaller nonprofits through her census of Indiana nonprofits. Others, such as John Kretzmann and his colleagues (1996), have tried visiting organizations as well as interviews to reach smaller nonprofits. Another approach is to ask individuals to name nonprofits that they may have some affiliation or interaction with, and the resulting pool of organizations then forms a database that can be sampled (Chaves 1999; McPherson 1982). If the focus needs to be on religious congregations, some scholars have even used the Yellow Pages to create a listing of congregations.

Stratifying the Survey Sample

We assumed that we would get a different response to questions about policy participation from nonprofits that use the IRS lobbying expenditure test than from those who do not. As described in other sections, the expenditure test requires a nonprofit to fill out IRS Form 5768, thus indicating a recognition that the organization can lobby.[145] It was important to us to include these types of organizations, since the governance styles and other information might prove informative. We refer to those who have "elected" as under the expenditure test; and to those "not electing" as under the substantial part test. Sometimes we refer to them as "electors" and "non-electors."

We also recognized as we proceeded with the development of the survey instrument that not all nonprofits under the expenditure test actually report lobbying expenditures on the Form 990. In fact, of the 4,928 electors in 1998, only 804 (16 percent) had any lobbying expenditures. The explanation for this must await further research, but several explanations seem likely. Organizations using the expenditure test may use volunteers to lobby so that no expenses are incurred. In addition, not all legislative advocacy is defined as lobbying under the expenditure test regulations. For example, testimony before legislative committees at the request of the committee chair, as well as conducting research and analysis that contains no public call to action, are exceptions to the definition of lobbying, even if they take a position on specific legislation. Another explanation may be that

[145] As a reminder, charities can choose – or "elect" – to be governed by section 501(h) of the tax code, which provide an expenditure limit on lobbying. These expenditure thresholds were identified in the previous chapter and are more thoroughly explained in Chapter 5. Charities that do not make this choice, by default, fall under a more ambiguous "no substantial part" test, where no substantial part of the activities can be devoted to lobbying.

these organizations lobby infrequently. Any combination of these or other factors could explain this phenomenon.

We were uncertain whether those who chose to be under the expenditure test but had no lobbying expenditures might be different from those under the expenditure test who had lobbying expenditures. To address the difference that might exist between those under the expenditure test and the substantial part test and the difference between those showing lobbying expenditures on the Form 990 and those not spending money, we stratified on all four variables. These served as some of the independent variables to test various policy participation questions.

Drawing the Survey Sample and Building the Database

The population studied consists of U.S. charities registered as 501(c)(3) organizations and filing IRS Form 990 *with the exception of universities and hospitals*. By definition, the population excludes hundreds of thousands of religious communities and small charities that are not required to file IRS Form 990.

The National Center for Charitable Statistics (NCCS) at the Urban Institute provided the survey sample. As we looked through the data, we learned that there were various errors or omissions we would have to address in order to have a high quality survey sample. The biggest problems had to do with the Form 990 data having incomplete or inaccurate addresses and omissions of the name of the executive director. We wanted the executive director's name so that we could personalize the survey mailing. Accordingly, we needed to establish a process to obtain correct addresses and the proper name of the person to receive the survey (the latter was important as mail addressed to "executive director" is less likely to receive attention than mail addressed by name). This involved checking other databases, Internet searching, and phone calling; this necessary step added many months to SNAP.

Of the 220,622 charities filing Form 990 in 1998, we excluded 14,591 based on the criteria described above. That left 204,298 charities without lobbying expenses and 1,024 charities with lobbying expenses. Because the number of charities with lobbying expenditures was so small, we compensated by sending surveys to more of them in order to ensure adequate cell sizes for our returns. For example, we sent the survey to 56 percent of the electors with lobbying expenditures versus 17 percent of electors without lobbying expenditures. Table 3-3 below summarizes the number of surveys we sent and to whom, along with the number returned.

Because we knew that the Form 990 data were of suspect quality, we also reserved a number of organizations from each of our strata to send surveys to in case some surveys were returned due to bad addresses or other reasons. These reserves were to be sent after several weeks, to allow time for returns to filter back to us through the postal system. This created a situation where, in effect, we were simultaneously running two surveys on two timetables (although one was much smaller than the other was).

NCCS drew the sample names from the 1998 Core File, which contains the Form 990 Return Transaction File. In addition to the names for our survey, it provided descriptive information and approximately 60 financial variables about the surveyed organizations. NCCS also used its 1998 Lobby Election Listing, which is a cumulative file produced from IRS data, that includes organizations that either opted to use the expenditure test by filling out IRS Form 5768 or answered "yes" to Question 1 on the Form 990, Schedule A, Part III. This listing provided additional information for the database about those we surveyed, including the total legislative expenses from Form 990,

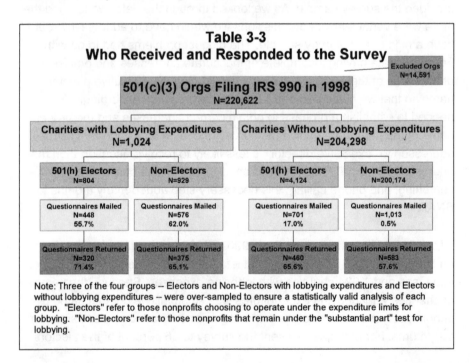

Table 3-3
Who Received and Responded to the Survey

Excluded Orgs
N=14,591

501(c)(3) Orgs Filing IRS 990 in 1998
N=220,622

Charities with Lobbying Expenditures N=1,024		Charities Without Lobbying Expenditures N=204,298	
501(h) Electors N=804	Non-Electors N=929	501(h) Electors N=4,124	Non-Electors N=200,174
Questionnaires Mailed N=448 55.7%	Questionnaires Mailed N=576 62.0%	Questionnaires Mailed N=701 17.0%	Questionnaires Mailed N=1,013 0.5%
Questionnaires Returned N=320 71.4%	Questionnaires Returned N=375 65.1%	Questionnaires Returned N=460 65.6%	Questionnaires Returned N=583 57.6%

Note: Three of the four groups -- Electors and Non-Electors with lobbying expenditures and Electors without lobbying expenditures -- were over-sampled to ensure a statistically valid analysis of each group. "Electors" refer to those nonprofits choosing to operate under the expenditure limits for lobbying. "Non-Electors" refer to those nonprofits that remain under the "substantial part" test for lobbying.

Schedule A, line 1, the variable indicating whether the organization uses the expenditure test, and the tax period selected of the Form 990.

The Form 990 information was put into an SPSS database and merged with the survey returns, providing a robust database for analysis. The merging process took considerable time and resources since there were a number of errors that needed to be cleaned, as well as merging difficulties caused by factors such as organizational name changes.

In sending the survey and subsequent follow-ups, we tried to follow the advice provided in Don Dillman's *Mail and Internet Surveys: The Tailored Design Method* (2000). We tested the survey instrument in the summer of 1999. The pretest went to 198 charities. We asked for feedback on the survey, allowing respondents to tell us if any of the questions were too confusing or intrusive. We also did an analysis of response rate on each question to determine if certain questions had under-responses; none did. The pretest also helped us understand what type of response rate we would receive on the final survey.

We made minor modifications to the survey based on the results of the pretest. Once the instrument was revised we sent it to 2,738 charities in January 2000, avoiding the Thanksgiving and Christmas holidays. We sent a cover letter, the questionnaire, and a business reply envelope, followed by reminders. The first reminder was a postcard one week after the initial mailing; it was followed by a letter, another questionnaire and a business reply envelope three weeks later; a letter, questionnaire and reply envelope was sent again after two and five months. The final reminder was sent by certified mail. By June 15, 2000, roughly six months after the initial mailing, we had received 1,738 responses, a 64 percent response rate.

Developing the Survey

It was very important to develop a survey that removed bias from the questions and addressed the sensitivity that public policy questions raised. We recognized that the limited number of charities reporting lobbying expenditures on the Form 990 might not accurately indicate the amount of actual policy participation taking place, since not all forms of advocacy are lobbying. We also knew that executive directors might say they engage in public policy when in practice they do not. In addition, we wanted to capture staff behavior that might be construed as engaging in public policy even if the board of directors or executive director did not condone lobbying in general. We had to develop questions that were specific enough to tease out the specific types of behavior we had defined as engaging in public policy.

The existing body of research did not offer much guidance. Past surveys on policy participation mostly focused on a general term called lobbying. But charities face a more precise tax code definition, creating doubts about how charities would react to questions about lobbying. We were concerned that if a charity said it did not engage in lobbying we would not know whether it was referring to the tax code definition or the colloquial meaning of the word. We first looked to the various organizational surveys (InterAction 1996; Council of Community Services of New York State 1997; Independent Sector 1997; OMB Watch 1997; National Council of Nonprofit Associations 1997). Some of these questions provided a starting point. We also looked to the literature and adapted questions. In the end, we used our best judgment.

We sent drafts of the survey to a number of people knowledgeable about nonprofit policy participation. Some were scholars, others practitioners, and others were involved in philanthropy. Many provided significant comments about the questions posed. This process was very instructive, as comments demonstrated a real split between the scholars and the practitioners concerning the best way to ask questions.

The response to one question, which asked how often the organization engages in lobbying activities, captured some of the differences in perspective. (The specific question – Question 5 – is provided below.) The answer key allowed the respondent to choose: Never; Once a month or less; Two, three times a month; or Four or more times a month. The scholars had no problem with the scale; the practitioners said that the scale made no sense. They noted that most nonprofits engage on an as-needed basis. Moreover, in most states legislatures are not in session year-round, so the use of a monthly scale made little sense.

Our research team's composition of both scholars and practitioners prompted a thorough discussion of the feedback we received on each survey question. This process of involving scholars and practitioners as part of the research team helped to ensure the best possible survey overall, and one that was useful and understandable to both researchers and practitioners. In the example above, we decided to keep the answer key as it was because the question was really designed as an experimental question, making the answers serve only as a benchmark to itself.

We had designed this experimental question because our experience had suggested that charities use different words interchangeably. Sometimes they use the word "lobby," at other times "advocacy," and still others use "public education." The use of the different words may, in fact, mean very different things to those who use them.

Since language was such a critical issue for this research, we decided to use this question as part of an experimental design to test the power of language. On this question, which dealt with self-reporting of the organization's engagement in public policy, we sent one-third of the sample the question using the word "lobby," another third the same question but substituting the word "advocacy," and for the final third, we substituted the word "educate." Thus, Question 5 read as follows for one-third (bold added here for emphasis):

> 5. For some nonprofits, there is a need to **lobby** those in government so that policymakers will have a better understanding of the problems facing the community. How often does your organization undertake an effort to **lobby** government officials at any level?

Another third of the sample got a Question 5 that removed the word "lobby" and replaced it with "advocate new policies before" government officials at any level. The last third of the sample got a Question 5 that removed "advocate new policies" and replaced it with "educate government officials at any level about specific policies."

The input from the practitioners helped us to provide descriptive characteristics of the activities we were trying to measure and modify language in other questions to make them more understandable to nonprofits. In addition to this question about whether the organization lobbies/advocates/educates, in Question 6, we asked a battery of questions about behavior including whether the organization testifies before governmental bodies. We also asked about frequency of such activities. This question helped us obtain information about organizational activities that the respondent might not consider to be engaging in public policy, but that we did. The question was structured as follows:

139

6. A variety of means of communicating and interacting with those in government are listed below. Please use the scale on the right to indicate how frequently, if at all, your organization engages in these activities. (By "your organization" we mean the executive director, other staff, volunteers, or members of the board.) In this scale, "0" means never, "1" is relatively infrequent interaction, and "4" is ongoing interaction.

	Frequency				
	Never	**Low**			**High**
Testifying at legislative or administrative hearings	0	1	2	3	4
Lobbying on behalf of or against a proposed bill or other policy pronouncement	0	1	2	3	4
Responding to requests for information from those in government	0	1	2	3	4
Working in a planning or advisory group that includes government officials	0	1	2	3	4
Meeting with government officials about the work we are doing	0	1	2	3	4
Encouraging members to write, call, fax or e-mail policymakers	0	1	2	3	4
Releasing research reports to the media, public or policymakers	0	1	2	3	4
Discussing obtaining grants or contracts with government officials	0	1	2	3	4
Interacting socially with government officials	0	1	2	3	4

We based Question 6 on items found in academic literature as well as the practical experience of reviewers. Despite the extensive input we received in developing the question, we failed, in retrospect, to ask about engaging in litigation either directly or through "friend of the court" briefs. This was noticeable as we proceeded into focus groups (described below): the subject was occasionally raised.

Based on input from practitioners, we also added a series of questions about whether charities can engage in certain types of activities, to better gauge nonprofits' understanding of statutory and regulatory requirements of government policy engagement. These questions were as follows:[146]

> 8. There is a good deal of confusion about whether various activities by nonprofits relating to the policymaking process are permissible. Based on your understanding, can your organization:

Support or oppose federal legislation under current IRS regulations	❑ Yes	❑ No
Take a policy position without reference to a specific bill under current regulations	❑ Yes	❑ No
Support or oppose federal regulations	❑ Yes	❑ No
Lobby if part of your budget comes from federal funds	❑ Yes	❑ No
Use government funds to lobby Congress	❑ Yes	❑ No
Endorse a candidate for elected office	❑ Yes	❑ No
Talk to elected public officials about public policy matters	❑ Yes	❑ No
Sponsor a forum or candidate debate for elected office	❑ Yes	❑ No

Once the survey was completed, we submitted a pretest as described above. We then mailed the final survey after making minor changes based on results of the pretest. Given that the survey received a 63.5 percent response rate, which is considered excellent for any social science survey and especially for a sensitive subject such as public policy participation, we believe that the collaboration between practitioner and scholar was very constructive. There were tensions, but the resolution of those tensions led to a stronger survey and a more robust research initiative.

---

[146] Except in very rare circumstances, such as where a statute specifically authorizes an activity, these items are universally controlled by federal law and regulation. Some states may require disclosure that goes beyond federal law and regulation, but our questions only addressed whether the 501(c)(3) entities could engage in the activity, not how much or what needs to be disclosed.

Preliminary Analysis

During the summer of 2000 survey responses were entered into a SPSS database created for this project. This was a lengthy process, involving the merging of three separate data sources – our survey data, IRS Form 990 data, and information about lobbying expenditures from the Form 990 – from two different software programs, SPSS and Microsoft Access. We also instituted an elaborate process of checking the quality of the data for input or merging errors. Once the data were entered, we were able to conduct a preliminary analysis based on all survey responses. Our first effort was to test the validity and reliability of the survey responses. We found that the responses yielded a parametric population and one that was similar to some of the demographics of the charitable sector as a whole.

Most of 2001 was used collecting other data either through telephone interviews or focus groups. At the end of 2001 and the beginning of 2002 we did basic descriptive statistics for the survey questions. Some useful and surprising information emerged in this process. For example, we learned that the vast majority of charities – 90 percent – use e-mail and have access to the Internet. Many of them use these tools for public policy work.

Additional special analyses were used for various presentations, such as those at Independent Sector's annual conference and at the Association for Research on Nonprofit Organizations and Voluntary Action. By Spring 2002, we developed a preliminary analysis, which was presented through a written summary and a more complete PowerPoint presentation.[147]

Phase II – The Interviews

The purpose of the interviews was to obtain a qualitative assessment of information provided in the survey, to ensure that the quantifiable survey results were consistent with what the respondents told us verbally. We developed questions asked during interviews with the advice of our team of researchers and practitioners who reviewed the survey instrument. The interview questions allowed us to gather qualitative data about nonprofits' attitudes and approach to advocacy work. The interview questions focused on the role of governance structures, definitions of public policy involvement, perceived barriers to involvement (including the role of

---

[147] The preliminary analysis is available at http://www.ombwatch.org/article/archive/101/.

foundations and other funders), perceived effectiveness in influencing policymaking matters, and other findings from the survey data.

We conducted a series of 45 telephone interviews, each 45 minutes to 60 minutes long. (The interview protocol is available in Appendix D.) The names of people to be interviewed were randomly selected from a subdivided pool of survey respondents who indicated a willingness to be interviewed. They were broken into groups of high, medium and low participators based on survey responses. Most were executive directors or senior staff persons with significant management authority. Usually the person was the same person who completed the survey.

The interviews provided extra texture to the written survey responses. For example, the survey asked about the types of lobbying and advocacy activities an organization conducts, as well as whom within the organization is delegated authority for decisions related to government relations. The interviews helped us better explore the use of language used by nonprofits, and what sector-related terms really mean. More specifically, we focused on words such as lobbying, advocacy, and public education, and what types of activities are really associated with these terms, information not readily apparent in the written survey. The interviews also provided insight into the decision-making processes that result from, or lead to, specific types of advocacy, and the support offered by associations, foundations and technical assistance providers that can be supportive in public policy efforts. Together the survey and interview data provided new insights about nonprofits' state of readiness to participate in public policy and what we, as supporting organizations, can do to facilitate their efforts.

Phase III – Focus and Discussion Groups

We conducted 17 focus groups of nonprofit executive directors and board members in 11 cities in seven states.[148] Each session was two hours, and the average size was nine to ten people. The smallest group was two people and the largest was 13.

---

[148] An 18th focus group in Detroit of religious leaders was cancelled at the last second as it was scheduled for 1:00 p.m. on September 11, 2001, the day of the terrorist attacks in New York, Washington, D.C., and Pennsylvania. The first session that day, of foundation leaders, occurred without full knowledge of what was occurring. However, by the later part of the morning it was clear what was occurring, and the religious leaders were called into action.

We identified lead nonprofit organizations in each state to help organize the focus groups for us.[149] The hosting organization had responsibility for selecting participants based on criteria we provided and handling logistics for the events. Depending on the arrangements with the host organization, we gave focus group participants a small honorarium.

For most focus groups, we asked host organizations to recruit executive directors. However, for three sessions, we asked that participants only be board members. In one focus group, we asked that participants include both executive directors and board members. In two others – one of state nonprofit associations and the other of private and community foundations – we asked for senior staff instead of the executive director.

We also asked host organizations to recruit different types of nonprofits. One criterion was level of policy participation. In some sessions we sought a mixture of groups known to be low and high participators. In others we only wanted high participators.

Another criterion dealt with the mission of the organization. We wanted to hear from nonprofits representing different aspects of the sector, including human services, arts and cultural institutions, environment, economic development, health, and other issues areas. Some focus groups had participants representing a mixture of issue areas. Some focused on particular issue areas, such as health or environment.

A final criterion related to rural groups and organizations representing minority issues. Accordingly, one session involved groups that provide rural services, another involved Asian-American groups, and another involved Hispanic groups.

Table 3-4 provides a list of the 17 focus groups, describing the target audience, where it was held, and who hosted the event. The host organizations were very important to this research since they believed, as we do, in strengthening nonprofit advocacy and were looking forward to using the results from this research.

---

[149] In most cases we provided a small stipend to the host organization. We also provided a script they could use for calling potential participants along with other types of support.

The interaction between participants during the focus groups gave our analysis much greater detail about policy participation than could be captured in a survey or even in telephone interviews. We used the focus groups to reach out to organizations and individuals that were not part of the survey or interview phase but were critical to the goal of understanding the factors that encourage nonprofit policy participation. They also allowed for specific topics, such as money and politics, to emerge even though the subject was not part of the survey questions, and to generate new thinking about these topics by participants – especially executive directors.

We used the focus groups to focus on three broad questions:

1. What does participation in the public policy process mean?
2. What motivates and deters public policy participation?
3. What will aid nonprofits as they make decisions and take action on public policy?

We also used the focus groups to help us develop a composite measure for what it means to be a "policy participator." In most of the focus groups, we handed out a form listing the types of public policy activities that were included in the survey and asked participants to rank those they considered good measures of participating in public policy. Only three of the measures unanimously were ranked as good measures of public policy participation. They were:

- Lobbying on behalf of or against a proposed bill or other policy pronouncement
- Encouraging members or others to write, call, fax or e-mail policymakers
- Testifying at legislative or administrative hearings

Accordingly, if a nonprofit organization engaged in any one of the three activities, regardless of the frequency, we counted that organization as a "participator" for purposes of this research.

Table 3-4 SNAP Focus Groups

Participants	Types of Groups	Level of Policy Activity	Location	Date	Host Organization
Executive Directors	Asian-American human services	Low & Medium	Chinatown/ Boston, MA	5/16/2001	Lincoln Filene Center at Tufts
Executive Directors	General	High	Minneapolis, MN	2/26/2001	MN Council of Nonprofits
Executive Directors	General	Medium & High	Sacramento, CA	6/20/2001	Nonprofit Resource Center
Executive Directors	General, mostly environmental	Medium	Lansing, MI	9/12/2001	MI Nonprofit Association
Executive Directors	Health	Low, Medium & High	Boston, MA	6/15/2001	MA Association of Community Health Centers
Executive Directors	Health & Disability	Low, Medium & High	Nashville, TN	3/28/2001	TN Conference on Social Welfare
Executive Directors	Health & Environmental Health	Medium & High	Lansing, MI	9/12/2001	MI Nonprofit Association
Executive Directors	Health, Human Services & Community Dvlpt	Low & Medium	Somerville/ Medford, MA	5/15/2001	Lincoln Filene Center at Tufts
Executive Directors	Hispanic Health & Human Services	Low	San Antonio, TX	8/9/2001	United Ways of TX
Executive Directors	Human services & Economic Development	Low & Medium	Austin, TX	8/10/2001	United Ways of TX
Executive Directors	Rural service groups	Low & Medium	Redding, CA	6/21/2001	McConnell Foundation
Executive Directors & Board Members	General	Low & Medium	Sacramento, CA	6/20/2001	Nonprofit Resource Center
Board Members	General	High	Minneapolis, MN	2/26/2001	MN Council of Nonprofits
Board Members	Hispanic health & human services	Low	San Antonio, TX	8/9/2001	United Ways of TX
Board Members	Human services	Low & Medium	Austin, TX	8/10/2001	United Ways of TX
Senior Level Staff	Foundations	Low & Medium	Detroit, MI	9/11/2001	MI Nonprofit Association
Senior Level Staff	State Nonprofit Associations	Medium & High	Warrenton, VA	7/12/2001	Charity Lobbying in the Public Interest
Senior Level Staff*	Religious organizations	Low, Medium & High	Detroit, MI	9/11/2001	MI Nonprofit Association

NOTES:
* Session cancelled because of terrorist attacks

Moving from Research to Action

From the start, SNAP was intended to move from research to action. There were three types of action activities envisioned from the start: creating an online resource center to provide information about nonprofit policy participation; disseminating the SNAP results through the online resource center, this publication, and other means; and convening practitioners and researchers to convey the results and identify types of actions that should be taken to strengthen nonprofit policy participation.

Role of NPAction.org

Prior to the start of SNAP, one of the research partners, OMB Watch, had been operating a multi-year initiative called the Nonprofits' Policy and Technology Project. The end of the NPT Project overlapped by a year with the start of SNAP. One strong recommendation of the 40-person NPT Advisory Committee was the need to create a Web-based, one-stop resource that would bring together existing information about nonprofit advocacy. The website would help draw attention to other organizations and websites rather than compete with them.

Starting in 1999, OMB Watch also began a daily e-mail distribution list called NPTalk, which went to roughly 1,000 people around the country. The daily e-mail provided a review of issues that covered nonprofit technology and public policy participation. Ryan Turner moderated the e-mail list and researched topics building on e-mail notices he received from list participants. Feedback from participants was extraordinarily positive, even from those who felt that they knew most of the information posted. NPTalk continued until 2003, when the website recommended by the NPT Project was initiated. The content from the NPTalk e-mails provided core content for the website.

The research team also saw SNAP as an opportunity to populate the website with key types of information that would help nonprofits. Throughout 2000 and part of 2001 (including through the SNAP focus groups) we sought input from various local, state and national organizations about whether an online resource center focused on advocacy would be helpful and, if so, what types of information should be on the website. Most indicated they would use the website if the information was "relevant." The type of information identified as "relevant" included:

- Information about promising practices on policy participation. Many wanted the information organized by type of participation (e.g., research, advocacy, lobbying, etc.);
- Linkages to groups working in similar policy areas and to sites with more detailed information on how to engage in research, advocacy, organizing, voter education, and other public policy endeavors;
- Federal and state laws and regulations on lobbying, including information about the "substantial part" test and the expenditure test, and examples of what is considered lobbying and what is not;
- Rules regarding lobbying when a nonprofit receives a government grant or contract;
- Tips on effective advocacy;
- Research on what works, why nonprofits engage in public policy, and more. The SNAP findings would fit into this category;
- Access to free technology tools to help nonprofits engage in public policy matters, along with reviews of newer technology and the cost for deploying such tools. For example, what type of cost is associated with using video phones over the Internet, and how valuable is the tool in the context of public policy matters;
- Information about organizational structures that facilitate policy involvement;
- Answers to frequently asked questions; and
- Opportunities to debate and discuss issues about the role of nonprofits in public policy matters.

Many also felt it was important to have a free service that allows users to send e-mail to Congress, state legislatures, local officials, government agencies, and news media.

The online resource center that OMB Watch developed was called NPAction. org. An advisory group was established to help move the site from beta to public release, focusing on content, design, and marketing. The site was fully launched in the fall of 2003 and can be found at http://www.NPAction.org. NPAction's primary goal is to increase the level and improve the quality of nonprofit public policy participation. This is to be done by:

- Providing access to information through an online resource center about rules governing policy participation, examples of successful and unsuccessful efforts, identification of key resources and people, and other resource materials;
- Increasing the awareness of groups already engaging in public policy participation; and
- Enhancing opportunities for building communities of interest among new and emerging and existing public policy participators.

Dissemination of SNAP Findings

Our focus was on disseminating SNAP results to nonprofit leaders, scholars, and advisers to nonprofits. We also planned to distribute the findings to policymakers and the news media, particularly to news sources that covered the nonprofit sector. We developed a plan for disseminating SNAP findings that went beyond posting information on NPAction. This publication would be a main vehicle, but also there were other publications planned. For example, we published preliminary findings in the *Nonprofit Quarterly* (Arons and Bass, 2002).[150] One member of the research team, Jeffrey Berry, also wrote a book[151] on the broad subject of nonprofit policy participation utilizing SNAP data.

Convening Practitioners to Use the Results

The SNAP data are worthwhile only if the findings are put to use. From the beginning, the research team indicated it would not be satisfied with simply publishing a book on the findings. Accordingly, we conceived of a series of steps to elevate the use of the data, assuming we can raise the resources to implement this phase of the initiative. First, we planned to work through nonprofit intermediaries, such as the state nonprofit associations, to convene strategy sessions to discuss the research findings and the implications for nonprofit leaders in the state. These types of meetings were intended to occur in the future, after publication of this book.

These strategy sessions will target: training and technical assistance providers, professionals (e.g., accountants, lawyers) providing services

---

[150] David F. Arons and Gary D. Bass, "Not Ready to Play the Game: Nonprofit Participation in Public Policy," *Nonprofit Quarterly* (Fall 2002).

[151] Jeffrey M. Berry (with David F. Arons), *A Voice for Nonprofits,* The Brookings Institution (2003).

to nonprofits, and researchers. Funders will be invited to them. These sessions will focus on:

- Priority areas for training and technical assistance to strengthen policy participation;
- How to best utilize limited resources to maximize policy participation;
- Identification of helpful tools and training methods for motivating nonprofits to engage in public policy matters;
- Organizational behavior changes that may help nonprofits become more engaged in public policy;
- How professional advisers can facilitate policy participation;
- Regulatory and other types of policy changes that should change to strengthen policy participation; and
- Research needs left unaddressed.

Additionally, one of the research partners, Center for Lobbying in the Public Interest (CLPI), planned to use the SNAP findings to help structure improved training and support services to strengthen nonprofit advocacy. CLPI has used the SNAP research in several ways. First, it has published materials, such as an article for the Alliance for Nonprofit Management, that emphasize the importance of public policy participation.[152] The article, by the head of CLPI, notes that a survey of members of the Alliance for Nonprofit Management found demand for capacity-building services in the public policy arena grew from 2002 to 2003. She liberally uses the SNAP data to help those who provide capacity-building services understand where the needs are. Furthermore, CLPI has used SNAP data to reconfigure its services to provide ongoing support and training on strengthening nonprofit advocacy. Hence, the findings from this research will live in the day-to-day activities of CLPI.

---

[152] Liz Baumgarten, "Building Capacity for Public Policy Advocacy," at http://www. allianceonline.org/Members/Enhance/enhance_-_june_2004.enh/building_capacity_for. epage

Chapter 4
Participation in the Policymaking Process:
Overview of Key Survey Findings

The SNAP study's chief finding is that, while most charitable nonprofits lobby and engage in other forms of advocacy, most of their advocacy is limited and intermittent. They fail to sustain their engagement over time. Usually, their efforts are aimed at policies to advance the purposes contained in their mission statements, which at times coincides with threats to their continued operation.

Charities' participation in the policy process takes many forms, but many leaders shy away from saying they "lobby." The survey uncovered a general distaste for "politics" and, to a lesser extent, government, and some nonprofits seem to prefer putting their energies into direct program delivery. Yet we found widespread recognition of the importance of advocacy, particularly when funds are available to support it either specifically or as part of the organization's core operations. Most charitable organizations find financial resources for policy insufficient to mount sustained advocacy programs staffed by people with the kinds of skills necessary to monitor the process and direct the kinds of activities that influence the debate.

Who responded to the survey?

Virtually any organization recognized as charitable and qualified to receive tax-deductible donations became a candidate to receive the survey as long as it was not a religious congregation, university, hospital or small organization excluded from the sample for reasons described in the previous chapter.

The 1,738 nonprofits that responded (64 percent of the random sample) run the gamut of group relationships in contemporary American society – Little Leagues, PTAs, United Way agencies, "friends of" various institutions and landmarks, professional associations from the local to the national level, mental health service groups, language institutes, shelters for the homeless, state associations of various types, conservation leagues and "special interest" groups of students, enthusiasts and advocates of many different subjects and activities. Figure 4-1 shows that, usually, the executive director answered the questionnaire (72 percent of respondents).

Figure 4-1. Who Completed the Written Survey

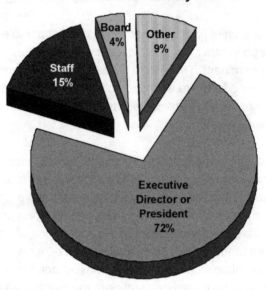

Organizations as different as a lighthouse museum and an international hall of fame were included. Table 4-1 shows the breakdown of respondents based on categories defined by the Nonprofit Taxonomy of Exempt Entities (NTEE) used in the federal Form 990. Within the nonprofit sector, the NTEE is used to discuss "sub-sector" or issue areas.

Table 4-1. Respondents by NTEE Categories

	Number	Percent
Human Services	493	29.1
Health	272	16.1
Education	216	12.8
Arts	164	9.7
Environment and animals	161	9.5
Social action, services	139	8.2
Recreation, sports and leisure	69	3.8
Philanthropy, grant making, foundations	59	3.5
Religion	35	2.1
Other	89	5.3
Total with NTEE information	1,692	100.0

As in most surveys, ours carries a potential selection bias in that those with a greater interest in the subject of public policy and those with greater staff capacity were more likely to complete and return the questionnaire.

We did not ask respondents to define the level at which they operate – national, state, regional or local – and the Form 990 does not explicitly provide that information. In some cases, as with a national or state association, it is possible to determine an organization's geographic scope from its name, but in most cases it is not. Because the sample was random, we believe that by and large it reflects the same mix found among charities as a whole: it's likely that the great majority of organizations in the sample and those who responded operate at the local level.

Because of the broad diversity of the sample we know we must be cautious about generalizing and making comparisons between the respondents. In addition to differences in size and scope, the nature of their mission statements spanned a wide range as well. While some goals clearly could be furthered by government action, others, such as those of self-improvement groups, might not find public policy to be as relevant to their cause. Still, one can see how a Girl Scout council, for example, might become interested in education policy, the rights of women or any number of other issue areas even though its main purpose is to teach girls to develop their skills and self-reliance. In fact, Girl Scouts are among the more active types of nonprofits in advocacy today. Other organizations with narrowly circumscribed goals might discover a common cause that they believed appropriate for government action. In the democratic ideal, ideas for public policy bubble up from groups of individuals who may have come together originally for other reasons.

Staff and budget

There was a tremendous range in the size of the organizations studied. Annual expenditures, obtained from the Form 990, ranged from a mere $500 to a whopping $458 million. Discounting for the size of largest organizations, we found that most have relatively modest budgets. The median annual budget was only $450,600. The mean, or average, was much higher ($4.1 million), reflecting the presence of a few very large organizations.

On average, respondent organizations got most of their revenue (26 percent) from individual donors or membership dues, 11 percent from fundraising events, and 14 percent from services they provide; these are all sources that afford maximum flexibility for engaging in public policy advocacy, since there are few restrictions placed on such funds. The typical respondent received 23 percent of its income from government sources, funding that cannot be used for lobbying, and 12 percent from foundations, which may or may not be limited by the philanthropy to non-lobbying activities.[153] (The law does not preclude advocacy using foundation funds, though some grant makers impose the restriction on their own accord.)

Staff size also was relatively modest though again the range was very wide. The median number of professional staff was six; clerical, three; and "other," four. The median number of volunteers was 20.

Nearly three-fourths of the respondent organizations delegated responsibility for government affairs or public policy to specific people in the organization; usually the executive director, who, of course, has many other important functions, is the person responsible. (See Table 4-2.) Less than a third of the organizations had some other staff person dedicated to advocacy or policy analysis.

Table 4-2. Staff Assigned to Government Relations
(Respondent could check more than one person)

	Number	Percentage
Executive director	978	57.8
Another staff member	533	31.6
Board member	451	26.7
Board committee	307	18.3
Lobbyist or paid consultant	307	18.3
Volunteer	152	9.0

Most are membership organizations

One of the main characteristics of the 1,738 respondent organizations is that a large majority (69 percent) had members. This is important for several reasons in considering their potential to influence policy. First, membership

---

[153] As mentioned in others parts of this book, nonprofits receive about one-third of revenue from government. Thus, our sample population, possibly because it excludes universities and hospitals, is below the norm.

implies that, to at least some degree, these organizations have the potential to speak for more people than only their boards and paid staff. To the extent that they represent large numbers of voters, policymakers tend to pay more attention to their views. Second, membership organizations have a built-in constituency to mobilize if they choose to engage in lobbying or other forms of advocacy.

Table 4-3. Types of Members*
(Respondent could check more than one member type)

	Percentage
Individuals	53.8
Other nonprofits	23.1
Corporations or business trade associations	15.8
Government agencies	8.1
No members	31.0

* Total exceeds 100 percent because some had more than one type of member.

The mobilization potential of the nonprofits studied is significant. The median number of individual members was 600 and the median number of organizational members was 45. Again, the range was very large, from 0 to 6 million, with the *average* number of individual members being 25,130; for organizational members, the range was 0 to 40,000 with an *average* of 365.

More than half of the organizations responding (51.1 percent) are themselves dues-paying members of other organizations and coalitions. Many of these affiliations (37.4 percent of all respondents) are with national organizations. Roughly one-fourth of the respondents (25.9 percent) belonged to state associations, and 9.7 percent held local memberships. While this presents a picture of a rather thick, intricate web of nonprofit alliances, it is important to note that nearly half (46.1 percent) reported belonging to no other organization.

Disseminators not researchers

Another indicator of potential to inform policy is the ability to generate and disseminate research. Most nonprofits in the survey reported they were not equipped to conduct research. Only 26.2 percent rated themselves high or moderately high in this area. However, considerably more of them are capable of disseminating information and research. Of all the respondents 41.6 percent rated themselves high or moderately high as disseminators of research information.

A lesson for national organizations, researchers, and funders is that local nonprofits, through their newsletters, websites, word of mouth, and other communications tools, represent a major outlet for research and analysis with policy implications. At the same time, it probably would be a mistake (as many of us have learned) to rely *carte blanche* on local nonprofits to collect data and do even rudimentary analysis of public policy issues.

Age and founding of organizations

The oldest group responding to the survey was founded in 1773, before the founding of the country, and several were founded in the 1800s. The average age of the groups was roughly 40 years, which would date them to 1966, near the beginning of the activist period in which there was a growth in government, a period that stretched into the seventies. It was the start of an era that saw the War on Poverty unfold and protests against the Vietnam War get into full swing. Organizations coming out of this time would be expected to be more sensitive to the importance of public policy and inclined to want to have an impact on it.

Table 4-4 shows that the two decades during which most organizations were started also showed a drop-off in policy participation (as defined as an organization either lobbying, encouraging others to lobby, or testifying). For groups formed during the 1970s and 1980s, policy participation dropped below 90 percent, even though homeless and anti-poverty groups were formed to fight the Reagan Administration's budget cuts and other policies affecting programs serving the poor.

Table 4-4. Decade Organization was Founded and Policy Participation

Decade	Number of Groups	Percentage that are Participators*
Pre-1950	349	90.4
1950-59	104	92.0
1960-69	184	90.1
1970-79	402	86.0
1980-89	404	86.8
1990-99	244	76.2

* "Participator" means that the organization indicated it either had lobbied, encouraged others to lobby, or testified

It is somewhat surprising that at an average age of 48, so many of the organizations that responded are still led by their founders. Four out of five of the respondents (82.9 percent) said their present executive directors were among the organization's founders. An even greater number (86.3 percent) said their board chairs were among the organization's founders. This correlation seems to indicate a very high degree of commitment and loyalty, along with the longevity, of nonprofit leaders, but it also indicates the potential for a leadership gap in the very near future.

We asked about the continued presence of a founder in a leadership role to determine whether it influenced policy participation rates. Survey results showed almost no difference in participation level based on whether or not a founder was still in a leadership position.

<u>In Talking About Policy Engagement, Language Matters</u>

The lack of uniform definitions and usage for common terms associated with nonprofit advocacy has led to confusion and inconsistency in overall knowledge of advocacy within the sector. Advocacy can include many types of activities, including grassroots organizing, litigation, submitting comments on proposed regulation or testifying before a legislative committee. The targets can be the general public or decision-makers in the executive, judicial, or legislative branches of government.

People use terms like "lobbying" and "advocacy" interchangeably, referring to the same set of activities. Yet others draw distinctions. For example, the colloquial definition of the term "lobbying" is often much broader than the legal definitions used by state or federal regulators. To truly understand the nature of nonprofit advocacy by charities, we need to be careful in making comparisons.

To address this issue, we had one survey question – described in the preceding chapter – designed to test if the words commonly used by nonprofits regarding engagement in the policymaking process made a difference. Three versions of the survey were sent out, each with a different phrasing on the experimental question. One third of the sample was asked:

> Q5. For some nonprofits, there is a need to **lobby those in government** so that policymakers will have a better understanding of the problems facing the community. How often

does your organization undertake an effort **to lobby** government officials at any level?

Another third of the sample got a Question 5 that asked:

Q5. For some nonprofits, there is a need to **advocate new policies before** those in government so that policymakers will have a better understanding of the problems facing the community. How often does your organization undertake an effort **to advocate new policies before** government officials at any level?

The last third of the sample's Question 5 read this way:

Q5. For some nonprofits, there is a need to **educate those in government about specific policies** so that policymakers will have a better understanding of the problems facing the community. How often does your organization undertake an effort **to educate government officials** at any level about specific policies?

Table 4-5 shows that those receiving the "lobby" question, compared with the other two-thirds of the sample, were at least twice as likely to answer that they "never" lobby. We then compared the three groups to ensure there were no major differences between the groups, and there were not. Simply changing the choice of word creates a different response.

Table 4-5. The Differences Language Makes*
(Percent of those asked using the word in column one)

Phrase survey used to ask about activities	Never	Once a Month or Less	2-3 Times a Month	Four or More Times a Month
Lobby those in government	29.3	36.4	14.1	20.2
Advocate new policies	14.9	40.2	19.6	25.3
Educate those in government	12.3	40.7	24.3	22.7

Q5. For some nonprofits, there is a need to lobby those in government so that policymakers will have a better understanding of the problems facing the community. How often does your organization undertake an effort to **lobby** [or "advocate new policies before" or "educate government officials at any level about specific policies"] government officials at any level?

We found that, for a variety of reasons, many nonprofit leaders either do not or will not use the term "lobby" to describe their activities. The head of a voluntary organization in Sacramento, for example, clearly acknowledged lobbying but said they never use the word. "We 'educate' legislators," she said. Some have said that the choice of words does not make a difference as long as nonprofits get more involved in public policy matters. Compare the frequencies in the "never" column in Table 4-5, above. Not surprisingly, "educating" policymakers, the activity most respondents admitted to, is the least controversial term. More than twice as many respondents admitted at least some activity in that vein as compared to "lobbying." Even "advocacy," a commonly used synonym for lobbying, is almost equally as palatable a descriptor as "education" in the nonprofit world.

Yet, as we will discuss in this chapter, we found that attitudes the staff, board, and public have regarding engaging in public policy are a good predictor of whether the organization lobbies, encourages others to lobby, or testifies. If the public expresses negative attitudes regarding lobbying, it may result in limiting the type of public policy activities undertaken by nonprofits. One objective should be to legitimize the importance of lobbying.

Our findings indicate that a good number of nonprofit leaders either do not understand the legal definition of lobbying or do not know that it is a perfectly permissible activity for nonprofits. In an interview, a human services director described an effort to get a bill passed that clearly fit the legal definition of lobbying. Yet this description was offered just after the director claimed his organization "doesn't lobby." Like him, other nonprofit executives may have consciously or unconsciously wiped the word out of their vocabularies because they know it is a red flag for some funders, whether public or philanthropic. Another reason might be a belief that lobbying has negative connotation in the general public.

In one focus group, someone described being very involved in lobbying. They had written about legislation in their newsletter and described their frustration with the state legislature because they often act on bills before the newsletter is distributed. At the same time, another participant claimed his group does not lobby and then proceeded to describe how the organization meets with state legislators to encourage them to put more money into programs serving those with disabilities.

The behavior of those respondents who say they never lobby, advocate or educate policymakers does not always follow the rhetoric (see Table 4-6). Although more than 150 respondents say they do not lobby, 15.5 percent of these report on the same survey that they have lobbied for or against a proposed bill or other policy pronouncement at least at a low frequency. Similarly, nearly half (48 percent) of those who say they have never lobbied report undertaking an activity we defined as being a "participator" (this includes lobbying, encouraging members to write, call fax, or e-mail policymakers, or testifying before a legislative or administrative hearing).

Table 4-6. Behavior Does Not Always Follow Rhetoric

Those Who Report They NEVER:	Percentage of Respondents		
	BUT report "Lobbying for or against a Proposed Bill or Other Policies"	BUT are a Participator	BUT Report Lobbying Expenditures to the IRS on Form 990
Lobby	15.5	47.5	10.7
Advocate	23.0	37.6	12.4
Educate on Policy	13.8	29.2	7.5
Those Who Report 4 or More Times a Month they:			
Lobby	98.2	100.0	69.0
Advocate	97.2	100.0	60.7
Educate on Policy	94.1	98.3	53.7

This disconnect between rhetoric and behavior drops with "advocacy" and even more so with "educate." Nonetheless, three in ten respondents who said they never educate government officials at any level about specific policies report on the same survey that they lobby, encouraging others to lobby, or testify, and our definition of a participator.

There is much less of a disconnect between those who say they actively lobby, advocate, or educate policymakers and their reported behavior. For example, all of those respondents who said they lobbied or advocated four or more times a month were also identified as being a participator (they lobbied, encouraged others to lobby or testified), and 98 percent of those who say they educate policymakers were considered participators.

Even among respondents who have chosen to use the expenditure test and have reported lobbying expenditures to the IRS under the annual Form 990, 6.5 percent of those asked about lobbying say they never do, while 2.8 percent of those asked about advocacy say they never do, and only 1 percent asked about educating policymakers say they never do. This is from a subset of the survey that has at the very least indicated some interest in lobbying by electing to come under an optional set of lobbying expenditure limits, and reported lobbying expenditures to the IRS. Still, they prefer not to refer to what they do as "lobbying."

The message this sends is loud and clear. Anyone who wants to encourage nonprofit involvement in policy would do better to call it anything but lobbying. But cloaking the behavior under different names may not be wise. We must remember that lobbying is a First Amendment right that should be cherished. We have fought to protect our form of democracy with its constitutional right to petition government. Yet recent news about disgraced lobbyist Jack Abramoff has further sullied the image of lobbying. What nonprofit leaders should remember is that lobbying is not disgraceful; Abramoff, who broke the law, is disgraceful.[154]

At the same time, we need to recognize that all advocacy is not lobbying and that other forms of policy participation, from mingling socially with policymakers to staging a protest, can have value. This confusion suggests a need for better definitions so nonprofits can properly label the different types of policy participation.

Participation In Policymaking Is Wide But Not Deep

The ambivalence shown toward the word lobbying should not obscure the clear finding that the great majority of charitable nonprofits are participants, at some level, in the policymaking process. More than four in five charities (86 percent) participate at least occasionally in one of three activities that we used to determine who was a "participator" in policymaking.

---

[154] Propelled by the Abramoff guilty plea and the possible indictment of members of Congress and senior staff, Congress is considering legislation to reform lobbying and ethics in Congress. While the legislative outcome is uncertain as this book goes to print, it is certain that Congress will not restrict the constitutional right of individuals or groups to lobby. Instead the focus is on greater disclosure.

In the survey, we asked about the frequency of nine kinds of interactions nonprofits might have with government. We chose not to ask questions in a form consistent with legal definitions. Instead, the questions address a variety of forms of advocacy. All of the activities we asked about are legal for charities, though several may not be paid for with government money. Indeed, a large number of activities we did not ask about that are commonly used to influence policy – from conducting a poll to writing letters to the editor – are not necessarily considered lobbying under the legal definition.

Table 4-7. Types of Policy Participation Considered in the Survey
Testifying at legislative or administrative hearings
Lobbying on behalf of or against a proposed bill or other policy pronouncement
Responding to requests for information from those in government
Working in a planning or advisory group that includes government officials
Meeting with officials about the work we are doing
Encouraging members to write, call, fax, or e-mail policymakers
Releasing research reports to the media, public, or policymakers
Discussing obtaining grants or contracts with government officials
Interacting socially with government officials

Since the literature in the nonprofit field does not agree on a common definition of the term advocacy, we answered the question of who is a policy "participator" by asking participants in the study's focus groups to tell us which of the nine activities they believe constitute "policy participation." We also asked how strongly they felt about their responses. Every person felt strongly that three items on the questionnaire (direct lobbying, asking members to lobby, and testifying) were acts of participation in the policy process. There were mixed reactions to the remaining six items, with some people feeling strongly that they were not examples of participation. The definition we ended up using is outlined in Table 4-8. It is very similar to the legal definition of lobbying (see Table 4-8 for our definition compared to the legal definition).

Table 4-8. SNAP Definition of "Participator" versus Lobbying Definition

"Participator" defined by focus groups	Legal definition of lobbying
• Testifies at legislative or administrative hearings; • Lobbies on behalf or against a proposed bill or policy; or • Encourages members to write, call, fax or e-mail policymakers.	• States position in support of or opposition to specific legislation to a legislator, or • Encourages the public to contact policymakers in support of or opposition to a specific legislative proposal.

Characterizing the overall response to the question about types and degree of participation is like trying to decide whether a cup is half full or half empty. Nonprofits recognize the importance of public policy to their mission and goals and do get involved, but only a minority are ready to be present at the policymaking table on a continuing basis. Involvement in advocacy appears wide but not deep.

Only a few (22 to 29 percent) *never* participate in policy under our definition that includes testifying, lobbying, and issuing grassroots calls to action (see Table 4-9). "We simply don't do those types of things," said a leader of a faith-based group in San Antonio, TX. "It's not in our mission to engage in public policy," said a director of an organization dealing with substance abuse in Sacramento, CA. Many non-participators said they felt advocacy took away time from the things they had to do each day – fundraising, dealing with staff issues, and a variety of other day-to-day crises.

More than three in four respondents encourage their members to contact decision-makers about specific policy measures. And, as the following table shows, nearly as many say that they directly lobby policymakers at least occasionally. However, only 15.9 percent said they lobby at the most frequent, or "ongoing," level.

Of those who said they do lobby, three in five reported doing so at a low level. Most of these reported the lowest frequency possible on our scale. Like those who do not lobby at all, many of them see it as "inappropriate" or "not our mission." Others said their board members fail to understand the role charities have to play in public policy formation. And some board members, we were told, view "advocacy" as well as lobbying in negative terms.

Testifying at hearings was rated the second least frequent of all the activities we asked about. This does not necessarily reflect a lack of interest by nonprofits in testifying. It probably reflects that lawmakers usually can invite only a limited number of witnesses to participate in hearings. As a result, only the best-known or the organizations known to have very high stakes in the issue at hand may be asked to testify.

Very frequently nonprofits simply talk with policymakers about what their organizations do. One in five had such conversations on an ongoing basis, while 63.4 percent communicated such information at least occasionally. These conversations may or may not have any influence on specific policy questions.

More than three in four nonprofits said government officials contact them with requests for information or help. Over 40 percent of them said this happens at least twice a month. Officials "view us as a resource, a resource for information about how their policies impact our members," said a spokesperson from an eldercare association. Furthermore, nonprofit opinions seem to be respected. More than two out of three of the survey respondents said government officials are "interested in what we have to say." Moreover, 26.4 percent said their government contacts are also interested in actively working with them toward common goals, a point that should encourage more groups to participate in policy.

Table 4-9. Frequency Of Different Types Of Policy Participation
(Percentage of respondents)

	Never	Low	High
Releasing research reports to the media, public or policymakers	31.0	47.1	21.8
Discussing obtaining grants or contracts with government officials	29.2	42.6	28.2
Testifying at legislative or administrative hearings	29.0	47.9	23.1
Lobbying on behalf or against a proposed bill or other policy pronouncement	26.3	42.8	31.0
Encouraging members to write, call fax or e-mail policy makers	22.3	40.8	36.8
Interacting socially with government officials	19.3	55.5	25.2
Working in a planning or advisory group that includes government officials	18.4	39.2	45.1
Meeting with government officials about the work we are doing	15.0	40.2	44.8
Responding to requests for information from those in government	12.9	26.0	41.0

Question 6: A variety of means of communicating and interacting with those in government are listed below. Please use the scale on the right to indicate how frequently, if at all, your organization engages in these activities. (By "your organizations" we mean the executive director, other staff, volunteers, or members of the board.) In this scale, "0" means never, "1" is relatively infrequently interaction, and "4" is ongoing.

"Low" combines 1 and 2; "High" combines 3 and 4.

Answers to the question about policy activities also hinted at the venues for communicating with officials. It appears there are frequent opportunities, at least at the state and local levels, for nonprofits to engage with policymakers somewhat as peers. Perhaps most surprisingly, our study showed that more than three-fourths of nonprofits interact socially with policymakers at least occasionally, and another eight percent do so regularly. It also appears that there are frequent occasions for nonprofit representatives to sit on planning bodies and study groups with public officials. This was the most frequently mentioned means of contact with policymakers.

Profile of a Participator

Despite wide differences among charitable nonprofits, the survey enabled us to draw a profile of those who are more likely than others to be participants in policy formation.

Compared with other nonprofits, policy participators are more likely to[155]:

- Be environmental, health, or social action groups (the least likely are those in the arts, recreation, religious, and philanthropic organizations).
- Have chosen to use the Internal Revenue Code's expenditure test limits on lobbying expenditures.[156]
- Have larger budgets and multiple funding sources.
- Regardless of staff size, have senior staff beyond the executive director or a board committee specifically assigned to government relations.
- Receive government *and/or* foundation funding.
- Be tech-savvy about e-mail and the Internet, especially where policy is concerned.
- Have members, particularly other nonprofits or government agencies.
- Be members of associations or coalitions (joining national and state associations strengthens the correlation in that order).
- Receive "calls to action" from associations or coalitions, the more frequent the better.
- Receive requests for information from public officials.

Using the IRS Expenditure Test Correlates with More Advocacy, But Is Not a Predictor

At the national level, much attention is paid to educating nonprofits about the importance of opting to use specific IRS lobbying expenditure limits rather than falling under the vague default standard that lobbying may not consume a "substantial" portion of an organization's resources. Therefore, an important question for us in conducting the study was to determine whether those who had chosen the expenditure test in Section (h) of the tax code were actually more likely to lobby.

---

[155] This is a bivariate analysis.
[156] See Internal Revenue Code §§501(h) and 4911. Discussion of the expenditure test is in Chapter 2 and Chapter 5.

As it turned out, there *was* a statistically significant correlation between opting to use the expenditure test and eight of the nine policy activities we asked about in the survey. The only activity for which the correlation was not statistically significant was in discussing government grants or contracts with officials.

We learned from this analysis that efforts to encourage use of the expenditure test as a way of bolstering nonprofit policy engagement is *not* off the mark. Nevertheless, a chicken-and-egg question remains about whether the choice of the expenditure test facilitates more engagement or whether the engagement leads groups to learn about and use the test.

Table 4-10. Differences Between Those Under the Expenditure Test and Substantial Part Test

	Reported Lobbying Expenditures on Form 990	Did Not Report Lobbying Expenditures on Form 990
Lobbying on behalf of or against a proposed bill or other policy pronouncement	NS	*
Encouraging members to write, call, fax, or e-mail policy makers	NS	NS
Testifying at legislative or administrative hearings	NS	***
Interacting socially with government officials	NS	NS
Working in a planning or advisory group that includes government officials	NS	*
Meeting with government officials about the work we are doing	NS	NS
Responding to requests for information from those in government	NS	NS
Releasing research reports to the media, public, or policymakers	NS	***
Discussing obtaining grants or contracts with government officials	*	**

NOTES:

* p<.05; ** p<.01; *** p<.000 – meaning that there is a significant difference between those under the expenditure test and those under the substantial part test.

NS= No significant difference between those electing under the expenditure test and those under the substantial part test.

An analysis of variance shows no significant difference using election of the expenditure test (dependent variable) as a predictor of any of the above variables for groups with lobbying expenses.

An analysis of variance shows a significant difference using election of the expenditure test (dependent variable) as a predictor of any of the above variables for groups without lobbying expenses (p<.000).

189

To further test whether use of the expenditure test results in more policy participation, we subdivided groups that chose the expenditure test and those under the substantial part test into two groups: one that reported lobbying expenses on their IRS Form 990 and one that did not. Using a statistical test, we tested whether there was a significant difference between expenditure test groups and substantial part test groups on various measure of policy participation when they had reported lobbying expenses on the IRS Form 990. We also did the same comparison for organizations that reported no lobbying expenses on Form 990. As Table 4-10 shows, there is a significant difference between them on many of the measures of policy participation when the organization reports no lobbying expenditure on the Form 990. However, there is little difference between them when the organization reports lobbying expenditure on the Form 990. This outcome reinforces the notion that the decision to use the expenditure test is not the critical factor in determining whether a nonprofit will engage in policy matters. Rather, the stronger predictor of participation is whether the organization spends money.

What Motivates Nonprofits To Participate?

The survey revealed that nonprofit involvement in the policy process is mostly mission-driven. Table 4-11 shows that 81 percent of respondents said that promoting government policies that support their mission was a key motivating factor for engaging in policy matters. Respondents told us they are motivated, in their words, to do things like preserve the environment, address community needs, eradicate homelessness, protect their clientele, make their communities better places, and give a voice to nonprofits and the voiceless in society. After goals specifically related to mission, the most frequently mentioned motivation was to "raise public awareness of important issues," with 76 percent of respondents saying it was a key motivating factor for engaging in public policy.

Sometimes nonprofits expressed advocacy's relationship to "mission" as one in which government help is a matter of self-preservation. If the organization gets the public help it needs to survive, it will be able to pursue its mission. The executive of a Girl Scout council in upstate New York, for example, said, "Our members do not get involved unless something threatens their existing operations." An extension of this rationale is the idea of government relations as a "necessary evil," as one executive director from Boston told us in a focus group. As an organization, he said they try to avoid having to deal with elected officials but must because their grants and contracts depend on solid relationships with them. He went on to say that every time he leaves a meeting with an elected official he feels "unclean."

Other than furthering the mission of the organization and its own survival, some interviewees expressed motivation more in terms of advocacy as a tool for the empowerment of members and clients. Those who talked about "giving voice" to the powerless, the elderly, kids, and disabled people seemed to believe the act of engaging, or the empowerment derived from it, is as valuable as the policy change itself.

Table 4-11. Factors Motivating Participation In Policy Process

	Percentage		Gamma[1]
	No Influence	Major Factor	Association with being a Participator[2]
Promoting government policies that support our mission	8.2	80.8	.729
Raising public awareness of important issues	8.2	75.7	.695
Protecting government programs that serve our clients, constituents, or community	13.4	71.8	.673
Defending nonprofits' advocacy rights	23.2	37.1	.477
Opportunities to gain government funding	35.5	40.0	.365

[1] Gamma is a measure of association. Gamma ranges from -1 to +1 with -1 indicating a perfect negative association, +1 a perfect positive association, and 0 indicating no association. Thus, a higher number indicates a greater association.

[2] Participator means the organization either lobbies, encourages others to lobby, or testifies.

Using a Chi-square statistic, there is a significant difference between participators and non-participators on each motivation factor. In each case, $p<.000$. N= 1,471 to 1,521, depending on question.

Q16. Turning from barriers to inducements, what factors motivate your organization to become involved in the public policymaking process?

0 = No Influence; 1 = Low Motivating Factor; 4 = High Motivating Factor

"Major Factor" combines scores of 3 and 4.

In interviews, passion and commitment came out as another type of motivation. "There are a lot of passionate people in this field," explained a childcare council executive in California. "The passion for the work we do gives us energy, tenacity and longevity." There is also a heightened sensitivity of what is perceived as wrong or inequitable. An arms control advocate asked what motivates their advocacy answered, "Right now, I feel an obligation because there is such a disturbing state of affairs."

For those who wish to encourage nonprofits to increase their level of engagement in public policy matters it may be more important to focus on mission-based motivation rather than topics such as the legal rules. Such an approach may help to foster sustained participation rather than the intermittent pattern we found in this study. Table 4-11 also compares those who are "participators" (they lobby, encourage members to lobby, or testify) with the inducements to participate by showing a measure of association. As the percentage of respondents who identify a factor as a major reason for engaging in public policy increases, the measure of association with being a participator also increases.

What Hinders Policy Participation?

When asked, nonprofits give lack of money as the main reason for not being more frequent and consistent participants in policy debates. Eighty-one percent of respondents mentioned it as a barrier. In a second tier of barriers were such reasons as the tax law (68 percent of respondents) and lack of skills (64 percent). A third tier (51 to 55 percent of respondents) pointed to organizational and public attitudes toward policy activity, their receipt of government funds and cautionary advice from accountants or attorneys as hindering policy participation.

The survey found lack of advocacy funding is not only a frequent barrier but also a large one. On a scale of from 0 to 4, nearly half (48.4 percent) ranked financial limits as a large barrier, which combined the responses to scores of 3 and 4.

In writing the survey, we made the mistake of not asking if lack of time was a barrier. This would have told us if, given the funding, nonprofits would spend it on public policy engagement. In focus groups, we asked executive directors if either giving them money to hire a dedicated policy person or another person to free up time for policy work could ameliorate the time barrier. Many said yes; they noted that because they are at capacity they did not know how they could reallocate or reorganize in order to create capacity for public policy. A few added that even if they had resources for additional staffing, they might address other high priority needs such as development and service delivery before public policy. There may be a need for technical assistance on staffing patterns and resource allocation to facilitate advocacy in addition to focusing on motivational factors discussed earlier. This need seems more prevalent among service-oriented agencies.

169

Table 4-12. Barriers to Policy Participation

	Percentage		Predictor of Participation	
	No Barrier	Major Barrier	Chi-square Test	Gamma[1]
Organization's limited financial resources	18.9	48.3	p<.000	.267
Tax law or IRS regulations	32.8	22.7	p<.001	.243
Staff or volunteer skills	35.4	21.3	p<.003	.208
Organization receives government funds	48.6	17.3	p<.000	.375
Board or staff's attitude toward involvement in the policymaking process	45.2	15.8	Not Significant	.007
The public's attitude toward involvement in the policymaking process	46.3	11.7	p<.002	.189
Organization receives foundation funds	58.8	6.1	p<.002	.248
Advice from attorneys or accountants	49.3	8.7	p<.000	.241

[1] Gamma is a measure of association. Gamma ranges from -1 to +1 with -1 indicating a perfect negative association, +1 a perfect positive association, and 0 indicating no association.

Q15. In the previous section we asked you about your direct involvement in the public policymaking process. Now we would like to know about factors that you feel are barriers to your organization's involvement in the policymaking process and how significant those barriers are. In the scale below, 0 represents no barrier, 1 a low barrier, and 4 represents a major barrier.

For purposes of this table, "Major Barrier" aggregates those marking 3 and 4 on the survey.

N= 1,423 to 1,465, depending on question.

We also compared the barriers respondents identified to whether those barriers played a significant role in limited participation as measured by whether the nonprofit has lobbied, encouraged members to lobby, or testified. Table 4-12 shows that limited financial resources, the number one identified barrier, is also a predictor of participation. Although attitudes of board and staff, as well as the public, regarding participating in the public policy process were not identified as a major barrier, it remains a good predictor of policy participation. To the extent that there is a negative attitude about lobbying, the organization is not likely to lobby. Similarly, while three out of five nonprofits said government funding is not a barrier to advocacy, it proves to be a significant predictor of participation.

In questions testing whether respondents understood the legal rules related to lobbying, we found almost all (82 to 94 percent) understood the most basic limits, such as not being able to lobby with federal funds or that there is no restriction on taking policy positions without referencing specific legislation. However, there was a troubling lack of knowledge on two issues. Half thought they could not lobby at all if only part of their budget comes from federal funds. Nearly as many (43 percent) thought nonprofits could not sponsor a forum or debate featuring candidates for office, even if it in no way favored one candidate over another.

In interviews and focus groups, retribution and intimidation also surfaced as issues that groups face when they decide to engage in policy. We were told of grant funds halted and campaign contributions expected because of positions groups had taken on public policy issues.

Nonprofits also feel discouraged by the overwhelming odds they experience when they go up against corporate or other well-healed lobbyists. One mentioned being outspent by opponents in the Right to Life Movement on a scale of "42 to one." An environmental executive said they work in a "conservative bastion where the development juggernaut is alive and well." A migrant worker aid society said the legislature was about to give in to opponents out to silence their lawsuit against corporate farmers in the state. A mental health advocate in Pennsylvania talked about a state lobbyist disclosure law that served as a "gag rule" because its reporting requirements were so confusing.

These barriers and others will be discussed in greater detail in later chapters. Different types of nonprofits experience these impediments in various ways. It makes a difference where an organization is in its life cycle, how big it is, and what are the effects of local attitudes and politics. In the chapter with recommendations (Chapter 7), we attempt to present a model to guide the kind of interventions that can reduce the roadblocks that stand in the way of full participation in American policymaking by a diverse group of charitable nonprofits – the sector that represents people from all walks of life in all their various pursuits.

Role of Associations

If an objective is to encourage nonprofit policy participation, a smart investment would be to support policy-oriented coalitions, associations, and similar alliances. Nonprofit organizations that belong to coalitions and associations – nonprofit organizations that have organizational members – emerged as the most active kinds of groups in the SNAP survey.

Organizational membership is highly associated with all forms of policy-oriented activity. A corollary to this finding is that nonprofits that belong to these larger umbrella groups are also more likely to be engaged in policy participation. (For the study's purpose, "participators" were defined as organizations that testified at hearings, lobbied for or against a bill or policy, and/or encouraged their members to lobby.)

Chapter 5
Legal Rules as a Factor Influencing Participation

Prior to SNAP, most research on nonprofit advocacy examined "interest groups" or other subsets of the sector, but few have segmented nonprofits based on tax-exempt status.[157] However, since the Internal Revenue Code imposes significant advocacy restrictions on the largest subset of the sector – public charities exempt under Section 501(c)(3) of the code – separate study of advocacy by these groups is necessary for a clear picture of advocacy in the sector and barriers and incentives that influence participation.

Currently confusion reigns. Elected officials, the general public, and many nonprofits do not understand the legal rules regarding lobbying and electioneering that apply to charities. In our survey question on legal rules respondents scored an overall C-, with especially low grades on the rules that apply to government grantees engaged in lobbying

> **Tax Status and Advocacy**
>
> Public charities, exempt under Sec. 501(c)(3) of the tax code, are the only nonprofits that:
>
> - Have limits on how much legislative lobbying they can do, and
> - Cannot endorse or oppose candidates for office.

and nonpartisan voter education. Combining this information with other results from the survey, interviews, and focus groups demonstrates that the complexity of the law is largely to blame. Nonprofits that consult experts, including attorneys and accountants, are more likely to be participators in public policy activities, as are groups that use the IRS expenditure test to measure their lobbying limits. However, choosing the IRS expenditure test is not as important as helping nonprofits understand why they should be involved in public policy issues in the first place.

---

[157] See for example, research conducted by Jeffrey M. Berry. A number of his publications are identified in the bibliography at the end of this book.

Differences Between 501(c)(3)s and Other Nonprofits

There are significant differences between interest groups and charities. For example, if a trade association representing chemical manufacturers was exempt under Section 501(c)(6) as a business league, the contributions it received would not be tax-deductible and there would be no restrictions on the amount of legislative lobbying it could do. A business league can also support or oppose candidates for office. But an environmental research and advocacy group exempt under 501(c)(3) is limited in the amount of legislative lobbying it can do, and it is absolutely prohibited from supporting or opposing candidates for office. Contributions to the 501(c)(3), however, are tax-deductible.[158]

The difference in tax treatment is significant when public policy issues are being debated in Congress, state legislatures, or local governments. If a bill to curb emissions from chemical plants is coming up for a vote, the chemical manufacturer's trade association can put significantly more resources into a lobbying campaign than can the environmental group. Often the chemical company contributed to the campaigns of legislators on key environmental committees, while the environmental group will not appear on the list of campaign contributors because they are prohibited from supporting or opposing candidates. Comparing advocacy of these different types of groups is like comparing apples and oranges.

A segmented examination of advocacy by public charities also helps illustrate the overall impact of legal restrictions arising from the tax code. Public charities include charitable, educational, scientific, religious, and artistic organizations. The SNAP research sample excluded large institutions like universities, hospitals, and religious organizations, so that the research was able to focus on the types of groups that are most typical of this portion of the sector.

The groups in our sample show a good general understanding of select legal principles, but confusion about specifics and, in some cases, confusion about basic principles. Participators are more likely to consult

---

[158] In Chapter 2 we discussed the Supreme Court decision in the 1983 *Regan v. Taxation with Representation* case in which the Court determined it was constitutional to limit the free speech of charities because of the tax subsidy created through tax deductibility. A key factor in the Court's decision was that a charity could establish a 501(c)(4) to provide unlimited lobbying.

experts and understand the law. Our study was also able to take a close look at the differences between respondents that have chosen to use the IRS expenditure test to measure their lobbying limit and those that use the default standard, which says "no substantial part" of a charity's activities can be used in attempts to influence legislation. In Chapter 2, we provided short descriptions of the expenditure test and the substantial part test.

Organizations that opt to use the expenditure test to measure their lobbying must follow detailed regulations. In the *Nonprofit Lobbying Guide*, Bob Smucker provides an easy-to-follow explanation of the lobby rules for organizations that choose to use the expenditure test. The lobby rules create two categories of lobbying: direct lobbying and grassroots lobbying. Direct lobbying is when an organization attempts to influence specific legislation by stating a position to a legislator or other government employee who participates in the formulation of legislation. Grassroots lobbying is when an organization urges the public to take action on specific legislation. To be grassroots lobbying, the communication must: (a) refer to specific legislation; (b) reflect a point of view on that legislation; and (c) carry a call to action that provides information about contacting legislators.

The lobby rules provide a number of exemptions from communications being considered lobbying. Some of these include:

- Attempting to influence executive branch actions;
- Nonpartisan analysis, study, or research;
- Discussion of broad social, economic, and similar policy issues;
- Providing technical assistance, such as testimony, in response to a written request; and
- Self-defense lobbying.

Table 5-1. An Overview of the Substantial Part Test and the Expenditure Test

Substantial Part Test	Expenditure Test
• No certain and definitely allowable amounts of lobbying expenditures	• Clear lobbying definitions
	• Definitely allowable amount of lobbying expenditures
• One-year violation may result in the loss of tax-exempt status	• Amount permitted for grassroots lobbying might be too low
	• Exceptions to what activities constitute lobbying
• Additional reporting burden on tax Form 990	• No jeopardy to tax-exempt status for one-year violation
	• Less reporting burden than substantial part test

The expenditure test provides a sliding scale on how much money can be spent on direct and grassroots lobbying depending on budget size of the organization. The amount that can be spent on grassroots lobbying is one-quarter the total amount permitted for lobbying. Table 5-2 shows that an organization with $500,000 in exempt purpose expenditures can spend up to 20 percent on lobbying, or $100,000. The organization can spend up to 25 percent of that ceiling on grassroots lobbying, or $25,000. An organization with $1 million in exempt purpose expenditures can spend up to $175,000 on lobbying ($100,000 + (($1 million - $500,000) x 15 percent)), with up to one-quarter, as much as $43,750, on grassroots lobbying. The maximum an organization can spend on lobbying is $1 million, of which $250,000 can be for grassroots lobbying; this maximum applies to an organization with more than $17 million in exempt purpose expenditures.

Table 5-2. Lobby Ceilings under the Expenditure Test

Exempt Purpose Expenditures	Allowable Lobbying Expenditures	Allowable Grassroots Lobbying
Up to $500,000	20%	25% of allowable lobbying amount
$500,000 - $1 million	$100,000 + 15% of excess over $500,000	$25,000 + 3.75% of excess over $500,000
$1 million - $1.5 million	$175,000 + 10% of excess over $1 million	$43,750 + 2.5% of excess over $1 million
$1.5 million - $17 million	$225,000 + 5% of excess over $1.5 million	$56,250 + 1.25% of excess over $1.5 million
Over $17 million	$1 million	$250,000

Confusion, Confusion – Everywhere Confusion

On our survey we provided an eight-question quiz on advocacy legal rules. Overall, respondents got 73 percent right, which would be a C- if we were grading the quiz. While respondents, especially participators[159], did well on certain questions that show a strong general understanding of some legal principles on advocacy, interviews and focus groups revealed that this level of understanding drops significantly when it comes to the details. Even in focus groups of high participators, most executives did not know basic information about lobby laws, such as how much they can lobby or

---

[159] We defined a "participator" as an organization that has at least once lobbied, encouraged members to call, write, fax or email policymakers, or testified before a legislative or administrative hearing.

Table 5-3.

HOW TO CALCULATE THE EXPENDITURE TEST LOBBYING BUDGET:

Step 1: Determine "Exempt Purpose Expenditures"

Annual budget amount	_____
Minus costs of outside fundraiser	_____
Subtotal	_____
Minus capital costs	_____
Total = Exempt Purpose Expenditures	_____

Step 2: Apply IRS Percentage Formula

Exempt Purpose Expenditure Amount		_____
20% of first $500,000	+	_____
15% of the next $500,000	+	_____
10% of the third $500,000	+	_____
5% of the remaining	+	_____

Total = Annual Lobbying Budget
(May not exceed $1 million)   _____

Step 3: Determine Grassroots Lobbying Budget

Annual Lobbying Budget	_____
Divide by 4 = Grassroots lobbying budget	_____

Source: IRS Reg. .4911-1(c)(1).

even what constitutes lobbying under IRS definitions. In fact, most did not know whether the organization had chosen to use the expenditure test or remained under the substantial part test.

The following is a sampling of the comments we got when we asked high participators about the details of the IRS limits on lobbying:

- "We can only do up to 15 percent of our budget on lobbying anyway because of the legal restrictions."
- "501(c)(3) groups can make an election and spend up to ten percent of their budget on lobbying."
- "We're under the limit. Ten percent or less is considered insubstantial."
- "The educational fund is a (c)(3) and we're not allowed to lobby; we're not allowed to influence public policy."

- "I have to wait until a legislator contacts us. I can't contact them because we are a 501(c)(3) and we can't do political lobbying. There is a very large risk we run for lobbying. That is why we keep our heads down and just do the work."

As noted in the discussion above, the first two statements make incorrect assumptions about the percentage of expenditures allowed. The IRS regulations use a sliding scale based on an organization's budget. It has been the same – not adjusted for inflation – since Section 501(h) was passed in 1976 (see Table 5-2 and 5-3 for details). The third statement assumes the substantial part test has an established percentage limit, but this has never been established. Moreover, the percentage is likely to be based on expenditures, and the substantial part test counts all activities such as the work of volunteers even when no money has been spent. The last two statements show that some nonprofits are still thoroughly confused. Some may even be confusing the ban on candidate electioneering with legislative lobbying.

Table 5-4. Understanding Advocacy Rules					
	Percentage with Correct Answers				
Based on your understanding, can your organization:	All Respon-dents	Those Under the Expenditure Test	Those Under the Substantial Part Test	Participators	Non-Participators
Use government funds to lobby Congress	93.6	94.2	93.1	93.0	96.3
Talk to elected public official about public policy matters	91.1	96.1	86.7	95.4	56.2
Endorse a candidate for elected office	87.4	88.3	86.7	86.9	90.7
Take a policy position without reference to a specific bill under current regulations	81.8	90.7	73.9	87.6	35.5
Support or oppose federal regulations	79.3	86.7	72.9	84.6	40.7
Support or oppose federal legislation under current IRS regulations	72.5	80.6	65.5	77.8	32.3
Sponsor a forum or candidate debate for elected office	56.5	63.1	50.7	60.6	26.2
Lobby if part of your budget comes form federal funds	50.4	60.8	42.0	55.1	17.3

For questions in italics there were significant differences between participators and non-participators, with participators more likely to get the correct answers. p < .000 in all cases.

N=1,368 to 1,586, depending on question.

The answers to all questions, except the first and third, are "yes."

Table 5-4 provides the percentage of correct responses for each question for all respondents, along with the percentage of correct responses for those under the expenditure test and substantial part test, as well as those identified as participators and non-participators. The table shows that respondents know the general principle that you cannot use federal funds to lobby and that you can talk to elected officials about public policy matters. Eighty-seven percent of respondents also knew that you cannot support or oppose a candidate for elected office.

Table 5-5 provides information about overall test scores; that is, of all respondents how many questions did they get correct. Sixty-five percent of all respondents scored 75 percent (a C grade) or better on the test. By comparison, 73 percent of those under the expenditure test scored 75 percent (a C grade) or better on the test, as did 71 percent of "participators." Participators are groups that have said they lobby on bills or other policy pronouncements, encourage members to call, write, fax, or e-mail policymakers, or testify at legislative or administrative hearings. Participators and those under the expenditure test did significantly better on the questions than did their counterparts. However, the relationship between status as a participator and knowledge of the law is stronger than the relationship between an organization under the expenditure test and status as a participator. The higher the degree of association, the greater the amount of variance that is accounted for.

Table 5-5. How Respondents Scored on a Test About Advocacy Rules

Out of 8 Questions, How Many Got:	All Respondents		Expenditure Test		Substantial Part Test		Participator		Non-Participator	
	N=	%	N=	%	N=	%	N=	%	N=	%
8 Correct	270	16.7	164	22.0	105	12.2	255	18.4	4	2.3
7 Correct	411	25.4	211	28.3	200	23.2	385	27.8	18	10.3
6 Correct	361	22.4	170	22.8	187	21.7	336	24.3	16	9.1
5 Correct	210	13.0	95	12.7	115	13.3	80	13.0	21	12.0
4 Correct	127	7.9	52	7.0	74	8.6	05	7.6	15	8.6
3 Correct	110	6.8	29	3.9	81	9.4	0	5.1	33	18.9
2 Correct	111	6.9	23	3.1	88	10.2	44	3.2	63	36.0
1 Correct	15	0.9	2	0.3	13	1.5	9	0.7	5	2.9
Total	1,615	100.0	746	100.0	863	100.0	1,384	100.0	175	100.0

* "Participators" are those organizations that lobby, encourage members to call, write, fax, or e-mail policymakers, or testify before legislative or administrative hearings.

Those under the expenditure test did significantly better than those under the substantial part test (p<.000). It was also true that "participators" did significantly better than non-participators on the test (p<.000). But unlike the expenditure-substantial part comparison, the degree of association is far greater for the comparison of participator to non-participator (Gamma=. 694) than for the expenditure-substantial part comparison (Gamma=.283).

Perhaps unsurprisingly, the older the organization is, the better the organization does on the advocacy test. This is part of a pattern of increasing sophistication with age.

Table 5-6. Older Organizations are More Knowledgeable About Advocacy Rules Average Number of Questions Correct out of 8	
Age of Organization	**Average Correct**
1-5 years	4.82
6-10 years	5.61
11-15 years	5.67
16-20 years	6.12
21 and over	6.19

Given the complexity of the rules on advocacy, it may not be surprising that nonprofit executives do not know them. If an organization lobbies, it needs to know the rules under the tax code. If that same organization receives a federal grant (or a pass-through grant from the state government), it needs to know the rules under OMB Circular A-122 or comparable rules that apply to universities and hospitals. If that same organization advocates for additional funding for itself, it needs to comply with yet another set of rules, commonly called the Byrd Rule. If that same organization lobbies "covered officials" at the federal level above specified thresholds, it needs to comply with the Lobbying Disclosure Act. Depending on the state in which the organization resides, it probably also needs to register and comply with additional disclosure requirements submitted at the state level.

To make matters worse, under each of these rules and requirements the definitions of lobbying or advocacy differ, some significantly and some in nuanced ways. Table 5-7 provides a side-by-side comparison of some of these rules. This labyrinth of rules can seem daunting, if not intimidating to nonprofit leaders. The solution is often simply to avoid advocacy.

Nonprofit organizations participating in the public policymaking process may identify with comments from a Lansing, MI nonprofit leader who represents human services organizations in the state:

> The people who are making the rules…really don't have an understanding of what's going on with… consumers themselves and the direct service providers. Some of the stuff, we have such

a difficult time balancing it that part of our job becomes an art of manipulation, of making sure that we can meet the terms of different policies and still do our jobs to the best of our ability. And those of us doing what we do for the love of what we do, sometimes we get really frustrated.

Frustrated may be an understatement. The legal rules were identified by survey participants as a major barrier to nonprofit participation in public policy matters. Chapter 4 provides greater detail on the SNAP findings on barriers and incentives to participation. Nonprofits moving past the barriers are working hard to follow the rules. But there are two areas where lack of knowledge is particularly troublesome. Half of respondents misunderstand the rules for government grantees, and too many (43 percent) do not think they can host candidate debates and forums. In addition, interviews and focus groups results indicate knowledge of the rules is even weaker than shown by the survey results.

Misunderstanding the Rules for Government Guarantees

Even among those who receive government funds, nearly four in ten (39 percent) did not know they could lobby if their organization receives federal funds. This is extremely problematic given that roughly one-third of all charity revenue comes from government, most of it from federal funds (including those passed through state and local governments). The fact that nonprofits do not understand the grant rules – particularly those dealing with public policy participation – has enormous consequences for the sector's role in public service. Government grantees are among those most likely to have the knowledge and experience needed for informed consideration of issues relating to their program areas, whether it is services for the homeless, research or other programs. Congress, state legislators, and the public are deprived of a valuable resource when grantees feel they are barred from sharing views based on their expertise and mission-driven perspective. When grantee nonprofits feel deterred from sharing policy concerns, it leaves disadvantaged people without an organized policy advocate to fight for them.

Table 5-7. Comparison of Major Advocacy Rules

	Expenditure Test: Section 501(h) of Tax Code[1]	Federal Grant Rules: OMB Circular A-122[2]	Lobbying for Grants: Byrd Provision[3]	Lobbying Disclosure Act[4]
Primary Purpose	Permit lobbying by charitable organizations (501(c)(3)) on a limited basis and clarify how much can be spent for such purposes.	Provide cost principles for nonprofit organizations to determine what activities are "allowable" for federal payment or reimbursement, and which are not. One section prohibits the use of federal funds for lobbying and partisan political activity.	Prohibit use of federal funds to influence anyone in a federal agency or Congress regarding the modification, renewal, or award of a grant, contract, loan or cooperative agreement.	Established criteria for determining whether an organization or firm should register their employees as lobbyists and disclose lobbying activities. It does not seek to restrict lobbying.
Definition of lobbying/ advocacy	Attempting to influence legislation at the federal, state, or local level – either directly or indirectly (e.g., encouraging the public to take action). It does not include attempts to influence administrative agency actions (but does include actions to get executive branch officials to influence legislation). Grassroots lobbying must: a) refer to specific legislation; b) reflect a view on that legislation; and c) contain a call to action with respect to that legislation. In addition to lobbying restrictions, charities are prohibited from supporting or opposing a candidate for elected office.	1) Attempting to influence legislation at the federal or state level – either directly or indirectly (e.g., influencing the opinions of the general public). It does not include attempts to influence administrative agency actions (but does include actions to get executive branch officials to influence legislation). 2) Participating or intervening in political campaign. 3) Legislative liaison activities (e.g., attending legislative hearings, gathering or analyzing legislative materials) when done to support efforts to engage in unallowable lobbying.	Attempting to influence the awarding of money by a federal agency or Congress.	Attempts to influence legislation, executive branch policy, administration of a federal program or policy, and nominations that require Senate confirmation. Only apply at federal level and does not include grassroots lobbying. Includes any action in support of lobbying contacts, including preparation or planning activities, research and other background work, and coordination with other lobbyists. 501(h) electors can use tax law definitions

Exceptions to Lobbying/ Advocacy	1) Nonpartisan analysis, study, or research 2) Providing technical assistance or advice (e.g., invited testimony) in response to a written request 3) Communications with members that discuss legislation but do not urge specific action 4) Self-defense activity, including matters that may affect the organization's own existence, powers, exempt status, and similar matters (self-defense exception does not apply to grassroots lobbying) 5) Discussion of broad policy issues that may require legislation, but the communication does not discuss specific legislative measures	1) Providing technical assistance or advice in response to a documented request (e.g., public notice of a hearing). 2) Attempts to influence state legislation that would directly reduce the cost of the federal assistance, or avoid material impairment of the grantee's authority to carry out the federal assistance. 3) Activities specifically authorized by statute to be undertaken.	1) Does not relate to the right to petition Congress or influence "legislative activities supporting or opposing programs." 2) Payment for agency or legislative liaison activities not directly related to the federal assistance. 3) Payment for professional and technical assistance related to preparing, submitting, or negotiating the federal assistance. 4) Direct cash assistance, settlement of claims against the government, and contractor profits are not covered.	Communications related to routine information-gathering Required communications (e.g., subpoena, required by a federal grant) Communications part of the public record such as testimony and comments on regulations Confidential communications
Who is Covered	Tax exempt 501(c)(3) organizations that have elected to be subject to the expenditure test.	All federal nonprofit grantees. Block grants are not subject to federal standards.	All recipients of federal assistance. Excluded: grants, cooperative agreements, and contracts under $100,000; loans and loan guarantees under $150,000; and subcontracts from loans and loan guarantees under $150,000	Organizations that spend at least $24,500 every six months on lobbying. Lobbying firms that spend more than $6,000 every six months on a client. Any lobbyist that fits the LDA definition.
Enforcement	Inaccurate reporting of lobbying expenses may result in penalties or other sanctions. Charities must also pay a 25% tax on lobbying expenditures beyond the permissible limit. Groups that spend more than 150% of these limits over four years may lose their tax-exempt status.	Depending on severity of violation, a nonprofit organization must repay all "associated" costs for lobbying, face immediate suspension or termination of grants, and/or debarment from all future federal funds. Nonprofits must follow Circulars A-110.	For making a prohibited payment: $10,000 to $100,000 per occurrence. For failing to report (or late reports): $10,000 to $100,000 per occurrence.	Civil fines of not more than $50,000.

Reporting Requirements	All charitable tax-exempt organizations must file an annual report to the IRS (Form 990) that includes information about lobbying, including how much was spent on direct and grassroots lobbying.	Federal grantees must comply with OMB Circular A-110, which establishes uniform grant administrative requirements, and A-133, which establishes audit requirements. They must submit narrative reports to the granting agency. Each direct-cost employee who expects to spend 25% of his/her time lobbying must keep a time log.	All applicants for federal assistance must submit two reports when reports submitted, received, and quarterly if material change. One report contains a statement that no federal funds were used for prohibited lobbying on that grant/contract. The second report contains a statement on whether anyone was paid non-federal funds for lobbying on that grant/contract.	If covered, must register and file reports semi-annually. Nonprofits under the expenditure test can opt to use content from IRS Form 990 instead.

NOTES:

[1] 501(c)(3) organizations are covered by lobbying definitions in section 4911 of tax code and may elect to be covered by section 501(h).

[2] OMB Circular A-122, "Cost Principles for Nonprofit Organizations," 49 Federal Register, 18276-77, April 27, 1984. Available at http://www.whitehouse.gov/omb/circulars/a122/a122_2004.html (see Attachment B25 for section on lobbying). Colleges and universities are governed by cost principles in OMB Circular A-21. Hospital cost principles can be found in 45 C.F.R. part 74, Appendix E, Principles for Determining Costs Applicable to Research and Development under Grants and Contracts with Hospitals.

[3] Section 319 of PL 101-121, the Interior and Related Agencies Appropriations Act of FY 1989, amends title 31, USC, by adding section 1352 entitled "Limitation on use of appropriated funds to influence certain Federal contracting and financial transactions." There are other detailed reporting requirements such as those under 42 U.S.C. §1490p(d) and 3537b (the "Housing and Urban Development Reform Act"). These have all been slightly modified since passage of the Lobbying Disclosure Act.

[4] The Lobbying Disclosure Act of 1995 (PL 104-65) can be found at http://www.senate.gov/reference/resources/pdf/contacting10465.pdf. The 1998 amendments can be found at http://www.senate.gov/reference/resources/pdf/contacting105166.pdf.

For more than 20 years, various federal officials and members of Congress have tried to shut down the civic participation of nonprofit organizations. As described in Chapter 2, the first of these attacks came in 1983 from the White House Office of Management and Budget, which attempted to prohibit nonprofit grantees from using non-federal funds for any "political advocacy" costs, defined as "attempting to influence a government decision" at any level of government.

Because nonprofits interact with government on a regular basis and influence many types of decisions, including administrative ones, this proposal drew a firestorm of protest. The final rule was vastly different, limited to a prohibition on use of federal funds for legislative lobbying purposes, a proposition supported by nonprofits – and one widely understood by nonprofits. However, the real issues underlying the OMB proposed rule – limiting the advocacy voice of charities – have never really died.

The threat reemerged in 1995-1997 when a small cadre of Congress members, led by Reps. Ernest Istook (R-OK), David McIntosh (R-IN), and Robert Ehrlich (R-MD), sought to severely restrict the advocacy voice of federal grantees. The proposal was nearly identical to the 1983 OMB proposed rule: broaden the definition of lobbying to include any discussion of public policy matters, severely limit the free speech advocacy rights of organizations receiving federal grants, limit grantees' rights of association with advocacy organizations, and provide rewards for "bounty hunters" who successfully sue grantees for alleged violations of the new restrictions. These Istook amendments were soundly defeated because of a vast mobilization effort in the nonprofit sector that was led by the Alliance for Justice, Independent Sector and OMB Watch.

The attacks continue to emerge – and to influence the public perception of charities. Similar proposals have been included in appropriations bills for individual federal programs in the past few years, but they have been pushed back by the same anti-Istook coalition. The SNAP results show that concerns about nonprofits mixing government funds and lobbying are unjustified. The vast majority – 93.6 percent – correctly answered "No" when asked if government funds can be used to lobby Congress. Those with and without government income were equally likely to answer the question correctly.

<u>Misunderstanding the Rules on Nonpartisan Voter Education</u>

The second troublesome finding is that a significant number of respondents (44 percent) incorrectly believe they cannot sponsor a candidate debate or forum. Such nonpartisan public education events are a crucial public resource in an election season. This result indicates that more education is needed to encourage nonprofits to undertake this important public service. Particularly when party message mills choose relatively few issues in comparison to the vast number of interests represented by the nonprofit sector, it is critical that nonprofits understand and implement the power they have to channel candidate and public focus to issues and needs that often get little attention.

As with the lobbying rules for government grantees, the vast majority of respondents understood what constitutes prohibited activities. In this case, 88 percent answered correctly that they are not allowed to endorse candidates for office. The combined results from the related questions show that respondents tend toward caution and a broad reading of any prohibition on advocacy activities.

How Subsector Groups Score on the Advocacy Test

Respondents' understanding of legal rules varied according to their mission and the subject matter of their work. Environmental, health, housing, social action, and human services groups all scored above the survey average. On the other hand, groups in the arts, education, recreation, crime and public safety, community improvement and capacity-building, philanthropy, or religion scored below the average, some well below the average. Table 5-8 and Chart 5-1 provide further information about how the sub-sector groups scored on the advocacy test.

Table 5-8. Understanding the Advocacy Rules by Subsector
Score Range: 0 to 8 Correct

Sorted by Subsector			Sorted from High to Low		
	N=	Mean		N=	Mean
All Respondents	1,516	5.78	Environment & Animals	151	6.21
Arts & Humanities	147	5.56	Health	251	6.09
Community Involvement & Capacity-Building	91	5.75	Social Action & Civil Rights	46	6.04
Crime & Public Safety	95	5.56	Human Services	277	6.03
Education	196	5.13	Other	140	6.03
Environment & Animals	151	6.21	Housing	58	5.93
Health	251	6.09	All Respondents	1,516	5.78
Housing	58	5.93	Community Involvement & Capacity-Building	91	5.75
Human Services	277	6.03	Philanthropy	55	5.60
Philanthropy	55	5.60	Arts & Humanities	147	5.56
Recreation	53	4.79	Crime & Public Safety	95	5.56
Religion	27	4.85	Education	196	5.13
Social Action & Civil Rights	46	6.04	Religion	27	4.85
Other	140	6.03	Recreation	53	4.79

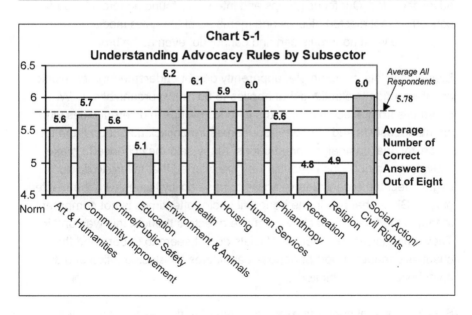

187

Table 5-9
Understanding Advocacy Rules
Broad understanding of some general laws and regulations
• 94% know they cannot use federal funds to lobby
• 91% know they can talk with elected officials about public policy matters
• 87% know they cannot endorse candidates for office
• 82% know they can take policy positions without referencing specific legislation
Areas in which education is still needed
• Only 72% know they can support or oppose federal legislation
• Only 79% know they can support or oppose federal regulations
Areas that need immediate attention
• 50% thought they could not lobby if part of their budget comes from federal funds
• 43% thought they could not sponsor a forum or debate featuring candidates for office

Confusion Goes Beyond Nonprofits

It is not simply leaders within nonprofit organizations who are confused about advocacy rules. Our focus groups and interviews found nonprofit leaders concerned that elected officials and members of the news media do not understand what nonprofits can and cannot do, even at the broadest levels.

Elected officials, for example, apparently do not understand the prohibition on intervention in elections that applies to 501(c)(3) organizations. We heard this from executive directors in focus groups in different cities who spontaneously raised concern about pressure politicians put on them for organizational campaign contributions. Many said they choose to make individual contributions because they are worried that failure to do so might affect the organization's ability to raise policy issues with the elected official. Given that pay in the nonprofit sector oftentimes is not comparable to that in the for-profit sector, executive directors thought this was unfair. They emphasized that elected officials do not seem to understand that charities cannot support or oppose candidates for elected office and that contributions are prohibited.

Similarly, several nonprofit executives noted that newspaper reporters often write inaccurate statements about what nonprofits can do regarding lobbying and advocacy. They note that many reporters seem to think that charities are not permitted to lobby; when charities lobby, reporters are confused. The problem is compounded when a reporter incorrectly notes in a story that 501(c)(3) organizations are not permitted to lobby. This further confuses the public, elected officials, and other charities.

Consulting Experts and Advocacy Activity

Because of the complexity of advocacy rules, we asked survey respondents about their use of experts, such as attorneys and accountants, to learn more about the impact these experts have on nonprofit advocacy. We found that the vast majority of respondents do consult experts, with 57 percent consulting with attorneys (see Table 5-10). Groups that participate in public policy consult lawyers at a higher rate than the general respondent. Similarly, organizations that elect to follow the expenditure test consult with attorneys more than those organizations remaining under the substantial part test.

Table 5-10. Types of Experts Nonprofits Consult

	All Respondents		Participators		Non-Participator		Expenditure Test		Substantial Part Test	
	N=	%	N=	%	N=	%	N=	%	N=	%
Attorney	962	57.4	895	63.7	34	16.1	521	68.7	439	48.2
Experts at other nonprofits	665	39.7	628	44.7	17	8.1	355	46.9	308	33.8
Accountant	455	27.1	414	29.4	25	11.8	245	32.3	329	22.9
Other	147	8.8	136	9.7	4	1.9	60	7.9	85	9.3

Q9. Does your organization consult experts about the legality of any efforts you make to influence government? Check all that apply.

There is a significant difference between participators and non-participators and between those organization under the expenditure test and those under the substantial part test with regard to consulting an attorney, experts at other nonprofits and accountants ($p<.000$).

Further analysis showed that, not surprisingly, respondents who consult experts know more about the law, whether they use attorneys or accountants (see Table 5-11). The advice they are getting does not steer them away from advocacy activity, dispelling the myth that legal advice deters advocacy. Our finding that the complexity of the law is a barrier seems to be a better explanation for reluctance to engage in policy matters. While experts may be the bearers of bad news in terms of the amount of time and effort a nonprofit must invest to understand the rules, their advice is not, in and of itself, a barrier to participation.

Nonprofits in our survey tended to consult with more than one expert (see Chart 5-2). Forty-two percent to respondents consulted with more than one expert; 29 percent with one consultant; and 29 percent did not consult with any experts.

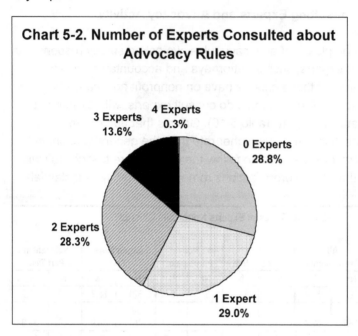

Chart 5-2. Number of Experts Consulted about Advocacy Rules

Table 5-11. Expert Advice Improves Understanding of Advocacy Rules

		Average Correct Answers to Advocacy Quiz (out of 8)	N=
Consult an Attorney	No	5.29	667
	Yes	6.13	940
Consult Accountants	No	5.62	1,166
	Yes	6.20	441

Those consulting attorneys and accountants did significantly better on the advocacy quiz than those who did not consult (p<.000)

Table 5-12 shows those organizations that consult an attorney, another nonprofit, or an accountant are significantly more likely to engage in different types of public policy activities.

Table 5-12. Consulting with Experts Leads to Greater Policy Participation
(Comparison of Means on a 0 to 4 Scale, with 4 Being High Frequency of Participation)

	All Respondents	Consult an Attorney		Consult an Accountant		Consult Experts at Other Nonprofits	
		Yes	No	Yes	No	Yes	No
Lobbying	1.721	2.083	1.231	2.170	1.554	2.157	1.431
Grassroots lobbying	1.899	2.236	1.443	2.338	1.734	2.346	1.603
Testifying	1.486	1.865	0.977	1.897	1.333	1.865	1.233
Respond to requests from those in government	2.154	2.519	1.231	2.506	2.022	2.464	1.947
Part of planning/advisory group with government officials	2.184	2.525	1.723	2.569	2.039	2.666	1.862
Release research reports to media, public, or policymakers	1.463	1.803	1.004	1.791	1.340	1.743	1.2759
Meet with government officials about work	2.198	2.601	1.657	2.575	2.057	2.609	1.928
Interacting socially with government officials	1.652	1.914	1.297	1.869	1.572	1.864	1.512
Discuss obtaining grants/contracts with government officials	1.603	1.816	1.316	1.802	1.529	1.839	1.450

In every case, participation is significantly greater when consulting any of the listed experts ($p<.000$).

Impact of IRS Lobbying Rules:
The Expenditure Test versus the Substantial Part Test

Significant resources have been invested in training, education and technical assistance aimed at increasing the number of groups that take advantage of the expenditure test.[160] Despite these vigorous efforts by national nonprofit infrastructure organizations, only a very small number of charities (approximately three percent) have chosen to use it. Based on 1998 data from IRS Form 990 we knew that only 1.5 percent of charities reported any lobbying expenditures. Less than half of those had chosen the expenditure test.

Many experts and proponents of nonprofit advocacy believe that use of the expenditure test increases legislative advocacy and lobbying by charities because of its many legal advantages and relatively generous limits. The SNAP research examined this assumption. Our sample design allowed us to compare groups that use the expenditure test and groups that do not.[161] We found there

---

[160] See discussion earlier in this chapter about the expenditure test and the substantial part test. Chapter 2 also provides a discussion of the topic.

[161] See Chapter 3 for a discussion of the research methodology we used.

was a statistically significant correlation between opting to use the expenditure test and eight of the nine policy activities we asked about in the survey (see Table 5-13). The only activity for which the correlation was not statistically significant was discussing government grants or contracts with officials.

Table 5-13. Policy Participation by Those Under the Expenditure Test vs. the Substantial Part Test

(Comparison of Means on a 0 to 4 Scale, with 4 Being High Frequency)

	Expenditure Test	Substantial Part Test
Lobbying	2.048	1.425
Grassroots lobbying	2.177	1.637
Testifying	1.810	1.194
Respond to requests from those in government	2.405	1.910
Part of planning/advisory group with government officials	2.490	1.898
Release research reports to media, public, or policymakers	1.779	1.172
Meet with government officials about work	2.521	1.899
Interacting socially with government officials	1.816	1.492
Discuss obtaining grants/contracts with government officials	1.655	1.531

Except for discussing obtaining grants and contracts with government officials, expenditure test groups are significantly more engaged in the above public policy items than groups under the substantial part test (p<.000)

For example, 14.2 percent of respondents using the expenditure test do not lobby, while more than twice as many – 36.2 percent – that are under the substantial part test do not lobby. Similarly, expenditure test groups lobby more often than groups under the substantial part test (see Chart 5-3).

For the most part, groups that use the expenditure test have a better understanding of the law and regulations based on the advocacy quiz in the survey. As Table 5-5 showed, organizations operating under the expenditure test did significantly better on the advocacy quiz than did those operating under the substantial part test. This was also true for each question, except the two questions on which most respondents knew the answer: that government funds cannot be used to lobby Congress and that charities cannot endorse a candidate for office.

This analysis demonstrates that efforts to encourage use of the expenditure test as a way of bolstering nonprofit policy engagement are *not* off the mark. Nevertheless, a question remains about whether the choice of the expenditure test facilitates more engagement or whether the engagement leads groups to learn about and use the test.

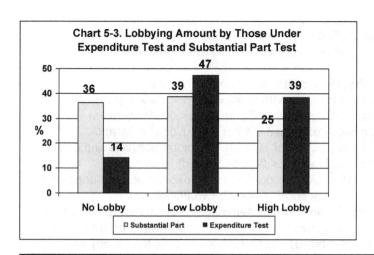

Chart 5-3. Lobbying Amount by Those Under Expenditure Test and Substantial Part Test

---

Table 5-14. Is the Expenditure Test a Predictor of Participation?

Whether an organization spends money on lobbying is a stronger predictor of policy participation than whether the organization elects to be under the expenditure test or the substantial part test

		Reported Lobbying Expenditures on IRS Form 990			
		Yes		No	
		N=	Mean	N=	Mean
Direct Lobbying	Expenditure Test	315	2.516	434	1.707
	Substantial Part Test	363	2.256	553	.879
Grassroots Lobbying	Expenditure Test	315	2.556	437	1.904
	Substantial Part Test	360	2.289	552	1.212
Testifying	Expenditure Test	315	2.181	438	1.543
	Substantial Part Test	361	2.008	555	.665

Those groups electing the expenditure test are significantly more likely to engage in each of the three measures of policy participation identified above than those in the substantial part test (p<.000). As might be expected, those groups reporting lobbying expenditures on Form 990 are significantly more likely to engage in the three identified measures of policy participation than those without expenditures (p<.000). However, the level of association is stronger when comparing groups that report lobbying expenditures and no expenditures than when comparing those under the expenditure test and substantial part test. This suggests that spending is a better predictor of participation than electing the expenditure test.

Gamma		
	Expenditure/ Substantial Part	Lobbying Expenditure/ No Expenditure
Direct Lobbying	.321	.554
Grassroots Lobbying	.272	.440
Testifying	.360	.564

193

Table 5-15. Comparison Groups under Expenditure Test Groups vs. Substantial Part Test

Expenditure Test Groups are *more* likely than others to:
- Participate in policy activities except discussing grants and contracts with government officials (p<.000; two-tailed)
- Have a better understanding of the advocacy law and regulations (except for allowable electoral activities and use of government funds) (p<.000; two-tailed)
- Consult attorneys, accountants, and experts at other nonprofits about advocacy efforts (p<.000; two-tailed)
- Conduct research and disseminate research (p<.000; two-tailed)
- Have an executive director (p<.000; two-tailed), board committee (p<.006; two-tailed), staff member (p<.000; two-tailed), or outside lobbyist (p<.001; two-tailed) responsible for government relations
- Have a paid staff (p<.002; two-tailed)
- Receive foundation funds (p<.000; two-tailed)
- Be a membership organization (p<.001; two-tailed))
- Get more interest from policymakers to their issues (p<.000; two-tailed)

Expenditure Test Groups are *less* likely to
- Have clerical support staff (p<.01; two-tailed)
- Have a founder as the current executive director (p<.007; two-tailed)
- Join associations that represent them before government (p<.008; two-tailed)

In Chapter 4 and in Table 5-14, we provide data that reveals that selection of the expenditure test over the substantial part test is less of a predictor of policy participation than if a group decides to spend money on engaging. The point is that choosing the expenditure test is not likely to suddenly make an organization engage in public policy. Rather, policy participation and the decision to engage is a more complex process that involves organizational motivation, board and staff understanding of the connection between advocacy and fulfilling the mission of the organization, and careful internal planning to structure staffing and funding to engage. It also requires getting past confusion over the complexity of the laws and regulations governing nonprofit advocacy. Consultation with experts seems to be a powerful tool in pushing past that barrier. To reiterate: *Those organizations that choose to fall under the expenditure test are clearly more engaged in public policy, but use of the expenditure test alone will not likely lead to greater participation.*

Characteristics of Groups that Choose the Expenditure Test

Expenditure test groups are less likely to have a founder as their current executive director than groups under the substantial part test. They are likely to have less clerical support staff. They are also more likely to have someone connected to their organization that is responsible for government relations. This person might be their executive director, a staff member, a board committee, or a lobbyist or other outsider.

Expenditure test groups are more likely to get income from foundations and corporations, and are less likely to get income from services provided to clients or others and from fundraising events. There is no difference between expenditure test groups and substantial part groups on receipt of government revenue.

Expenditure test groups are slightly more likely to be membership organizations (and are more likely to have all types of members asked about in our survey). They are less likely to be dues-paying members of associations that represent them before government. If they belong to an association, however, they are more likely to be contacted to take action, but no more likely to act on the request than groups under the substantial part test.

Expenditure test groups are more likely to use e-mail, the Web, fax machines, and telephone conferencing in the policymaking process than groups under the substantial part test.

Chapter 6
Money: The Critical Factor

There is no question it takes money to participate in the policy process. In the SNAP survey, we found having financial resources to be *the* critical factor. The more money an organization has, and from more different sources, the more likely it can employ policy staff and be heavily engaged in advocacy. The larger the organization's budget, the more likely it is to testify and lobby both directly and through its members (SNAP's definition of a "participator").

Our research also found that the more money an organization receives from government and foundations, the more perceived barriers there are to public policy participation. Strikingly, although there are greater barriers, organizations that receive revenue from government or foundations are more likely to participate in public policy, and with greater frequency, than those that do not receive such revenue.

While money is a major factor in assessing nonprofit policy participation, it is not the solution to inducing or encouraging participation. Even if an organization were to receive additional funds, it would not necessarily mean that the organization would suddenly get involved in advocacy. The SNAP survey data and interviews convincingly show that the critical issue remains motivating nonprofit staff and boards to participate in policy matters. Once they are convinced of the importance of engaging in public policy to achieve their mission, then other factors, such as money and understanding statutory and regulatory requirements, become more critical when trying to encourage participation.

The Link Between Money and Participation

Table 6-1 shows that 90 percent of organizations that are not participators – they do not lobby, encourage members to lobby, or testify – have annual budgets of $1 million or less. As organizational budgets increase, so does policy participation, as demonstrated in Table 6-2. The table shows that 68 percent of groups with budgets of under $25,000 are participators. That percentage steadily increases within each budget size category; 98 percent of respondents say they are participators in the category with the largest budgets, which is an annual budget of more than $10 million.

Table 6-1. Organizations that Do Not Participate in Public Policy by Budget Size

Budget Size	N=	Cumulative Percent
Under $25,000	25	11.1
$25,000 to $99,999	78	45.8
$100,000 to $499,999	76	79.6
$500,000 to $999,999	23	89.8
$1 million to $2.49 million	13	95.6
$2.5 million to $4.9 million	1	96.0
$5 million to $10 million	7	99.1
Over $10 million	2	100.0
Total	225	

Table 6-2. Percentage of Organizations Engaged in Policy Activity By Budget Size

Budget Size	Lobbying	Grassroots Lobbying	Testifying	Participator[1]
Under $25,000	48.7	54.4	44.9	67.9
$25,000 to $99,999	57.6	69.1	53.2	74.5
$100,000 to $499,999	70.8	77.4	67.5	83.2
$500,000 to $999,999	79.3	81.5	74.9	88.8
$1 million to $2.49 million	81.9	84.4	84.0	94.7
$2.5 million to $4.9 million	87.8	88.0	87.2	99.2
$5 million to $10 million	89.4	81.7	76.2	91.4
Over $10 million	90.2	82.6	92.6	98.3

[1] Participator means an organization lobbies for or against a proposed bill or policy pronouncement, encourages members to write, call, fax, or e-mail policymakers, or testifies at legislative or administrative hearings

In each case, there are significantly more groups engaged in public policy within larger organizations than smaller ones (p<.000).

This trend holds for each major type of public policy activity. Table 6-2 and Chart 6-1 show that as organizational budget size increases, the percentage of organizations that say they lobby for or against legislation or other policies steadily climbs. For example, 49 percent of organizations with budgets of less than $25,000 say that they lobby. Among organizations with annual budgets over $10 million, 90 percent say they lobby. The same trend holds for testifying at legislative and administrative hearings, and for encouraging members to write, call, fax, or e-mail policymakers, although there is a slight drop-off for grassroots lobbying among the largest organizations.

Frequency of Policy Participation and Money

Not only are groups with large budgets more likely to be involved, the are more likely to engage with greater frequency. In our survey, we asked the frequency of undertaking various policy activities, such as lobbying;

197

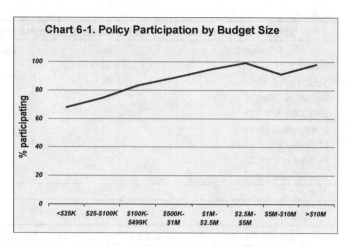

Chart 6-1. Policy Participation by Budget Size

Respondents with annual expenses of $1 million or more are significantly more likely to participate in policy than those with expenses below $1 million

releasing research reports to the media, public, and policymakers; and working in a planning or advisory group that includes government officials. We used a 0 to 4 scale, with 0 being not involved, 1 being a low frequency, and 4 being a high frequency. The nine policy activities we monitored are listed in Table 6-3 along with the average participation levels by organization budget size. In every activity, the larger organizations are significantly more engaged than the smaller organizations.

Chart 6-2 provides a line chart showing that for lobbying, grassroots lobbying, and testifying, there is a nearly direct line correlation between budget size and increased frequency of participation until an organization has a budget of $2.5 million or more. Both Chart 6-2 and Table 6-3 show that for organizations with annual budgets of $2.5 million or more, the frequency of encouraging members to lobby begins to drop slightly. For organizations with budgets of $10 million or more it begins to rebound, but still does not reach the grassroots lobbying level of organizations with budgets between $1 million and $2.5 million. This may be a result of larger organizations having more professional staff and thus having more capacity for direct lobbying without relying on members. A number of people, including Theda Skocpol, have written extensively about how national organizations' operations are becoming less membership-based and more professional.[162]

---

[162] For example, Theda Skocpol, "How Americans Became Civic" in *Civic Engagement in American Democracy*, Theda Skocpol and Fiorina Morris, eds. (Washington, DC: The Brookings Institution Press, 1999).

Table 6-3. Average Frequency of Policy Participation by Budget Size

Measured on a 0 to 4 scale, with 0 being none, 1 being low frequency and 4 being high frequency of participation

Budget Size	Lobby		Grassroots Lobbying		Testify at Hearings		Respond to Information Requests from Govt Officials		Part of Planning Group w/ Govt Officials		Release Research Reports to Media & Public		Meet w/ Govt. Officials About Work		Discuss Obtaining Grants with Govt Officials		Socialize with Govt Officials	
	N=	Means	N=	Means	N=	Means	N=	Means	N=	Means	N=	Means	N=	Means	N=	Means	N=	Means
Under $25,000	782	.910	79	1.114	78	.744	77	1.351	78	1.308	76	.671	79	1.203	78	.833	78	1.192
$25,000 to $99,999	311	1.302	311	1.659	314	1.029	312	1.577	308	1.623	311	1.080	315	1.603	309	1.100	307	1.316
$100,000 to $499,999	459	1.606	461	1.892	456	1.415	458	2.031	454	2.115	452	1.334	458	2.079	457	1.414	453	1.523
$500,000 to $999,999	213	1.822	211	2.028	215	1.567	216	2.194	214	2.407	216	1.514	213	2.329	214	1.682	217	1.673
$1million to $2,499,999	249	2.032	250	2.152	250	1.816	250	2.504	248	2.504	247	1.672	249	2.598	245	1.955	250	1.948
$2.5 million to $4.9 million	123	2.008	125	2.080	125	1.728	127	2.591	128	2.413	126	1.786	127	2.583	127	1.882	126	1.786
$5 million to $9,999,999	85	2.106	82	1.720	84	1.619	84	2.631	86	2.721	84	1.964	84	2.810	85	2.200	85	1.918
$10 million or higher	122	2.107	121	1.926	122	2.000	122	2.754	122	2.549	120	1.967	122	2.713	120	2.308	121	2.074

All are significant at p<.000

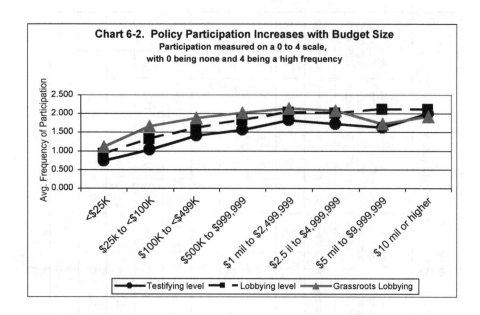

Chart 6-2. Policy Participation Increases with Budget Size
Participation measured on a 0 to 4 scale,
with 0 being none and 4 being a high frequency

The level of direct lobbying also drops slightly for organizations with budgets between $2.5 million and $5 million. However, for organizations with budgets of $5 million or greater, the linear increase in lobbying with budget size picks up again.

While there is no magical budget size at which the frequency of policy participation is optimal, there is a significant difference between organizations with budgets of $1 million or more as compared to those with less than $1 million. It also appears that policy participation in organizations with budgets over $2.5 million begin to stabilize; and in certain areas, such as grassroots lobbying, it slightly dips.

Organizations with Larger Budgets Having Public Policy Staff

The larger an organization's budget, the more likely the group is to charge someone with government relations responsibilities, whether through additional staff or professional consultants (see Sidebar Table 1). Organizations that delegate day-to-day government relations responsibilities to anyone other than the executive director are significantly more involved in public policy activities than groups that delegate the responsibility to the executive director or do not assign anyone the responsibility. This is true for organizations of all budget sizes. Hiring staff to tackle these organizational responsibilities results in groups more engaged than delegating the responsibilities to board members, volunteers, or outside lobbyists.[163]

Sidebar Table 1.
Presence of Government Relations Staff
By Budget Size

Budget Size	% With Someone Responsible
Under $25,000	45.7%
$25,000 to $999,999	55.9%
$100,000 to $499,999	70.3%
$500,000 to $999,999	75.6%
$1 million to $2,499,999	81.4%
$2.5 million to $4.9 million	88.1%
$5 million to $10 million	88.2%
Over $10 million	95.9%

Sig = .000; Gamma = .447

72.9% of all respondents had someone responsible for government relations.

---

[163] It is also true that having an executive director responsible for making overall decisions regarding government relations is also a critical factor in nonprofit participation. This makes sense since it provides an organizational rudder and sends a message that policy engagement is an organizational priority. However, the data suggest that the executive director should not have primary responsibility for day-to-day governmental relations.

Funding Sources

Individual donors and government are, overall, the two largest sources of income for our survey respondents.[164] As Chart 6-3 shows, on average, they together provide 48 percent of nonprofit revenue, with individual donors accounting for 25 percent of revenue and government 23 percent. Just over half of survey respondents receive some form of government income (51.8 percent).

While individual donors and government funds represent the two largest sources of respondent revenue, government funding is the largest source overall for organizations with budgets over $1 million. Individual donors comprise the largest source of income for organizations with budgets of under $1 million (see Chart 6-4).

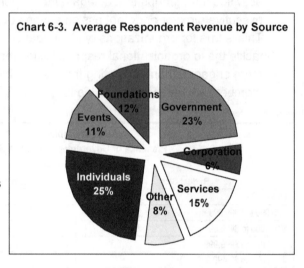

Chart 6-3. Average Respondent Revenue by Source

Foundations 12%
Events 11%
Government 23%
Corporation 6%
Individuals 25%
Other 8%
Services 15%

Chart 6-5 shows for policy participators and non-participators the percentage of revenue each derives from various sources. For participators, roughly one-half of organizational revenue comes from the combination of individuals and government, generally split between the two (individuals provide on average 26 percent of revenue, and government provides 24 percent). The largest gap between non-participators and participators is on government funding; participators receive 15 percentage points more

---

[164] For the purpose of the discussion, government funding is used to denote grants and contracts, and other funding arrangements between nonprofits and government entities at the federal, state, and local levels. Because the sample did not include groups, such as universities and hospitals that enter into contractual arrangements more often than other types of organizations with government agencies there may be discrepancies between our findings and patterns within the overall nonprofit sector in the United States. For example, government revenue was 31.3 percent of all nonprofit revenue in 1997, according to *The New Nonprofit Almanac and Desk Reference*; in our survey, however, it was 23 percent.

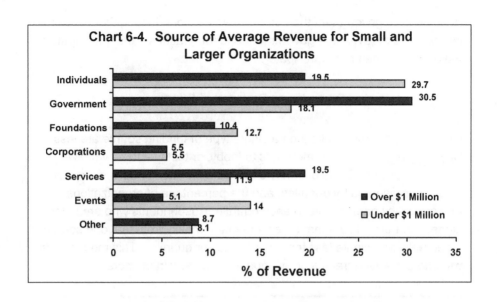

Chart 6-4. Source of Average Revenue for Small and Larger Organizations

Individuals: Over $1 Million 19.5, Under $1 Million 29.7
Government: Over $1 Million 30.5, Under $1 Million 18.1
Foundations: Over $1 Million 10.4, Under $1 Million 12.7
Corporations: Over $1 Million 5.5, Under $1 Million 5.5
Services: Over $1 Million 19.5, Under $1 Million 11.9
Events: Over $1 Million 5.1, Under $1 Million 14
Other: Over $1 Million 8.7, Under $1 Million 8.1

■ Over $1 Million
□ Under $1 Million

% of Revenue

Chart 6-5. Sources of Organizational Revenue for Policy Participators and Non-Participators

Income Source

Individuals: Participator 25.9, Non-Participator 31.3
Government: Participator 24.3, Non-Participator 9.1
Foundations: Participator 12.5, Non-Participator 7.9
Corporations: Participator 5.3, Non-Participator 6.4
Services: Participator 14.1, Non-Participator 14.8
Events: Participator 9.9, Non-Participator 17
Other: Participator 7.8, Non-Participator 12.9

■ Participator
□ Non-Participator

% of Revenue

203

revenue from government than do non-participators. In fact, there are only two sources of revenue – government and foundations – that participators have more of than non-participators.

Diversifying Sources of Funding

Groups that are more reliant on a single type of funding source are less likely to lobby, encourage members to lobby, or testify – to be what we call "participators." Table 6-4 shows the concentration of each source of revenue, presented by quartiles, and the percentage of organizations that are policy participators in each quartile. Respondents who are in the highest quartile – those that receive revenue mostly from that one source – generally participate less than those in lower quartiles. This means those with more diverse streams of revenue tend to participate more.

Table 6-4. Percentage of Organizations that are Participators by Concentration of Revenue Source

	Lowest Quartile	2nd Quartile	3rd Quartile	Highest Quartile
Income from Donors (p<.000)	92.4%	87.7%	85.5%	83.1%
Income from Government (p<.733)	94.1	96.4	94.5	93.8
Income from Foundations (p<.702)	93.9	90.2	88.0	92.6
Income from Corporations (p<.000)	93.6	91.3	84.5	82.2
Income from Services (p<.000)	96.3	90.9	85.2	85.1
Income from Events (p<.000)	94.8	89.5	82.5	77.3

An organization that is a "participator" is one that lobbies, encourages others to lobby, or testifies.

Except for revenue from government and foundations, as income becomes more concentrated, policy participation drops.

For most income sources (with the exception of government and foundation funding), the more a respondent relies on a single source of income, the less likely they are to participate. For example, 92 percent of organizations that are in the lowest quartile of revenue from individual donors – meaning they receive diverse funding streams – are participators. Conversely, 83 percent of organizations in the highest quartile are participators. As a greater share of revenue is derived from individual donors, public policy participation drops. This is especially striking for those who derive a high percentage of their income from fundraising events. These organizations also happen to be smaller organizations, which, as discussed above, are less likely to be engaged in public policy.

These data suggest the importance of diversifying revenue sources if an objective is to increase nonprofit public policy participation. Because government and foundation sources present an anomaly to this trend, and because nonprofits are heavily dependent on each source for revenue, the next two sections explore the impact of government and foundation revenue on nonprofit policy participation.

Government Revenue

Given that participators received far more of their average income from government (24.3 percent) than non-participators (9.1 percent), it is striking that government funding was perceived to be a major barrier to participating in public policy. Chart 6-6 shows that as the percentage of an organization's income from government sources goes up, so does the perception that government money is a barrier to participation. Instead of becoming more comfortable with lobbying while getting government money, most respondents view it as a hindrance to advocacy. Overall, 76 percent of those groups that receive government funds perceive that funding as a barrier to participation, and one-quarter view such funding as a high barrier (see Table 6-5).

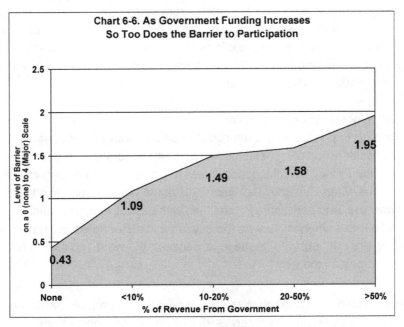

Table 6-5. Government Funding and Barriers to Participation

	No Barrier to Participation		Low Barrier to Participation		High Barrier to Participation	
	N=	Percent	N=	Percent	N=	Percent
All Respondents	701	48.7%	495	34.4%	243	16.9%
Receives Government Grants	191	23.8	414	51.6	198	24.7
Receives No Government Grants	510	80.2	81	12.8	45	7.1

Low Barrier includes scores of 1 and 2 on the survey; High Barrier includes scores of 3 and 4.
p<.000; Gamma=.729

Lobbying is not allowed with federal government money except when specifically authorized by law. This is discussed more fully in the earlier chapters. This does not mean, however, that groups are precluded from involvement in public policy matters – and it does not mean they cannot lobby; it only means they cannot use government money to lobby. Yet there is a widespread perception that if an organization receives government funds, the organization can no longer engage in any type of advocacy even with its private funding. As noted in an earlier chapter, half of SNAP survey respondents incorrectly thought you could not be an advocate if you receive federal grants. As we described in Chapter 2, this may not be surprising given the number of failed federal initiatives to enact laws and regulations that would prohibit government grantees from using private funds to engage in advocacy. Researchers do not know whether this is because respondents did not know the outcome of the efforts to impose restrictions or were simply unaware of their rights. These attacks on nonprofit advocacy, starting in the early 1980s, have had a lasting chilling impact.

Obviously, not all groups that receive government funds feel inhibited from participating in public policy matters. An executive with a Pennsylvania mental health association described what many nonprofits that get government money do: take opportunities to participate in advisory panels or sessions when invited by legislators, distribute relevant research to policymakers, and participate in meetings with executive branch and elected officials when invited. As the executive director noted, most of these activities are not "lobbying" in the legal sense of the word, "so there's not much that gets in the way."

Others we interviewed emphasized the importance of properly allocating staff time. One person who receives 95 percent of her funding from government sources, for example, told us that her organization is very adept at ensuring that the government funds are restricted to carrying out the grants and contracts, and a very small percentage of their own time and resources are used for legislative advocacy. Several old hands at advocacy told us that if there is a possibility that an employee might lobby, then that person should not bill 100 percent of his or her time to the government grant. This, of course, requires having multiple revenue sources (as discussed above).

There are many reasons why nonprofit executives report that government funding creates barriers to policy participation. Many indicate the government grants are not only difficult to obtain, but also to sustain, given the difficulty in understanding and following guidelines from a host of agencies responsible for one grant. And given that many groups are dependent upon government funds to further their missions, they might not want to "rock the boat" by participating, either directly or indirectly, in advocacy activities. In a Michigan focus group, many supported the comment made by a participant that "government grants can dilute advocacy." This was echoed in other interviews and focus groups. The executive director of a Pennsylvania organization delivering services to persons with mental retardation found that high dependency on government contracts changed the culture within the organization. He notes that staff and board members became increasingly focused on protecting the government revenue to the point of downgrading the importance of advocating on behalf of the clients. Even the idea of lobbying for more money for programs they were implementing was not looked upon favorably after awhile. This situation reinforces the growing divide between service delivery and advocacy discussed in Chapter 2.

In focus groups, two themes emerged with regard to government funding and policy engagement. First, many felt that an increased reliance on government revenues allowed government agencies to shape what the organization could and could not do. "If you [receive] government funding, then there are subtle ways government can coerce you," said an executive from a Pennsylvania nonprofit. "When this happens, our Board begins to tremble."

A West Coast nonprofit executive described in an interview being asked by government agencies "to perform services not in our contract," a common refrain during focus groups. When asked what this means for policy participation, participants explained that these additional tasks crowd out the opportunity to tackle advocacy activities. There simply are not enough resources. And organizations fear that if they do not act on these extra "requests" from the government agencies, their grants or contracts will not be renewed.

Second, many groups voiced concern about government retribution for nonprofit advocacy activities. A human services director in Texas noted that he expected his group's state grant to be eliminated or cut because the group lobbied a point in opposition of the view of a legislative staffer who now works in the state agency that provides the grants. As he spoke, a number of other people in the focus group giggled and nodded their heads in knowing acknowledgement of the cost for speaking out on policy issues. An official of a large voluntary organization in another state claimed the group "lost 80 percent of their state grants because of lobbying."

Some groups noted with great consternation that government agencies imply or directly threaten audits on use of the government funds when the group speaks out on policy matters, particularly when they do so in disagreement with those in political control. Several people told us that grant audits they faced – as opposed to IRS tax audits – were politically motivated, adding that such action chills policy activity within the organization. "Literally, you take a position critical [of a policy], the next day the special audit team from the state, they're in all your records.... [I]t's very hard to be an advocate when you're dependent upon state money," lamented a director of a health care provider in Massachusetts.

One lawyer for a state-based nonprofit described a story of her organization successfully defending itself against claims of improper activity with grant funds. But that took years and considerable legal expense. Even though the organization was vindicated, it sapped enormous energy, leaving the staff and board a little gun-shy about further advocacy activities.

A surprising number of people in nonprofit leadership positions think politically motivated audits of grant funds are common. While many of these stories may be apocryphal, their overall impact is quite profound. One board member of a San Antonio, TX nonprofit posed a rhetorical question: Why should our group engage in public policy matters when it is likely simply to anger some local politician who will force more scrutiny of the organization? He added that as part of his fiduciary responsibility he must be sure that revenue for the organization's work is secure. It is safer, he added, not to advocate since it might disrupt this funding by triggering unnecessary investigations.

Given the breadth of the perceived barriers to policy participation, it seems inconceivable that the survey data would show that those groups that receive government revenue actually get more involved in public policy than those that do not receive such funding. But that is precisely what the survey results show.

Table 6-6. Government Revenue and Impact on Policy Participation		Not Participator	Participator	Total
No Government Revenue	Number	173	593	766
	%	22.6%	77.4%	100.0%
Gets Government Revenue	Number	44	781	825
	%	5.3%	94.7%	100.0%

Policy participation includes lobbying, encouraging others to lobby, or testifying.

p<.000; Gamma=.676

Table 6-6 and Chart 6-7 show that 95 percent of those organizations that receive government revenue are participators – they lobby, encourage others to lobby, or they testify – while only 77 percent of those organizations that do not received government revenue are participators. Not only are

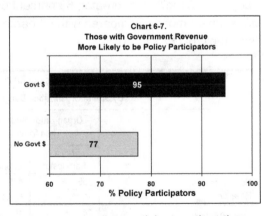

Chart 6-7.
Those with Government Revenue
More Likely to be Policy Participators

groups significantly more likely to engage as a policy participator when they receive government funding, but the frequency of engagement also goes up.

Chart 6-8 shows the frequency of lobbying, encouraging others to lobby (grassroots lobbying), and testifying goes up as government revenue as a percentage of overall budget goes up. The only exception is grassroots

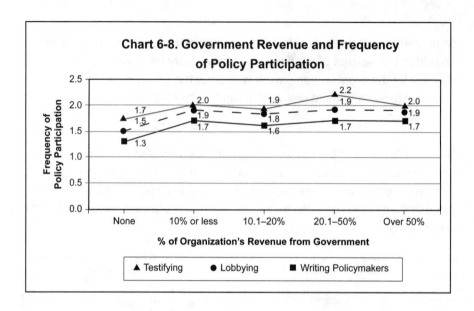

Chart 6-8. Government Revenue and Frequency of Policy Participation

% of Organization's Revenue from Government

▲ Testifying   ● Lobbying   ■ Writing Policymakers

lobbying, which drops when government revenue exceeds 50 percent of the organization's budget.

Among respondents with organizational budgets of less than $1 million, non-participators are far less likely to get government money (18 percent) than participators (49.1 percent). Among those organizations with budgets of $1 million or greater, 69 percent of participators received some government money, compared with 43 percent of non-participators groups (see Table 6-7).

Table 6-7. Policy Participation and Government Revenue
By Size of Organization Budget

		Organization Budget Less Than $1 million		Organization Budget $1 million or Greater	
		Not a Participator	Participator	Not a Participator	Participator
No Government Revenue	Number	159	415	12	161
	Percent	82.4%	50.9%	57.1%	30.3%
Gets Government Revenue	Number	34	400	9	371
	Percent	17.6	49.1	42.9	69.7
Total	Number	193	815	21	532
	Percent	100%	100%	100%	100%
		Sig=.000 Gamma=.637		*Sig=.009 Gamma=.509*	

Foundation Revenue

Out of a list of eight items, foundation funding presented the smallest barrier to policy participation, according to survey respondents. Nearly six of ten respondents (59 percent) said they do not perceive receipt of foundation funding as a barrier to policy participation at all. Another 35 percent saw the barrier presented by foundation funding as low.

That picture changes substantially when looking at foundation funding as a barrier through the eyes of groups that receive foundation funding versus those that do not. While 59 percent of all respondents say that foundation funding presents no barrier, that number drops to 47 percent for those that receive foundation grants and it jumps to 74 percent for those that do not receive foundation grants. And while 35 percent of all respondents say foundation funding presents a low barrier to participation, that number jumps to 46 percent for those receiving foundation grants, and it drops to 20 percent for those not receiving foundation grants (see Table 6-8).

Table 6-8. Foundation Funding and Barriers to Participation

	No Barrier to Participation		Low Barrier to Participation	
	Number	Percent	Number	Percent
All Respondents	850	58.6%	502	35.2%
Receives Foundation Grants	380	47.0	375	46.4
Receives No Foundation Grants	470	74.2	127	20.0

Low Barrier includes scores of 1 and 2 on the survey

p<.000; Gamma=.431

Table 6-9 compares government funding to foundation funding as a barrier to policy participation. Nonprofits identified the barrier each funding source on a scale from no barrier to a major barrier. Slightly more than three-quarters of the respondents viewed government funding as a barrier, with one-quarter calling such funding a major barrier to participation. A little over half of the respondents identified foundation funding as a barrier, with only seven percent calling it a major barrier.

Table 6-9. Comparing Government and Foundation Funding as a Barrier to Policy Participation			
Is the Funding Source a Barrier?	No Barrier	Low Barrier	Major Barrier
Organization receives government funds (p<.000; Gamma=.729)	23.8%	51.6%	24.7%
Organization receives foundation funds (p<.000; Gamma=.431)	47.0%	46.4%	6.6%

While foundation funding does not present a major barrier, especially when compared with government funding, it is still a barrier to policy participation. Moreover, the perception of foundation funding being a barrier grows significantly as the percentage of foundation revenue increases in relation to the organization's overall budget (see Chart 6-9).

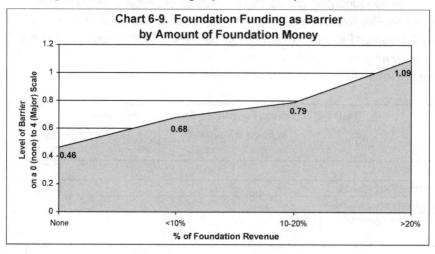

As is the case with government revenue, policy participators get more of their revenue (12.5 percent) from foundations than non-participators (7.9 percent), despite complaints from nonprofits that foundations often discourage lobbying and advocacy. In virtually all the focus groups we conducted, participants talked about the antipathy foundation staff showed toward advocacy. Many talked about the grant award letters containing language that restricts use of grant funds for lobbying. As the head of a Tennessee human services group said, "All the major foundations have a clause [in grant letters] that says you cannot do any lobbying with their money, every one of them." Those familiar with these grant restrictions thought the restrictions extended far beyond the tax code definition of lobbying to include restrictions on general advocacy.

Nonprofit executives also note that foundation employees send contradictory messages about advocacy. On the one hand, program officers emphasize the importance of the grant having an impact, often in terms of social change that involves regulatory and legislative changes. On the other hand, they discourage grant proposals that directly address advocacy. An executive of a West Coast human services organization said, "Family foundations are interested in programs but not in advocacy," even when that advocacy is to protect the ability for organizations to deliver services. The director of a health group in Pennsylvania summed it up as: "Foundations are interested in national advocacy but not in supporting it locally.... They want to have a national impact." Yet national groups that were interviewed also said foundations do not support advocacy. Thus, national, state, and local groups seem to assume that someone else is receiving foundation support for advocacy, but it is not them. This assumption may derive from a general belief that some foundations must be supporting advocacy, but not the ones that support us, especially since foundations continue to emphasize having an impact on broad social issues.

Foundation program officers acknowledge the mixed signals sent by foundations about advocacy. In a Detroit focus group of foundation staff, several said they encourage grantees to engage in public policy, on the sly. They talked about how difficult it is to get proposals that include advocacy activities through their grant clearance processes. Several described foundation trustees who do not want to fund proposals that support advocacy, even as they want foundation funds to shape local, state, or federal policy directions. For one reason or another, there seems to be a disconnect between the overall trustee objectives and the types of activities they want to support. One solution these program officers employed was to support grantee advocacy with a wink and a nod; it is not directly funded, but the program officers do not discourage use of their funds for these types of activities. These foundation program officers acknowledged that this sends a confusing message to the grantees.

Many foundation grantees described foundation funding as "fickle"; when a topic is in vogue, foundations will fund it for a few years and then move on. Foundation inconsistency in funding was described as the top concern for those nonprofit leaders wishing to engage in advocacy. The head of a national arms control organization argued that even when foundations do provide support for advocacy or lobbying, they do not understand the need for continued support. "Foundations will fund something for a few years. ...Unfortunately, two or three years are not how change works. They want

213

instant gratification. ... Foundations think there is an instant solution for social problems." An executive with an association of engineers echoed that "foundations want instant gratification," and added that they "get disappointed if you haven't done the entire mission in three years."

A few participants in focus groups said that lessons could be learned from conservative foundations. Conservative funders such as the Olin Foundation, they said, provided consistent general support in order to create change.[165] They understood that change does not occur overnight and that the leaders of change need steady support. The nonprofit leaders we talked with felt that the lesson to be learned from foundations such as the Olin Foundation was that foundations across ideological interests should emulate the success of the conservative funders. But few were optimistic that things would change.

Several noted that when foundation leaders provide support for advocacy it is usually in reaction to a crisis situation. For example, the director of a Minnesota housing program echoed a common refrain, "In the past, they [foundations] have denied us [grants]. But now the housing situation here is getting so desperate that they realize that they need to get behind the advocates." Those engaged in advocacy stressed that effective advocacy is often done preventively – working with policymakers to avoid a crisis situation. Thus, when funders see a crisis, it is often too late for effective advocacy. Instead, it is crisis management.

In other chapters we have described some new developments undertaken by foundation leaders to support nonprofit advocacy. For example, the Northern California Grantmakers Association has developed a Public Policy Grantmaking Toolkit "to encourage and help you [foundations] incorporate long-term change and policy-related work into your funding portfolio. This toolkit

---

[165] Upon the closing of the Olin Foundation, the New York Times published an opinion piece by John J. Miller, the author of "A Gift of Freedom: How the John M. Olin Foundation Changed America," (November 28, 2005, "The Very Foundation of Conservatism") that covered this subject. "The Olin Foundation's leaders understood that success is often unplanned, and so they focused on creating the conditions for success rather than thrusting a set of detailed agendas and goals upon grant recipients.... What's more, philanthropists must have Job-like patience, because in the war of ideas there are few quick payoffs.... The idea was simply to provide a steady source of assistance to conservative thinkers, who could devote themselves to writing books and articles rather than to raising cash for next year's budget."

provides resources for
funders new to public
policy as well as those
with more experience."[166]
These types of actions
are directly responsive to
the concerns expressed
by nonprofit leaders and
may hold hope for the
future.

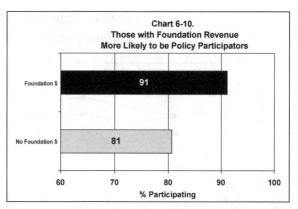

Chart 6-10.
Those with Foundation Revenue
More Likely to be Policy Participators

Chart 6-10 and Table 6-10 show that 91 percent of organizations that receive
foundation revenue are participators – they lobby, encourage others to lobby,
or they testify – while 81 percent of organizations that do not receive foundation
revenue are participators. Not only are groups significantly more likely to
engage as a policy participator when they receive foundation funding, but the
frequency of engagement also goes up.

Table 6-10. Foundation Revenue and Impact on Policy Participation		Non-Participator	Participator	Total
No Foundation Revenue	Number	141	591	732
	%	19.3%	80.7%	100.0%
Gets Foundation Revenue	Number	76	780	825
	%	8.9%	91.1%	100.0%
Policy participation includes lobbying, encouraging others to lobby, or testifying.				
P<.000; Gamma=.260				

Chart 6-11 shows the frequency of lobbying, encouraging others to lobby
(grassroots lobbying), and testifying goes up as foundation revenue as a
percentage of the organization's overall budget goes up. For some reason,
however, the frequency of each of these advocacy activities drops for
organizations that have between ten and 20 percent of their revenue from
foundations. Nonetheless, the frequency of these three types of policy
activities is significantly higher for organizations with foundation funding
than without.

---

[166] http://www.ncg.org/toolkit/home.html

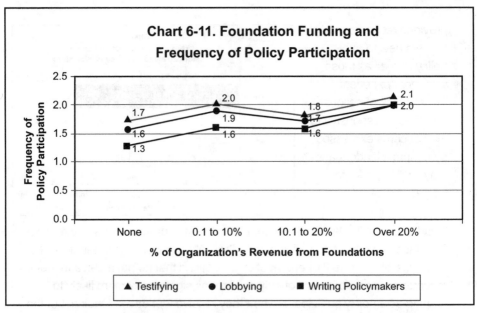

Chart 6-11. Foundation Funding and Frequency of Policy Participation

% of Organization's Revenue from Foundations

▲ Testifying ● Lobbying ■ Writing Policymakers

For respondents with organizational budgets of less than $1 million, non-participators are less likely to get foundation money (34 percent) than participators (52 percent). For those organizations with budgets of $1 million or greater, 66 percent of participators received some foundation money, compared to 43 percent of non-participators groups (see Table 6-11).

Table 6-11. Policy Participation and Foundation Revenue
By Size of Organization Budget

	Organization Budget Less Than $1 million				Organization Budget $1 million or Greater			
	Not a Participator		Participator		Not a Participator		Participator	
	N=	Percent	N=	Percent	N=	Percent	N=	Percent
No Foundation Revenue	127	65.8%	395	48.5%	12	57.1	176	33.3
Gets Foundation Revenue	66	34.2	420	51.5	9	42.9	353	66.7
Total	193	100%	815	100%	21	100%	529	100%
	Sig=.000 Gamma=.343				*Sig=.024 Gamma=.456*			

Like government funding, foundation funding has a significant impact on policy participation. In the Table 6-12, we compare the strength of correlation between funding source and nonprofit policy participation. The table shows that foundation funding is more closely correlated with increased frequency of testifying and lobbying than is government funding. The bottom line, though, is that funding from either foundations or government is a good predictor of not only nonprofits engaging in public policy, but also of engaging with greater frequency.

**Table 6-12. Comparing Frequency of Policy Participation
and Sources of Organization Revenue**
(Using Correlation Coefficients Controlling for Budget Size)

	Foundation Funding	Government Funding
Frequency of Testifying (n=1,619)	.208	.134
Frequency of Lobbying (n=1,618)	.132	.118
Frequency of Grassroots Lobbying (n=1,615)	.096	.101

All are significant at the .000 level, 2-tailed. Figures in the table are Pearson's correlation coefficients, which is a measure of linear association. Correlations measure how variables or rank orders are related. This analysis controlled for the organization's budget size using a means for addressing large budget skews since size of budget influences policy participation.

Conclusion

There is little doubt that money has an impact on nonprofit policy participation. The more money an organization has, the greater the likelihood the organization will be engaged in public policy. However, money does not ensure that an organization will engage in public policy. Instead motivation and management structure, in combination, tend to be greater predictors of policy participation than an organization's budget size.

Source of revenue is very important when looking at nonprofit participation. In particular, government and foundation revenue are important. Each is perceived as a barrier to participation; yet nonprofits that receive government and foundation revenue are more involved in public policy matters than those groups not receiving either source of revenue. Additionally, as the amount of revenue from each of these sources increases, so too does the frequency of policy participation by the nonprofit group.

Chapter 7
Using SNAP as a Springboard to Strengthening Nonprofit Advocacy:
Conclusions and Recommendations

The paradigm at the beginning of the 21st century is a vast and growing population of nonprofits whose participation in the policy debate is wide but not deep. The pattern is for organizations to jump in and jump out of the policy process. The nonprofit infrastructure and support field then responds with whatever intervention seems to fit the need of the moment or that is immediately available. This intervention includes legal training on what amount of lobbying the tax law will allow or stark exhortations to advocate on the crisis du jour. We have learned that this response is not nearly enough to create a framework for consistent, ongoing nonprofit policy engagement.

At a time when nonprofit organizations are adopting ever more sophisticated management and governance practices, it is a major weakness that more have not also made public policy a core activity. We need to step back and look at the entire life cycle of a nonprofit's public policy involvement to determine what kinds of external support are needed along the way.

Nonprofits are likely to be "in" the debate when they are under attack; and when there is a threat to their organizational existence, to the programs that serve their clients and those in similar circumstances, or to the advocacy rights of the sector itself. The causes and communities served by nonprofits have too much at stake for their representatives to wait patiently on the sidelines until the next crisis arises. Just as it is expected that organizations will raise funds almost all year around to maintain organizational viability, it should also be expected that nonprofits will partner with, influence, and challenge government throughout the year because laws and policies affect lives long after nonprofit programs have faded.

What can we who desire a truly engaged, democratic society realistically envision in today's world? In this time of overextended workers, overscheduled families, unlimited leisure possibilities, and an all-pervasive media, is it reasonable to expect a revival of what we imagine was the deep involvement of masses of citizens in the movements for abolition, suffrage, temperance, civil rights, peace, and women's rights? Is it possible for every little nonprofit in America to be involved in matters beyond the immediate crisis and provide an ongoing forum for their members to discuss the issues of the day? Probably not, but what can we realistically expect of charities in bringing people together to consider their common cause and express their collective will to their elected representatives. And what resources will they need to do it?

Realistically, we believe it is possible for nonprofits to do more of what they do now in the policy arena. We also see more nonprofits joining in the "doing" of policy, if only sporadically and on issues narrowly tied to their mission and organizational sustainability. In short, we need to promote both a deepening and widening of policy participation. Our challenge is to make the extraordinary the ordinary.[167]

With the right incentives and leadership, more nonprofits can be expected to leave the sidelines and enter the policy arena. We believe that with the right support, more of those currently involved will be able to devote increased time and energy to public policy and, in turn, become more effective advocates. And, with the right support, some may even become motivated to address additional public issues that are now viewed as only tangential to the mission of the organization. Added together, policy engagement such as this by all the various individuals associated with nonprofits – members, clients, donors, volunteers, board members and staff – will foster an even more vibrant democracy and assure that more voices now unheard by policymakers have a place at the decision-making table.

If we are to move toward this broader vision of nonprofits' role in a democratic society, everyone who has anything to do with the sector needs to play a role. Funders need to put up the resources and provide other encouragement. Educators need to expand public policy curricula and develop skills and leadership for policy work. Management support organizations also need to broaden their training content and pay attention to how policy can support organizational effectiveness and how organizations can be structured to make ongoing policy participation an essential function. Nonprofits need to take steps: make the time to advocate, join coalitions that we know help stimulate policy participation, monitor policy developments, alert their members. As our study found, government also has an interest in receiving input and information from the nonprofit sector. The process of creating

---

[167] Shifting nonprofit advocacy from being "extraordinary to ordinary" is a phrase we first heard used by Florence Green, the executive director of the California Association of Nonprofits.

government procedures, and public laws and regulations should be tailored to encourage more of such participation.

Motivation

Motivation is needed to make any of this happen. Each one of the actors mentioned above needs to be motivated by the institutions and groups to whom they most readily respond – private and community foundations, their peers, individual donors, and the public. Motivation comes in many forms – professional expectations, pleas for compassion, monetary incentive, the promise of success, the dire consequences of inaction, demystification of the process, and recognition of achievement.

First and foremost, people working in the nonprofit world and the public at large need to be disabused of the notion that lobbying is "unclean," as one executive director put it. We cannot afford to let the scandals of money in politics sour us to the point where we throw up our hands and avoid engagement in the democratic process altogether.[168] We need to convince people that only the involvement of many more will save our system from being controlled by the few lobbyists who represent only the narrow special interests of their clients. All of us concerned with the nonprofit sector should take steps to portray the policy process, including lobbying, as an honorable activity, one that should not be compromised or apologized for. Indeed, the interaction between nonprofits and government is crucial to the successful functioning of democratic government. By lobbying for policy change, we can improve lives and society.[169]

---

[168] The scandal surrounding convicted lobbyist Jack Abramoff will likely further sully the image of lobbying. It will likely leave the impression that lobbying is simply the process of "buying" access to elected leaders and using money to influence their actions. There is no question that money has a corrupting influence in the policy-making process and plays a critical role in making an unleveled playing field, but we should remember that Abramoff violated the law and was caught.

[169] Some of the important contributions of nonprofit lobbying throughout American history are described in Chapter 2. Some might argue that nonprofits should simply abandon the word "lobbying" and instead talk about "advocacy" since it appears to be a more acceptable word to boards, funders, and others. While the data from our research shows many nonprofit leaders do that now, we believe that lobbying is not only honorable but an essential democratic activity embedded in our constitution. To abandon the term would be to abandon an American belief that the public has a right to petition our government.

Educators and support organizations in the nonprofit sector should encourage nonprofits to think about advocacy, lobbying, and other forms of policy participation as tools for achieving their mission. A proactive approach that seeks long-range policy solutions to community problems or needs can do as much, if not more, than other organizational activities to help a nonprofit achieve its goals. For example, in addition to providing homeless shelters, a housing group could work toward fairer housing laws or funding for job training programs.[170]

In addition to mission, most nonprofits would find ample reason in their values statements to get involved on a broader set of policies that might range from budget and tax issues, to war and peace, civil rights, the environment, and programs affecting populations other than their strictly defined client group. In a typical statement of values, for example, one might find commitments to social justice, pluralism, diversity, and the dignity of individuals. Such values, which many nonprofits share, could easily justify advocating for, say, equitable tax policy, affirmative action policies, hate crimes legislation, and other causes.[171] The possibilities for involvement in the policy process could become endless – some organizations might consider adopting a periodic review of mission and how policy changes can strengthen that mission.

Those that provide support services to nonprofit organizations need to heighten the comfort level staff and board members have with the policy process. Information about what we and other researchers have found about the benefits of policy participation need to be shared with nonprofit leaders. Most nonprofits told us they encounter public officials who are interested in their ideas and the information they have. Some even want to work with nonprofits toward mutual goals. Learning this will help other nonprofits see that contact with policymakers is not always threatening or intimidating. We need to show that government policy helps control what happens in the real world. Policy can help organizations become more effective and efficient. With nonprofit input, laws and program rules can be tailored, for example, to make government proposal-writing and performance evaluation more meaningful and less onerous as management tools.

---

[170] Nonprofit leaders need to see themselves as a resource to the community and to policymakers.

[171] These actions are equally important whether from a conservative or progressive perspective. This diversity of ideology within the nonprofit sector is what adds to the value of the sector.

Probably nothing could motivate the entire nonprofit sector as effectively as a pronouncement by powerful institutions, including universities and foundations that advocacy is an expected nonprofit activity. Every nonprofit executive should be taught that policy is something she or he needs to understand, appreciate and use to further an organization's mission and world vision. With policy participation given this sort of respectability and priority, directors would be able to confront recalcitrant boards. They would be able to train and sensitize staff, donors, and volunteers. They would be able to engage community members not just as consumers, donors, and service-only volunteers, but also as advocates.

University nonprofit centers must begin to emphasize policy as one of the most important tools that a nonprofit leader can possess.[172] We need to teach future nonprofit managers that policy can not only advance their missions, such as making people healthier by expanding health coverage, but also enhance the effectiveness of the organization itself. Being involved in public policy can yield tangible benefits. It can help raise nonprofits' profile and money. It can bring media attention and show the public they are out there fighting for people. It would be hard to imagine the Harvard Business School or National Federation of Independent Business downplaying the importance of public policy to its students and members. So should it be impossible to think of the nonprofit sector with a hands-off attitude toward public policy.

Passion also plays a part in motivation. Our study revealed that nonprofits often act *with* passion and *out of* compassion. Yet it sometimes feels like nonprofit associations have professionalized and toned down their rhetoric to such a degree that we are not reaching our audience the way we could. We know from our study that workers in nonprofit organizations are people who are moved when they hear about the gravity of a situation or the scale of human suffering involved.

An example of this passion in action is seen in nonprofits that are motivated to oppose budget cuts that continue to come at every level of government. Such fiscal changes should motivate groups focused on direct service

---

[172] They can rely on faculty in public policy or public affairs departments who are familiar with teaching about policy participation. However, the general rules about the policy process also need to be tailored to nonprofits, which often require certain adjustments to participate in the policy process.

programs, not just those already known for their advocacy. Communicating the human suffering that budget cuts entail will help motivate more direct service groups. An example of this is the Minnesota Council of Nonprofits' "Think Twice" campaign, which provided advertising materials picturing, for example, somber children holding signs saying, "If we cut funding for nonprofits, will you let me come to your house after school?"

Passion and motivation for policy participation should be demonstrated anytime there is an opportunity to make government work better for a particular cause, not just when there is a crisis. How would a junior softball league be able to stop a city from zoning vacant land for industrial use unless they spoke to city council members? How would health organizations be able to successfully lobby for restaurant smoking bans without educating elected officials about the dangers of secondhand smoke? Indeed potential for mutual education between nonprofits and government is endless and should be ongoing rather than seasonal.

Resources

Budgetary strain was by far the most significant barrier to policy participation found in our survey. If we are to see a flowering of civic engagement led by nonprofits, we need to look to those who have the resources – foundations, both public and private, large donors and donor-advised funds. There are a variety of avenues they can pursue, all legal, if they can be persuaded that democratic participation is good and necessary.

First and foremost, foundations should stop using language in grant letters that unnecessarily prohibits the use of grant money for public policy activities that are perfectly legal. Foundation leaders themselves should seek out the training needed to explain the legalities to their legal and accounting departments.

Second, more funders should think hard about the importance of policy not only to their own charitable causes but also to the stability and health of the nation. If public policy matters to them for any of these reasons, funders should consider creating initiatives aimed specifically at advocacy on specific policy issues. If the money is there, people will come.

Every few years, some foundations have shown renewed interest in funding voter education and registration. Such initiatives are needed on an ongoing basis, and they should be directed at teaching the techniques and methods of democratic participation. Foundations should consider launching initiatives to support advocacy in the areas where they now support direct services, that is, advocacy for policy changes that would improve health, education, and family functioning and, by promoting solutions, reduce the need for services in the long term.

A third approach is for foundations to shift emphasis to core operating grants as opposed to special project grants that must be dedicated to activities that often are more tangential to the organization's mission than public policy. The need to go after special project funding, in fact, reduces the time and resources an organization can devote to public policy. The Independent Sector has endorsed a statement calling for foundations to give core operating support rather than project grants "whenever appropriate and feasible" to "organizations whose goals are substantially aligned with their own.[173] "The statement, authored by Paul Brest of the Hewlett Foundation, grew out of extensive study and discussion by nonprofit and philanthropic leaders. The Council on Foundations has not endorsed the Brest statement. They should.

Since 1999, the California Wellness Foundation has acknowledged the benefits of core support for its grantees. The foundation learned that "with the aid of unrestricted grants, nonprofit organizations can strengthen their infrastructures, reevaluate missions, and otherwise set themselves on a strategic course for long-term success." They can also have the flexibility to strengthen their public policy work, as did the Children's Environmental Health Network when it used a California Wellness Foundation grant to take its national public education and advocacy campaign to the state level in California. "Public policy-focused organizations have access to an especially limited pool of funding," the network said about the importance of the foundation's core operating support.[174]

---

[173] "Guidelines for the Funding of Nonprofit Organizations," Paul Brest, http://independentsector.org/issues/buildingvalue/opsupport.html.

[174] "Ensuring Flexibility for Health Advocates," the California Wellness Foundation, 1999, http://www.tcwf.org/annual_1999/content/policy.html

Finally, foundations could fund and otherwise promote their grantees' participation in training workshops and coalition activities that build skills or provide information on public policy and the policymaking process. For example, in 2001-2002 the Ford Foundation funded training workshops for their grantees to learn about the lobby laws from the Alliance for Justice. The Robert Wood Johnson Foundation's Connect Project is an ongoing program that organizes meetings between grantee health service organizations and legislators.

The Northern California Grantmakers Association launched an online Public Policy Grantmaking Toolkit in 2005.[175] The website provides success stories of foundations providing grant support for public policy work. The site notes, "Foundations have historically supported public policy efforts for two reasons: to leverage their resources, and to advance their mission. ... By supporting advocacy efforts and policy change, foundations can leverage their dollars to create the community and governmental support that is often needed to achieve substantive change. In addition, public policy grant making can have a ripple effect in a community. Impacting and achieving real policy change can often be an empowering experience that will encourage longer-term community engagement in policy advocacy."

The toolkit also provides a review of legal issues concerning foundation funding of public policy, ways to assess policy grant making, links to foundation colleagues who support policy grant making, and best practices for such funding. The best practices include general operating support and multi-year funding, all items included in the Brest statement.

Both private and community foundations will find examples of how they might invest in public policy work as well as effectively engage in policy and civic activities themselves in a book by Fieldstone Alliance called *Power in Policy: A Guide to Advocacy and Civic Participation*. This book shares insights for foundations on the topics of motivation for advocacy, mission-relatedness, building internal capacity, and finding effective strategies in the policy arena.

Organizational structure

Internal characteristics and processes of an organization can both benefit from and, in the end, influence an organization's effectiveness in the

---

[175] http://www.ncg.org/toolkit/home.html

public policy arena. These include staff and resource allocation, board responsibilities and development. Management support organizations should encourage nonprofits to adopt these features through their conferences, publications, and training programs. Funders should support these features by making core operating grants or by allowing these costs to be covered in overhead.

Nonprofits themselves could start by taking baby steps along these lines. For example, they could have bake sales or other events and dedicate proceeds to advocacy. They could join an advocacy coalition. They could make personnel changes so that key employees are not paid 100 percent with government funds so they can have some time for advocacy if needed. Some of these baby steps may also become an opportunity for future fundraising, highlighting the importance of policy issues.

Staff and Board Responsibilities

Organizations should have staff, apart from the executive director, *specifically assigned* to policy work. Our survey showed that this is one of the most powerful predictors of an organization's engagement in policy matters. Typically executive directors have many job responsibilities. The day-to-day tasks of following legislation or regulatory rulemaking can often get lost or be overshadowed by more immediate needs. The organization needs to put someone in charge of scanning the policy scene for threats and opportunities that can affect the organization's mission and interests, even if only three hours a week. Having this information is essential if other members of the organization are to know when and how their participation is needed.[176] People who are not lobbyists, policy wonks or professional advocates usually do not look at day-to-day situations as grist for the policy mill, amenable to policy intervention. They also do not know where to find out what policymakers are really thinking and planning on issues outside of those currently on the table.

The sector's management and infrastructure support network needs to promote knowledge of the policymaking process among nonprofit professionals. We must train nonprofit executives about how to recruit and integrate into their staff people who know the policy process and have the skills to influence it.

---

[176] See "Make a Difference for Your Cause in Three Hours Per Week," Charity Lobbying in the Public Interest http://www.clpi.org/Getting_Started_Rvsd.aspx.

Boards must dedicate time and attention to public policy involvement. Their participation is vital, because boards take positions and give staff authority to take strategic action in the legislative, regulatory, and judicial arenas. To help achieve this, at least one board member or committee should be assigned to monitor and increase policy participation. Respondents indicated that having boards involved in both policy planning and direct advocacy could be a way of using board members' leadership skills, clout, and passion for the mission of the organization.

Recruiting and developing board members with experience in the public policy arena can bring immediate support to staff and tangible expertise when beginning to get involved in policy issues. Indeed, even one policy savvy board member can dramatically help beat the learning curve for organizations new to lobbying and advocacy.

Time

Focus groups cited time or the lack thereof as a major barrier to policy participation. We heard it is very difficult for executive directors to devote staff time to policy advocacy when competing time demands force hard choices. This is where organizational development experts and seasoned nonprofit managers can help. We need to help nonprofits with overall resource allocation models that enable policy participation and do not force executive directors to make a choice between service and advocacy.

Lobbying and advocacy skills

The sector needs to promote the development of stronger lobbying and advocacy skills among nonprofit managers and other policy staff. They need to know more about substantive policy issues in their areas, but also the kinds of information that are persuasive to lawmakers. They need to know the nuts and bolts of direct and grassroots lobbying. They need to be introduced to the technology networks that will help them become more effective communicators on policy issues.

Nonprofits need to be encouraged to join active advocacy coalitions because we know that ties to such umbrella alliances generate more involvement by nonprofits. Coalitions in different fields and at the various levels of government need support so they can fill this important role.

Associations can play a big role in connecting local and state organizations to coalitions and even encourage joining. The sector needs to recognize that participating in coalitions, although time-consuming, is an effective and efficient way to advocate on policy issues – and that joining associations leads to greater policy participation.

Once these key ingredients are in place, other factors can deepen the ability of nonprofits to influence public policy. A more thorough knowledge of lobbying laws, for example, can help enlarge the involvement of an engaged organization that has reached a point at which it is worrying about lobbying expenditure limits.

Another entire body of legal expertise on nonpartisan voter engagement activities should be presented to nonprofits. By encouraging educated voter participation among clients and members, nonprofits help shape the governing environment, which, in turn, affects the success of their programs. Ultimately, elected officials respond to constituents who vote, and they know that nonprofits are, or can be, in touch with considerable numbers of voting constituents to discuss issues. During an election season, charitable nonprofits can conduct voter registration drives, hold candidate forums, distribute candidate questionnaires on their issues and publish voter guides. All of this can take place as long as the actions cannot be construed as an endorsement of or opposition to a particular candidate or party, and are consistent with the type of activities done annually.

Ongoing engagement

Nonprofits that engage in policy participation for the long haul have the opportunity to proactively shape the systems in which they operate. The benefits are much more rewarding than maintaining a reactive posture and merely responding to budget cuts and threats. Through this kind of sustained involvement, for example, the Children's Defense Fund and its allies succeeded in getting the State Child Health Insurance Program (SCHIP) enacted in 1997. SCHIP was arguably the most significant expansion of health coverage since Medicare. However, SCHIP did not happen overnight. The effective advocate is a persistent one. Ongoing engagement in public policy is an essential ingredient to successful advocacy.

We should not downplay the tremendous opportunity for policy input that nonprofit leaders possess when they serve on advisory and planning boards with government officials. New venues for such deliberation can be initiated by either the executive or legislative branch or by nonprofits themselves. Larger nonprofits, for example, should consider establishing blue-ribbon commissions to examine pressing issues at the state, local, or national level. Membership could include a bipartisan mix of government officials, and nonprofit, academic, and other experts who are known to have looked seriously at the problem at hand.

North Carolina has established a system of state agency liaisons to create ongoing mechanisms for two-way communication between state departments and nonprofits that share the same interests. Among other things, the liaisons identify nonprofit leaders for appointment to state boards and commissions participate in statewide nonprofit conferences, invite nonprofits to bid on state contracts and seek other ways to strengthen public-nonprofit partnerships. The North Carolina Center for Nonprofits helped instigate the liaison system and says it has resulted in program improvements and streamlining of the government grants and contracts process.[177]

Level the playing field

Certainly national infrastructure and nonprofit support organizations need to continue to educate the sector about their legal rights to lobby, advocate, and conduct voter education. In particular, the fact that nonprofits that receive government funds can lobby with other revenue needs to be communicated more widely. In addition to education on the rules, the nonprofit support groups need to promote legislative changes that would make it even easier for nonprofits to engage in policy.

Nonprofits, which in many ways are like small businesses, operate at a considerable disadvantage when it comes to dealing with government. Financially, they are usually not as well-capitalized (or have no reserves at all) and operate much closer to the margin. In nonprofits, staff time is stretched thin, the mission never seems to get smaller, and their leaders are extremely vulnerable to intimidation or retribution for their involvement

---

[177] "Nonprofit and Volunteer Liaisons in State Government – What They Do," http://www. ncnonprofits.org/laisroles.html.

in policy debates. For these reasons, and because government officials generally value the information and opinions of nonprofits, nonprofits and government should work together to find ways to make it easier for them to participate in the policymaking process.

Although our study did not ask about money in politics, comments by participants in interviews and focus groups shed light on the chilling effect that funder intimidation can have on nonprofit advocacy. Such charges merit more intensive research. How widespread is this phenomenon? How feasible is it for action to be taken in such cases under current law? What kinds of legal changes would be needed to curb abuses of this kind?

Conclusion

Nonprofits and the organizations that support them must refine their appreciation for the extent to which policy sets the stage for what can be achieved by organized public interests. Then they can move from a model of occasional advocacy to a new nonprofit business model that places policy participation co-equal with other management, governance, and service responsibilities. Once motivated, nonprofits need the leadership, training, and financial resources necessary to make their policy role a reality. With most organizations currently participating at a minimal level, if at all, there is a need for policy education and support from every quarter that cares about nonprofit charities and the democratic process.

Increased and consistent nonprofit engagement in public policy matters will immeasurably improve the quality of decisions that government makes. In a very real sense, the nonprofit sector is a vast reservoir of untapped expertise that should be harnessed to help policymakers improve upon decision making. Nonprofit leaders have enormous insight about a range of programs and services that elected leaders would find invaluable as they make decisions about funding and legislative and regulatory changes. Too often, policymakers only hear one side of the story – and it often does not have the important lessons that the nonprofit sector has learned. Once nonprofit leaders recognize they have a wealth of knowledge, it will be an important first step to speaking out and improving the laws of the land. It is our hope that this book advances and promotes ongoing dialogue, research and development within the nonprofit sector about the role public policy plays in achieving our missions.

Bibliography

Abramson, Alan J., and Rachel McCarthy. 2002. "Infrastructure Organizations." In *The State of Nonprofit America*, ed. Lester M. Salamon, 331. Washington, DC: The Brookings Institution Press.

Alexander, Jennifer, Renee Nank, and Camilla Stivers. 2001. "Implications of Welfare Reform: Do Nonprofit Survival Strategies Threaten Civil Society?" In *Understanding Nonprofit Organizations*, ed. J. Steven Ott. Boulder, CO: Westview.

Amidei, Nancy. 2000. "So You Want to Make a Difference." 13th ed., Appendix. Washington, DC: OMB Watch.

Arons, David F., ed. 2007. *Power in Policy: A Funder's Guide to Advocacy and Civic Participation.* St. Paul, MN: Fieldstone Alliance.

Arons, David F. "Nonprofit Management and Advocacy: Examining Barriers to Democracy." Paper delivered at the annual meeting of the Association for Research on Nonprofit Organizations and Voluntary Action, Washington, DC, November 4-6, 1999.

Arons, David F. *Holding Back Our Democracy: Nonprofits and Participation in the Public Policy Process.* Master's Thesis, Tufts Department of Urban and Environmental Policy, Tufts University Press, 1999.

Arons, David F. and Gary D. Bass. Fall 2002. "Not Ready to Play the Game: Nonprofit Participation in Public Policy," *The Nonprofit Quarterly*.

Asher, Thomas R. 1995. *Myth V. Fact: Foundation Support of Advocacy.* Washington, DC: Alliance for Justice.

Baumgarten, Liz. 2004. "Building Capacity for Public Policy Advocacy." Alliance for Nonprofit Management. http://www.allianceonline.org/Members/Enhance/enhance_-_june_2004.enh/building_capacity_for.epage.

Baumgarten, Liz and Michael Cortes. "The State of Teaching Nonprofit Advocacy." Paper presented at the ARNOVA conference, Montreal, Canada, November 14, 2002.

Baumgartner, Frank R., and Beth L. Leech. 1998. *Basic Interests.* Princeton, NJ: Princeton University Press.

Bass, Gary D., Shannon Ferguson, and David Plocher. 1995. *Living with A-122: A Handbook for Nonprofit Organizations*. Washington, DC: OMB Watch.

Bass, Gary D. 1996. "A Case Study of Nonprofit Advocacy in the U.S." Washington, DC: OMB Watch.

Burns, Nancy, Kay Lehman Schlozman and Sidney Verba. 2001. *Private Roots of Public Action: Gender, Equality, and Political Participation*. Cambridge: Harvard University Press.

Berry, Jeffrey M. "Building an Effective Lobby." Paper delivered at the annual meeting of the American Political Science Association, San Francisco, September, 2001.

Berry, Jeffrey M. 1999. *The New Liberalism: The Rising Power of Citizen Groups*. Washington, DC: Brookings Institution Press.

Berry, Jeffrey M. 1997. *The Interest Group Society*. 3rd ed. New York: Longman.

Berry Jeffrey M. 1977. *Lobbying for the People*. Princeton, NJ: Princeton University Press.

Berry, Jeffrey M., with David Arons. 2003. *A Voice for Nonprofits*. Washington, DC: Brookings Institution Press.

Berry, Jeffrey M., David F. Arons, Gary D. Bass, Matthew F. Carter, and Kent E. Portney. 2003. *Surveying Nonprofits: A Methods Handbook,* Washington, D.C.: Aspen Institute.

Boardsource website. 2004. www.boardsource.org.

Boris, Elizabeth T. and Jeff Krehely. 2002. "Civic Participation and Advocacy." In *The State of Nonprofit America*, ed. Lester M. Salamon. Washington, D.C.: Brookings Institution Press.

Boris, Elizabeth T., and Rachel Mosher-Williams. 1998. "Nonprofit Advocacy Organizations: Assessing the Definitions, Classifications, and Data." *Nonprofit and Voluntary Sector Quarterly* 27: 488-506.

Boris, Elizabeth T., and Eugene Steuerle, eds. 1999. *Nonprofits and Government: Collaboration and Conflict*. Washington, DC: The Urban Institute Press.

Brest, Paul. 2004. *Guidelines for the Funding of Nonprofit Organizations.* Independent Sector.

Brody, Evelyn. 1999. "Charities in Tax Reform: Threats to Subsidies Overt and Covert." *Tennessee Law Review* 66: 687-763.

Brody, Evelyn and Joseph J. Cordes. 1999. "Tax Treatment of Nonprofit Organizations: A Two-Edged Sword?" In *Nonprofits and Government: Collaboration and Conflict,* eds. Elizabeth T. Boris and Eugene Steuerle. Washington, DC: The Urban Institute Press.

Browne, William P. 1998. *Groups, Interests, and U.S. Public Policy.* Washington, DC: Georgetown University Press.

Burns, Nancy., Kay Lehman Schlozman, and Sidney Verba. 2001. *The Private Roots of Public Action: Gender, Equality, and Political Participation.* Cambridge: Harvard University Press.

Carver, John. 1997. "Board Members as Fundraisers, Advisors, and Lobbyists." Booklet #11, *The CarverGuide Series on Effective Board Governance.* San Francisco: Jossey-Bass.

Charity Lobbying in the Public Interest. 2003. "Foundations and Public Policy: Illustrations of High-Impact Grantmaking." www.clpi.org

Chaves, Mark. 1999. "Religious Congregations and Welfare Reform: Who Will Take Advantage of 'Charitable Choice?'" *American Sociological Review* 64: 836-846.

Chisholm, Laura B. 1995. "Accountability of Nonprofit Organizations and Those Who Control Them: The Legal Framework." *Nonprofit Management and Leadership* 6: 141-156.

Cohen, Michael. 1988.The *History of the Sierra Club: 1892 to 1970.* Random House.

Cohen, Rick. 2004. "The ACLU and the Combined Federal Campaign." *The Nonprofit Quarterly* (11) 3.

Colvin, Gregory L. and Lowell Finley. 1996. *The Rules of the Game: An Election Year Guide for Nonprofit Organizations,* Washington, D.C.: Alliance for Justice.

Council of Community Services of New York State, and the Nonprofit Coordinating Committee of New York. 1998. *Advocacy and Lobbying: What Charitable Nonprofits Know and Do in New York State*. Albany.

Covington, Sally. 1998. "Moving a Public Policy Agenda: The Strategic Philanthropy of Conservative Foundations." Washington, D.C.: National Committee for Responsive Philanthropy.

Covington, Sally. 1998. "How Conservative Philanthropies and Think Tanks Transform U.S. Policy." *Covert Action Quarterly* Winter (63): 6-16.

Crenson, Matthew A., and Benjamin Ginsberg. 2002. *Downsizing Democracy: How America Sidelined it's Citizens and Privatized Its Public*. Baltimore, MD: The Johns Hopkins University Press.

Dillman, Don A. 2000. *Mail and Internet Surveys: The Tailored Design Method*. New York: Wiley-Interscience.

Drucker Foundation. 1999. *The Drucker Foundation Self-Assessment Tool*. San Francisco, CA: The Drucker Foundation and Jossey-Bass Inc.

Egbert, Marcia, and Susan Hoechstetter. 2006. "Mission Impossible: Evaluating Advocacy Grants." *Foundation News & Commentary* January/ February: 38.

Fishman, James J., and Stephen Schwarz. 1995. *Nonprofit Organizations: Cases and Materials*. Westbury, NY: The Foundation Press.

Fremont-Smith, Marion. 2004. *Governing Nonprofit Organizations*. Cambridge, MA: Belknap Press of Harvard University Press.

Froelich, Karen A. 1997. "The 990 Return: Beyond the Internal Revenue Service." *Nonprofit Management and Leadership* 8: 141-155.

Froelich, Karen A. and Terry W. Knoepfle. 1996. "Internal Revenue Service 990 Data: Fact or Fiction?" *Nonprofit and Voluntary Sector Quarterly*. 25: 40-52.

Frumkin, Peter. 1997. "Private Foundations as Public Institutions." In *Philanthropic Foundations: New Scholarship, New Possibilities*, ed., Ellen Condliffe Lagemann. Bloomington, IN: Indiana University Press.

Galaskiewicz, Joseph, and Wolfgang Bielefeld. 1998. *Nonprofit Organizations in an Age of Uncertainty*. New York: Aldine de Gruyter.

Galston, Miriam. 1993. "Lobbying and the Public Interest: Rethinking the Internal Revenue Code's Treatment of Legislative Activities." *Texas Law Review* 71: 1269-1354.

Georges, Christopher. 1995. "Republicans Take Aim at Left-Leaning Groups That Get Federal Grants for Assistance Programs." *Wall Street Journal*, May 17.

Whitmann, Marshall and Charles P. Griffin. 1995. "There's No 'Gag Rule' on Nonprofits." *The Washington Post*, September 1.

Graziano, Luigi. 2001. *Lobbying, Pluralism and Democracy*. New York: Palgrave.

Grønbjerg, Kirsten A. 2002. "Evaluating Nonprofit Databases." *American Behavioral Scientist* 45: 1741-1777.

Grønbjerg, Kirsten A. 1994. "The NTEE: Human Service and Regional Applications." *Voluntas* 5: 301-328.

Grønbjerg, Kirsten A. and Laurie Paarlberg. 2001. "Community Variations in the Size and Scope of the Nonprofit Sector: Theory and Preliminary Findings." *Nonprofit and Voluntary Sector Quarterly* 30: 684-706.

Grønbjerg, Kristen A. and Steven Smith, "Nonprofit Organizations and Public Policies in the Delivery of Human Services." In *Philanthropy and the Nonprofit Sector in a Changing America,* eds. Clotfelter, Charles T. and Thomas Ehrlich. Bloomington: Indiana University Press, 1999.

Guthrie, Kendall, Justin Louie, Tom David, and Catherine Crystal Foster. October 2005. "The Challenge of Assessing Advocacy: Strategies for a Prospective Approach to Evaluating Policy Change and Advocacy." San Francisco, CA: Blueprint Research & Design.

Hall, Peter Dobkin. 1987. "A Historical Overview of the Private Nonprofit Sector." In *The Nonprofit Sector: A Research Handbook*, ed. Walter W. Powell. New Haven, CT: Yale University Press.

Hansmann, Henry. 1987. "Economic Theories of Nonprofit Organization." In *The Nonprofit Sector: A Research Handbook*, ed., Walter W. Powell. New Haven, CT: Yale University Press.

Harmon, Gail M., Jessica A. Ladd, and Eleanor A. Evans. 1991, 1995. "Being a Player: A Guide to the IRS Lobbying Regulations for Advocacy Charities." Alliance for Justice and Advocacy Forum.

Heatherly, Charles L., ed. 1981. *Mandate for Leadership: Policy Management in a Conservative Administration*. Washington D.C.: The Heritage Foundation.

Herman, Tom. 1999. "Nonprofit Groups Ordered to Open Their Books." *Wall Street Journal,* April 9, A2.

Hoefer, Richard. 2000. "Making a Difference: Human Service Interest Group Influence on Social Welfare Program Regulations." *Journal of Sociology and Social Welfare* 27: 21-38.

Hodgkinson, Virginia A., Thomas A. Pollak, and Lester M. Salamon. 1995. *The Impact of Federal Budget Proposals upon the Activities of Charitable Organizations and the People They Serve, 1996-2002: The 100 Organizations Study*. Washington, D.C.: Independent Sector.

Holton, Ruth and Gary Yates. 2002. "How Foundations Can Help in Tough Times." *The Chronicle of Philanthropy*, December 12.

Hopkins, Bruce R. 1992. *Charity, Advocacy, and the Law*. New York: John Wiley.

Huebler, John. 2003. *Philanthropy Described in Democracy in America by de Tocqueville,* Grand Valley State University. http://www.learningtogive.org/papers/concepts/americatocqueville.htm

Independent Sector. 2001. *Giving and Volunteering*, 2, Key findings. www.independentsector.org

InterAction. 1996. *InterAction Survey of CEOs of Members*. Washington, DC.

Isaacson, Walter. 2003. *Benjamin Franklin: An American Life*. New York, NY: Simon & Schuster.

Internal Revenue Service. 1986. "Lobbying by Public Charities.*" Federal Register* November 5: 40211-32

Internal Revenue Service, Publication 557

Johnston, David Cay. 1998. "Tax Returns of Charities to be Posted on the Web." *New York Times,* October 18, C1.

Kindell, Judith E., and John Francis Reilly. 1996. "Lobbying Issues," Internal Revenue Service, July (Exempt Organizations Continuing Professional Education Technical Instruction Program for FY 1997). http://www.irs.gov/pub/irs-tege/topic-p.pdf.

Kindell, Judith E., and John Francis Reilly. 1998. "Election Year Issues," Internal Revenue Service (Exempt Organizations Continuing Professional Education Technical Instruction Program).

Kopecki, Dawn. 2005. "US House GOP Conservatives Dismiss Compromise On GSE Bill." *Dow Jones Newswires*, June 29.

Krehely, Jeff, and Kendall Golladay. 2002. "The Scope and Activities of 501c)(4) Social Welfare Organizations: Fact versus Fantasy." Paper delivered at the annual meeting of the Association for Research on Nonprofit Organizations and Voluntary Action, Miami, FL, November.

Krehely, Jeff, Meaghan House and Emily Kernan. 2004. "Conservative Foundations and Public Policy. " Washington, D.C.: National Committee for Responsive Philanthropy, March.

Kretzmann, John P., John L. McKnight, and Nicol Turner. 1996. "Voluntary Associations in Low-Income Neighborhoods: An Unexplored Community Resource." Evanston, IL: Institute for Policy Research, Northwestern University. http://www.nwu.edu/IPR/publications/papers/grandblvd.pdf.

Lagemann, Ellen Condliffe. 1999. *Philanthropic Foundation: New Scholarship, New Possibilities.* Bloomington, IN: Indiana University Press.

Larson, R. Sam., and Mark Wilson. 2001. Survey of Nonprofit Management Students, Part 3 of 3, Building Bridges Cluster Evaluation, Center Point Institute. http://centerpointinstitute.org/bridges/PapersReports/StudentSurvey3.htm#Table%203.

Leech, Beth L. 1998. "Federal Funding and Interest Group Lobbying Behavior." Paper delivered at the annual meeting of the American Political Science Association, Boston, MA, September 3-6.

Lemann, Nicholas.1988, 1989. "The Unfinished War.*" Atlantic Monthly.*

Let America Speak website. http://www.ombwatch.org/article/articleview/399/1/51?TopicID=1

Levesque, Peter N. and Chopyak, Jill M. 2001. "Managing Multi-Sector Research Projects: Developing Models for Effective Movement from Problem Identification to Problem Solving." Paper presented at the Fifth International Research Symposium on Public Management, Barcelona, Spain, April. http://www.loka.org/crn/pubs/Managing_multisector. Final.8.2.01.

Linden, Russell, 2002. *Working Across Boundaries: Making Collaboration Work in Government and Nonprofit Organizations*. San Francisco, CA: John Wiley & Sons.

McPherson, J. Miller. 1982. "Hypernetwork Sampling: Duality and Differentiation among Voluntary Organizations." *Social Network* 3: 225-250.

Mirabella, Rosanne M. 2001. "Master List of All Universities Offering Nonprofit Management Education Courses." Department of Political Science, Seton Hall University, February.

Mothers Against Drunk Driving. 1995. "Istook-McIntosh-Ehrlich 'Nonprofit Gag Order' Would Cripple MADD's Lifesaving Advocacy Work and Establish a Big New Bureaucracy to Harass Charities." Press Release.

National Center for Charitable Statistics, Urban Institute. "Guide to the NTEE Classification System: The National Taxonomy of Exempt Entities." Washington, DC.

National Committee for Responsive Philanthropy and the Let America Speak Coalition. 1998. "Impartial Government Analyses Indicate Charities Affected by Proposition 226," Washington, D.C. http://www.ombwatch.org/las/1998/prop226report.html

National Committee for Responsive Philanthropy, "History of the CFC," http://www.ncrp.org/afap/cfc.htm

National Council of Nonprofit Associations. 1997. *A Greater Voice: Nonprofit Organizations, Communications Technology and Advocacy*. Washington, D.C.

Nownes, Anthony J., and Patricia Freeman. 1998. "Interest Group Activity in the States." *Journal of Politics* 60: 86-112.

O'Connell, Brian. 1994. *People Power: Service, Advocacy, Empowerment*. New York, NY: Foundation Center.

OMB Watch. 1986. *New IRS Rules: The End of Nonprofit Advocacy.*

OMB Watch. 1995. "Handcuffing America's Charities.".

OMB Watch. 1997. *Building Blocks for the Future: Findings and Recommendations for Strengthening Public Policy Communications and Collaboration in the Nonprofit Sector.* Washington, D.C.

OMB Watch. 1998. *Democracy at Work: Nonprofit Use of Internet Technology for Public Policy Purposes.* Washington, DC.

OMB Watch. 2003. "An Attack on Nonprofit Speech: Death by a Thousand Cuts," July. http://www.ombwatch.org/npadv/PDF/ANSjul03es.pdf

Paget, Karen, M. 1999. "The Big Chill." *The American Prospect* May-June: 30-31.

Pidgeon Jr., Walter. 2001. *Legislative Labyrinth: A Map for Not-for-Profits.* San Francisco, CA: John Wiley & Sons.

Powell, Walter W., ed. 1987. *The Nonprofit Sector: A Research Handbook.* New Haven, CT: Yale University Press.

Putnam, Robert D. 2000, *Bowling Alone: The Collapse and Revival of American Community.* New York: Simon and Schuster.

Rees, Susan. 1998. *Effective Nonprofit Advocacy.* Washington, DC: Aspen Institute Nonprofit Sector Research Fund.

Reid, Elizabeth, J. 1999. "Nonprofit Advocacy and Political Participation," in *Nonprofits & Government: Collaboration and Conflict,* eds. Boris, Elizabeth T. and Eugene Steuerle. Washington, D.C.: Urban Institute Press. See also http://www.urban.org/advocacyresearch/.

Rossiter, Clinton, ed. 1961. *The Federalist Papers: Hamilton, Madison, Jay.* New York: Penguin Books.

Saidel, Judith R. 1998. "Expanding the Governance Construct: Functions and Contributions of Nonprofit Advisory Groups." *Nonprofit and Voluntary Sector Quarterly* 27: 421-436.

Salamon, Lester M. 1987. "Partners in Public Service: The Scope and Theory of Government-Nonprofit Relations." In *The Nonprofit Sector: A Research Handbook,* ed. Walter W. Powell, 99-117. New Haven: Yale University Press.

Salamon, Lester M. 1995. *Partners in Public Service: Government-Nonprofit Relations in the Modern Welfare State*. Baltimore, MD: Johns Hopkins University Press.

Salamon, Lester M. 1998. "Explaining Nonprofit Advocacy: An Exploratory Analysis." Paper delivered at the Independent Sector Spring Research Forum, 1995. Updated 1998.

Salamon, Lester M., ed., 2002. *The State of Nonprofit America*. Washington, D.C.: The Brookings Institution Press.

Schadler, B. Holly. 1998. *The Connection: Strategies for Creating and Operating 501(c)(3)s, 501(c)(4)s, and PACs*. Washington, DC: Alliance for Justice.

Schlozman, Kay Lehman, and John T. Tierney. 1986. *Organized Interests and American Democracy*. New York: Harper and Row.

Schmitz, Paul, President and Chief Executive Officer, Public Allies (Interview, March 27, 2002).

Schudson, Michael. 1998. *The Good Citizen*, 98-109. New York: The Free Press,.

Sclove, Richard E., Madeleine L. Scammell, and Breena Holland. 1998. *Community-Based Research in the United States*. Amherst, MA: Loka Institute.

Sen, Rinku, and Kim Klein. 2003. *Stir it Up: Lessons in Community Organizing and Advocacy*. San Francisco, CA: John Wiley & Sons.

Shaiko, Ronald. 1999. *Voices and Echoes for the Environment*. New York: Columbia University Press.

Shear, Jeff. 1995. "The Ax Files." *National Journal*.

Simon, John. 1987. "The Tax Treatment of Nonprofit Organizations: A Review of Federal and State Policies." In *The Nonprofit Sector: A Research Handbook*, ed., Walter W. Powell. New Haven, CT.: Yale University Press.

Skocpol, Theda. 1999. "How Americans Became Civic." In *Civic Engagement in American Democracy*, eds. Theda Skocpol, and Morris Fiorina. Washington, DC: The Brookings Institution Press.

Skocpol, Theda, and Morris P. Fiorina, eds. 1999. *Civic Engagement in American Democracy*. Washington, DC: Brookings Institution Press.

Smith, David Horton. 1997. "The Rest of the Nonprofit Sector: Grassroots Associations as the Dark Matter Ignored in Prevailing 'Flat Earth' Maps of the Sector." *Nonprofit and Voluntary Sector Quarterly* 26:114-131.

Smith, Jackie. 1997. "Nonresponse Bias in Organizational Surveys: Evidence from a Survey of Groups and Organizations Working for Peace." *Nonprofit and Voluntary Sector Quarterly* 26: 359-368.

Smith, Steven Rathgeb. 1999. "Government Financing of Nonprofit Activity." In *Nonprofits and Government: Collaboration and Conflict*, eds. Elizabeth T. Boris and Eugene Steuerle. Washington, DC: Urban Institute Press.

Smith, Steven Rathgeb and Michael Lipsky. 1993. *Nonprofits for Hire: The Welfare State in the Age of Contracting*. Cambridge, MA: Harvard University Press.

Smucker, Bob. 1999. *The Nonprofit Lobbying Guide*. 2nd ed. Washington, DC: Independent Sector.

Sparks, John D. 1997. *Lobbying, Advocacy and Nonprofit Boards*. Washington D.C: National Council of Nonprofit Boards.

Stehle, Vince. 1995 "Welfare for Lobbyists?" *The Chronicle of Philanthropy* July 15.

Tocqueville, Alexis. 1969. *Democracy in America*. George Lawrence, trans., ed. J.P. Mayer, 509-524. New York: Harper and Row.

Troyer, Thomas A. 2000. "The 1969 Private Foundation Law: Historical Perspective on Its Origins and Underpinnings." *Council on Foundations.*

U.S. General Accounting Office. 1982. "Restrictions on Abortions and Lobbying Activities in Family Planning Programs Need Clarification," HRD-82-106, September 24.

U.S. General Accounting Office Report No. AFMD-82-123, September 29, 1982.

U.S. Office of Management and Budget. OMB Circular A-122, Cost Principles for Nonprofit Organizations, 48 *Federal Register*, 3348-50, January 24, 1983.

Van Til, Jon. 2000. *Growing Civil Society.* Bloomington: Indiana University Press, Bloomington.

Verba, Sidney, Kay Lehman Schlozman, and Henry E. Brady. 1995. *Voice and Equality: Civic Voluntarism in American Politics.* Cambridge: Harvard University Press.

Vogel, David. 1995. *Trading Up.* Cambridge, MA: Harvard University Press.

Yamane, Taro. 1967. *Elementary Sampling Theory.* Englewood Cliffs, NJ: Prentice-Hall.

Walker, Jack L. 1991. *Mobilizing Interest Groups in America.* Ann Arbor, MI: University of Michigan Press.

Weitzman, Murray S., Nadine T. Jalandoni, Linda M. Lampkin, and Thomas H. Pollak. 2002. *The New Nonprofit Almanac and Desk Reference.* New York: Jossey-Bass.

List of Appendices

Appendix A
IRS Form 5768

Form **5768** (Rev. December 2004) Department of the Treasury Internal Revenue Service	**Election/Revocation of Election by an Eligible Section 501(c)(3) Organization To Make Expenditures To Influence Legislation** (Under Section 501(h) of the Internal Revenue Code)	For IRS Use Only ▶
Name of organization		Employer identification number
Number and street (or P.O. box no., if mail is not delivered to street address)		Room/suite
City, town or post office, and state	ZIP + 4	

1 Election—As an eligible organization, we hereby elect to have the provisions of section 501(h) of the Code, relating to expenditures to influence legislation, apply to our tax year ending...and all subsequent tax years until revoked.

(Month, day, and year)

Note: *This election must be signed and postmarked within the first taxable year to which it applies.*

2 Revocation—As an eligible organization, we hereby revoke our election to have the provisions of section 501(h) of the Code, relating to expenditures to influence legislation, apply to our tax year ending...

(Month, day, and year)

Note: *This revocation must be signed and postmarked before the first day of the tax year to which it applies.*

Under penalties of perjury, I declare that I am authorized to make this (check applicable box) ▶ ☐ election ☐ revocation on behalf of the above named organization.

(Signature of officer or trustee)	(Type or print name and title)	(Date)

General Instructions

Section references are to the Internal Revenue Code.

Section 501(c)(3) states that an organization exempt under that section will lose its tax-exempt status and its qualification to receive deductible charitable contributions if a substantial part of its activities are carried on to influence legislation. Section 501(h), however, permits certain eligible 501(c)(3) organizations to elect to make limited expenditures to influence legislation. An organization making the election will, however, be subject to an excise tax under section 4911 if it spends more than the amounts permitted by that section. Also, the organization may lose its exempt status if its lobbying expenditures exceed the permitted amounts by more than 50% over a 4-year period. For any tax year in which an election under section 501(h) is in effect, an electing organization must report the actual and permitted amounts of its lobbying expenditures and grass roots expenditures (as defined in section 4911(c)) on its annual return if required under section 6033. See Schedule A (Form 990 or Form 990-EZ). Each electing member of an affiliated group must report these amounts for both itself and the affiliated group as a whole.

To make or revoke the election, enter the ending date of the tax year to which the election or revocation applies in item 1 or 2, as applicable, and sign and date the form in the spaces provided.

Eligible Organizations.—A section 501(c)(3) organization is permitted to make the election if it is not a disqualified organization (see below) and is described in:

1. Section 170(b)(1)(A)(ii) (relating to educational institutions),
2. Section 170(b)(1)(A)(iii) (relating to hospitals and medical research organizations),
3. Section 170(b)(1)(A)(iv) (relating to organizations supporting government schools),
4. Section 170(b)(1)(A)(vi) (relating to organizations publicly supported by charitable contributions),
5. Section 509(a)(2) (relating to organizations publicly supported by admissions, sales, etc.), or
6. Section 509(a)(3) (relating to organizations supporting certain types of public charities other than those section 509(a)(3) organizations that support section 501(c)(4), (5), or (6) organizations).

Disqualified Organizations.—The following types of organizations are not permitted to make the election:

a. Section 170(b)(1)(A)(i) organizations (relating to churches),

b. An integrated auxiliary of a church or of a convention or association of churches, or

c. A member of an affiliated group of organizations if one or more members of such group is described in **a** or **b** of this paragraph.

Affiliated Organizations.—Organizations are members of an affiliated group of organizations only if **(1)** the governing instrument of one such organization requires it to be bound by the decisions of the other organization on legislative issues, or **(2)** the governing board of one such organization includes persons (i) who are specifically designated representatives of another such organization or are members of the governing board, officers, or paid executive staff members of such other organization, and (ii) who, by aggregating their votes, have sufficient voting power to cause or prevent action on legislative issues by the first such organization.

For more details, see section 4911 and section 501(h).

Note: *A private foundation (including a private operating foundation) is not an eligible organization.*

Where To File.—Mail Form 5768 to the Internal Revenue Service Center, Ogden, UT 84201-0027.

Cat. No. 12125M

Form **5768** (Rev. 12-2004)

Appendix B
List of Advisors

We would like to thank the following people for their help on this research project:

Jim Abernathy, formerly with the Environmental Support Center

Audrey Alvarado, National Council of Nonprofit Associations

Nancy Amidei, University of Washington, School of Social Work

Marcia Avner, Minnesota Council of Nonprofits

Srilatha Batliwala, formerly of the Ford Foundation

Robert A. Boisture, Caplin & Drysdale

Neil Carlson, formerly with the National Committee for Responsive Philanthropy and now a consultant

Porthira Chhim, Cambodian American Project for Empowerment at the Cambodian Community Development, Inc.

Rick Cohen, National Committee for Responsive Philanthropy

Rev. Patrick Conover, United Church of Christ's Washington office for Justice and Witness Ministries

Pablo Eisenberg, Georgetown University Public Policy Institute

DeeAnn Friedholm, Children's Defense Fund of Texas

Joe Geiger, Pennsylvania Association of Nonprofit Organizations

Matthew Hamill, formerly with Independent Sector and now with National Association of College and University Business Officers

Kim Hsieh, formerly with the David and Lucile Packard Foundation

Frances Kunreuther, formerly with Harvard University and now with Demos

Jeff Kirsch, formerly with Families USA and now with Fight Crime: Invest in Kids

Sharon Ladin, National Association of Children's Hospitals and Related Institutions

Jim Masters, Center for Community Futures

John McNutt, University of South Carolina, College of Social Work

Debra Minkoff, University of Washington, Department of Sociology

Rick Moyers, formerly with the Ohio Association of Nonprofit Organizations and now with Meyer Foundation

Thomas P. Pollak, Urban Institute's National Center on Nonprofit Charitable Statistics

Susan Rees, formerly with the McAuley Institute and now a consultant

Elizabeth Reid, Urban Institute

Judith Saidel, University at Albany, Center for Women in Government and Civil Society

Doug Sauer, Council of Community Services in New York State

Margery Saunders, State University of New York, Brockport

Cinthia H. Schuman, Aspen Institute's Nonprofit Sector Research Fund

Peter Shiras, formerly with Independent Sector and now with International Youth Foundation

Vince Stehle, Surdna Foundation

Debbie Stein, formerly with the Voices for America's Children and now with the Hatcher Group

Carmen Delgado Votaw, formerly with the Alliance for Children and Families

Susan Weiner, Children's Cause of Cancer Advocacy

Appendix C
The Survey And Responses

Facing the Next Century

Strengthening America's Nonprofits

Thank you for taking the time to help us learn more about the nonprofit world. As noted in our cover letter, your answers will be held in the strictest confidence.

Part I
We start by asking for some basic background on your organization.

1. In what year was the organization founded? **1966** (mean)

2. Is the current executive director or board chair the founder or one of the founders of this organization?

Executive Director   ❏ Yes **82.9%**   Board Chair   ❏ Yes **86.3%**
                           ❏ No **17.1%**   ❏ No **13.7%**

3. If your organization has a membership, is that membership comprised of any of the following?
(Check all that apply.)

❏ Individuals **53.8%**   *Estimate number of individual members* **25130** **(mean)**

❏ Other nonprofits **23.1%**   *Estimate number of all organizations that are members* **365**

❏ Government agencies **8.1%**

❏ Corporations or business trade associations **15.8%**

❏ No membership **31.0%**

Part II

We'd like to learn a little about any interaction your organization has with government. By "government" we mean officials at any level (local, state, federal) who work at any government institution (legislative, executive, administrative agency, boards and commissions, judicial, etc.)

4. In some cases contact with those in government comes about at the initiative of the policymakers themselves. How often on average would you say that people in government approach the executive director, staff, or members of the board to discuss matters of mutual interest?

❑ Never **21.9%**   ❑ Two, three times a month **19.3%**
❑ Once a month or less **36.1%**   ❑ Four or more times a month **22.6%**

5.**(Experimental Design Question)** For some nonprofits, there is a need to advocate new policies before those in government so that policymakers will have a better understanding of the problems facing the community. How often does your organization undertake an effort to advocate with government officials at any level? **(See end of document for explanation)**

❑ Never   ❑ Two, three times a month
❑ Once a month or less   ❑ Four or more times a month

6. A variety of means of communicating and interacting with those in government are listed below. Please use the scale on the right to indicate how frequently, if at all, your organization engages in these activities. (By "your organization" we mean the executive director, other staff, volunteers, or members of the board.) In this scale, "0" means never, "1" is relatively infrequent interaction, and "4" is ongoing interaction. **Results are percent giving each answer on a 0-4 scale**

	Never	Low		High		
	0	1	2	3	4	*(means)*
Testifying at legislative or administrative hearings	29.0	29.2	18.7	12.2	10.9	*1.47*
Lobbying on behalf of or against a proposed bill or other policy pronouncement	26.3	23.9	18.9	15.1	15.9	*1.70*
Responding to requests for information from those in government	12.9	21.6	24.4	21.4	19.6	*2.13*
Working in a planning or advisory group that includes government officials	18.4	16.9	19.6	20.1	25.0	*2.16*

	Never	Low		Frequency High		
	0	1	2	3	4	*(means)*
Meeting with government officials about the work we are doing	**15.0**	**18.5**	**21.7**	**3.2**	**21.6**	*2.18*
Encouraging members to write, call, fax or email policymakers	**22.3**	**22.2**	**18.6**	**19.3**	**17.5**	*1.88*
Releasing research reports to the media, public or policymakers	**31.0**	**25.2**	**21.9**	**12.1**	**9.7**	*1.44*
Discussing obtaining grants or contracts with government officials	**29.2**	**23.8**	**18.8**	**16.0**	**12.2**	*1.58*
Interacting socially with government officials	**19.3**	**31.0**	**24.5**	**17.0**	**8.2**	*1.64*

7. Thinking generally about those in government that your organization deals with, please select the description below that typically describes those officials' attitudes.

5.2% ❑ Not really interested in hearing our views
27.5% ❑ Sometimes interested in what we have to say
41.0% ❑ Usually interested in what we have to say
26.4% ❑ Interested in what we have to say and interested in actively working with us to achieve a common goal

8. There is a good deal of confusion about whether various activities by nonprofits relating to the policymaking process are permissible. Based on your understanding, can your organization:

Support or oppose federal legislation under current IRS regulations	❑ Yes **72.5%**	❑ No **27.5%**
Take a policy position without reference to a specific bill under current regulations	❑ Yes **81.8%**	❑ No **18.2%**
Support or oppose federal regulations	❑ Yes **79.3%**	❑ No **20.7%**
Lobby if part of your budget comes from federal funds	❑ Yes **50.4%**	❑ No **49.6%**
Use government funds to lobby Congress	❑ Yes **6.4%**	❑ No **93.6%**
Endorse a candidate for elected office	❑ Yes **12.6%**	❑ No **87.4%**
Talk to elected public officials about public policy matters	❑ Yes **91.1%**	❑ No **8.9%**
Sponsor a forum or candidate debate for elected office	❑ Yes **56.5%**	❑ No **43.5%**

9. Does your organization consult experts about the legality of any efforts you make to influence government? Check all that apply.

❏ Attorney **57.4%**   ❏ Accountant **27.1%**

❏ Experts at other nonprofits **39.7%** ❏ Never make any effort to influence government **11.6%**

❏ None **15.9%**   ❏ Other **8.8%**

Part III

These questions are about your organization's capacity.

10. How many full-time equivalent staff members does your organization employ? *(mean)*

31 Professionals   **22** Clerical/support staff
2084 Volunteers   **41** Other

11. Does your organization have one or more persons who have responsibility for government relations or public policy? *If "yes" please check all that apply.*

❏ No **27.1%** ❏ Yes **72.9%**
❏ Executive Director **57.8%**
❏ Staff Member **31.6%**
❏ Volunteer **9.0%**
❏ Board Member **26.7%**
❏ Board Committee **18.2%**
❏ Lobbyist or other outside professional on retainer **18.3%**

12. What are the sources of your organization's annual income? *Rough estimates are perfectly fine – you don't need to consult your organization's records for a precise answer.*

Percent	*(mean)*
26%	Individual donors or membership dues
22%	Government (any level)
12%	Foundations
5%	Corporate Contributions
14%	Income from services provided to clients or others
11%	Fundraising Events
8%	Other _____
100%	Total

13. Is your organization a dues-paying member of one or more associations that represent you before government?

❏ Yes **51.1%**   ❏ No **46.1%**   ❏ Don't Know **2.7%**
If yes (check all that apply):
❏ Local Associations **9.7%**   ❏ State **25.9%**   ❏ National **37.4%**

14. (If you answered "no" to the previous question, skip to #15). How often do these associations contact you and urge you to contact policymakers about pending matters of importance? And how often do you respond to these requests?

We're contacted by Associations:	*We act upon these requests:*
Never **7.5%**	Never **11.2%**
Once a month or less **57.1%**	Once a month or less **66.6%**
Two or three times a month **23.1%**	Two or three times a month **16.2%**
Four times a month or more **12.2%**	Four times a month or more **6.0%**

15. In the previous section we asked you about your direct involvement in the public policymaking process. Now we would like to know about factors that you feel are barriers to your organization's involvement in the policymaking process and how significant those barriers are. In the scale below, 0 represents no barrier, 1 a low barrier, and 4 represents a major barrier.

Results are percent giving each answer on a 0-4 scale

	Size of Barrier					
	No Barrier	*Low*		*Major*		
	0	*1*	*2*	*3*	*4*	*(mean)*
Tax law or IRS regulations	**32.5**	**27.5**	**17.1**	**10.9**	**12.0**	*1.42*
Organization receives government funds	**48.4**	**21.6**	**12.9**	**7.7**	**9.5**	*1.08*
Organization receives foundation funds	**58.6**	**24.5**	**10.7**	**3.6**	**2.5**	*0.67*
Staff (or volunteer) skills	**35.6**	**21.8**	**21.5**	**14.8**	**6.3**	*1.34*
Organization's limited financial resources	**18.8**	**14.**	**18.0**	**22.3**	**26.1**	*2.22*
Advice from attorneys or accountants	**49.2**	**27.5**	**14.8**	**5.3**	**3.3**	*0.86*
Your board or staff's attitude toward involvement in the policymaking process	**45.2**	**23.1**	**16.0**	**10.6**	**5.1**	*1.07*
The public's attitude toward involvement in the policymaking process	**46.6**	**22.9**	**18.5**	**8.4**	**3.6**	*0.99*
Other_____	**37.9**	**4.2**	**10.4**	**15.8**	**31.7**	*1.99*

16. Turning from barriers to inducements, what factors motivate your organization to become involved in the public policymaking process? **Results are percent giving each answer on a 0-4 scale**

	No Influence	Low			High	(mean)
	0	*1*	*2*	*3*	*4*	*(mean)*
Opportunities to obtain government funding	35.4	12.4	12.4	15.3	24.6	1.81
Protecting government programs that serve our clients, constituents or community	13.1	5.1	9.9	20.3	51.6	2.92
Promoting government policies that support our mission	8.1	3.4	7.6	23.1	57.8	
Raising public awareness of important issues	8.1	4.4	12.0	23.4	52.1	3.07
Defending nonprofits' advocacy rights	23.2	20.2	19.6	17.8	19.1	1.89
Other_____	48.9	6.3	9.8	9.2	25.9	1.57

Heading over columns: *Significance of Motivating Factors*

17. How would you describe the capacity of your organization to conduct and disseminate research? **Results are percent giving each answer on a 0-4 scale**

	None	Low			High	(mean)
	0	*1*	*2*	*3*	*4*	*(mean)*
Conduct issue research	19.1	32.6	22.1	14.8	11.4	1.67
Disseminate research	15.2	23.2	20.0	23.2	18.4	2.06

Heading over columns: *Capacity*

18. Do you use any of these communications tools? Do you use them in your involvement in the public policymaking process?

Use?		*Used in policymaking process?*
Email	❏ Yes **90.4%** ❏ No **9.6%**	❏ Yes **63.4%** ❏ No **36.6%**
World Wide Web	❏ Yes **84.0%** ❏ No **16.0%**	❏ Yes **44.6%** ❏ No **55.4%**
Fax	❏ Yes **93.7%** ❏ No **6.3%**	❏ Yes **68.4%** ❏ No **31.6%**
Video conferencing	❏ Yes **14.0%** ❏ No **86.0%**	❏ Yes **5.6%** ❏ No **94.4%**
Telephone conferencing	❏ Yes **73.3%** No **26.7%**	❏ Yes **43.8%** ❏ No **56.2%**
Internet video phone	❏ Yes **2.4%** ❏ No **97.6%**	❏ Yes **1.0%** ❏ No **99.0%**

19. In thinking about the major decisions your organization makes *concerning government relations,* how would you estimate the relative influence of the following participants? **Results are percent giving each answer on a 0-4 scale**

Influence	None	Low			High	
	0	*1*	*2*	*3*	*4*	*(mean)*
Executive Director	**9.2**	**5.8**	**11.3**	**22.0**	**51.7**	**3.01**
Chair of the Board of Directors	**9.5**	**10.9**	**20.5**	**26.6**	**32.4**	**2.61**
Board of Directors or Board Committee	**8.7**	**10.5**	**20.5**	**30.9**	**29.3**	**2.61**
Professional staff	**17.2**	**11.3**	**22.0**	**28.2**	**21.3**	**2.25**
Important donors and funders	**32.9**	**24.4**	**20.5**	**14.4**	**7.8**	**1.40**
Other_____	**47.4**	**5.8**	**6.2**	**14.6**	**25.9**	**1.66**

20. In thinking about the major decisions your organization makes *concerning program strategy or implementation,* how would you estimate the relative influence of the following participants? **Results are percent giving each answer on a 0-4 scale**

Influence	None 0	Low 1	2	3	High 4	*(mean)*
Executive Director	4.6	1.8	4.8	18.2	70.6	3.48
Chair of the Board of Directors	3.7	7.8	18.2	32.6	37.7	2.92
Board of Directors or Board Committee	3.1	7.2	17.2	35.7	36.8	2.96
Professional staff	11.0	5.2	13.9	32.0	37.9	2.80
Important donors and funders	26.2	22.5	26.0	16.8	8.4	1.59
Other_____	46.9	9.2	8.2	14.5	21.3	1.54

21. What is your title?
  ❏ Executive Director/President **72.9%**
  ❏ Staff (specify position) **14.5%**
  ❏ Board Member **4.0%**
  ❏ Other **8.3%**
  ❏ Volunteer (other than Board) **0.4%**

Thank you for taking the time to help us. To further our understanding of nonprofits we will be interviewing some of the people who filled out this questionnaire. If you would be willing to be interviewed, please give us the following information:

Name of person filling out the questionnaire_____

Organization_____

Phone Number_____

Experimental Design Question (#5)

One of the questions on the survey was designed to test if the words used to refer to the act of presenting a case for or against an issue to government made a difference. Three versions of the survey were sent out, with a different phrasing on one question, to test this theory. The question was not designed to produce meaningful data about how often lobbying, advocacy or education are engaged in, but only to test the difference between the terms.

One third of the sample was asked:

5. For some nonprofits, there is a need to **lobby those in government** so that policymakers will have a better understanding of the problems facing the community. How often does your organization undertake an effort to lobby government officials at any level?

Never **29.3%**   Two, three times a month **14.1%**
Once a month or less **36.4%**   Four or more times a month **20.2%**

Another third of the sample got a question #5 that asked:

5. *For some nonprofits, there is a need to **advocate new policies** before those in government so that policymakers will have a better understanding of the problems facing the community. How often does your organization undertake an effort to advocate new policies before government officials at any level?*

Never **14.9%**   Two, three times a month **19.6%**
*Once a month or less **40.2%***   *Four or more times a month **25.3%***

The last third of the sample's question #5 read this way:

5. For some nonprofits, there is a need to **educate those in government** about specific policies so that policymakers will have a better understanding of the problems facing the community. How often does your organization undertake an effort to educate government officials at any level about specific policies?

Never **12.3%**   Two, three times a month **24.3%**
Once a month or less **40.7%**   Four or more times a **22.7%**

Appendix D
Interview Protocols

Interviews were conducted with a small sample of survey respondents that indicated on their survey a willingness to be interviewed. They were divided into "high participators," "medium participators," and "low participators." All received questions about what policy participation means plus questions about one of the following topics: legal advice and advisors, management and governance, or sources of revenue. The questions for each group about policy participation were the same with slightly different questions for the "low participators." The interview protocol is below and lasted about 45 minutes for each interview.

Interviewers were given the following instructions:

1. Review the list of questions and the organization's survey prior to the interview.
2. Feel free to slightly tailor the wording of the interview questions to fit your style
3. Use conversational tone. Be friendly.
4. State that the interview is confidential.
5. Don't leave important questions until the end.
6. Don't let the interviewee wander.
7. Re-ask unanswered questions in a different way.
8. Reaffirm the interviewee's answers with "yes" and "uh-huhs."

Interviewers were given the following information regarding recording the interview:

1. Block out 2–2.5 hours for the interview and the write-up.
2. The write-up has to be done immediately following the interview.
3. Don't edit during the interview.
4. Record key words and phrases – try to record key quotes.
5. Indicate whether the organization is a high/medium/low participator.
6. Indicate the name of the organization and their ID number on the back.
7. Type in your name by each interview.

The interview questions were:

QUESTIONS ABOUT PUBLIC POLICY PARTICIPATION

Thank you for taking the time for this interview

Questions of High and Medium Participators

Q. I wonder if you could talk a little about your organization's activities on public policy issues? Please describe the activities.

Probes:
- ✓ Work on legislation?
- ✓ Court cases?
- ✓ Regulations?
- ✓ Voter and candidate education?
- ✓ Community organizing on a public issue?
- ✓ Media education about a public problem?
- ✓ Serving on committees and commissions?

Q. When your organization is highly involved in a public policy matter what is it doing? Feel free to use an example.

Probes:
- ✓ Write newsletters?
- ✓ Hold special board meetings?
- ✓ Write letters to the editor of the newspaper?
- ✓ Lobby the legislature?
- ✓ Organize citizens for a rally?
- ✓ Join a coalition or association of other concerned groups?
- ✓ Attend public meetings?
- ✓ Comment on proposed ordinances or regulations?

Questions for Low Participators

Q. Would you tell me a little about your organization's mission or purpose?

Q. Does your organization get involved in public policy issues?

Q. When an organization is involved and active on public policy issues what is it doing?

Probes:
- ✓ Write newsletters?
- ✓ Hold special board meetings?
- ✓ Write letters to the editor of the newspaper?
- ✓ Lobby the legislature?
- ✓ Organize citizens for a rally?
- ✓ Join a coalition or association of other concerned groups?
- ✓ Attend public meetings?
- ✓ Comment on proposed ordinances or regulations?

Probe:

Please walk me through how your organization handled a recent public policy issue when it came up. What did you do or decide about it?

Segue to Factors that do or would serve to motivate or deter participation

Q. What motivates your organization to get involved in the first place?

✓ Mission?
✓ To secure funding?
✓ To change laws affecting those you serve?
✓ To develop relationships?
✓ Crisis?
✓ To be part of a coalition?
✓ Other reasons?

(interviewer note Q.16)

Q. What do you feel limits your organization's involvement in public policy matters? What barriers are present that hold you back from your potential?

Probes:
✓ Time
✓ Money
✓ Attitudes of board or staff or others
✓ Expertise
✓ The law

Segue to Factors that do or would serve to motivate or deter participation

Q. What keeps your organization from being more involved in public policy matters?

✓ Mission?
✓ Sources of funding?
✓ The law?
✓ Time?
✓ Knowledge of how to get involved?
✓ Technology?
✓ Other reasons?

(interviewer note Q.16)

✓ Technology
✓ Importance among your
organization's supporters?
✓ Other?

(interviewer note Q.15)

Q. What factors would have to
change for your organization to
become more involved?

✓ Direct impact of policy to those
you serve?
✓ More knowledge of the law?
✓ More staff/volunteer expertise?
✓ Funding?
✓ Board involvement?
✓ Technology?
✓ Time?

Q. What would be helpful to you in
your public policy work?

Q. How does emerging information
and communications technology
influence your public policy work?
(interviewer note Q.18)

Probe:
Would training and education
about Internet technology for
public policy be helpful?

What has been successful and
what has not worked?

Q. What factors would have to
change for your organization to
become more involved?

✓ Direct impact of policy to those
you serve?
✓ More knowledge of the law?
✓ More staff/volunteer expertise?
✓ Funding?
✓ Board involvement?
✓ Technology?
✓ Time?

Q. What would be helpful to you?

Q. Could emerging information
and communications technology
including the Internet aid your
work? If so, how?

Probes:
Is anything presently limiting your
organization's use of the Internet
for public policy work? e.g.,
knowledge of available resources,
training, etc?

Would training and education
about communications technology
for public policy be helpful?

QUESTIONS ABOUT LEGAL ADVISORS AND ADVICE

Segue to impact of legal advisers and advice
Q. Does your organization receive advice about the legality of involvement on public policy issues?

Probes:
What is the nature of their advice?
• Do they give you advice on lobbying vs. other types of advocacy?
• Is the advice about internal operations or external issues such as writing testimony, court briefs or letters to legislators?

Q. Do attorneys advocate on behalf of your organization?

Probe: Is there an attorney on your board? If so, do they give you legal advice?

Q. Do you get guidance from an accountant about public policy-related activity? If so, what is the nature of their advice?

Probes:
Do you get the same or different advice from attorneys vs. accountants?
Who else advises you on legal matters related to public policy?

Q. (If they don't get advice from legal advisers) Is legal advice about the legality of public policy work available to you?

Q. How available is legal advice for nonprofit such as yourself in your area?

Q. What would help your legal knowledge of public policy related work?

Thank you for your time for this interview, we will send you a copy of the report when it is finished.

QUESTIONS ABOUT MANAGEMENT AND GOVERNANCE QUESTIONS

Segue to questions about management/governance decision-making

(Interviewer note Q.19 & 20)

Q. Let's discuss a related scenario. Say a public policy issue comes up such as a new government regulation or court case, or legislation that might affect your programs. How do you generally hear about it? What happens when you do hear about it? And, how are decisions made about how to better understand it and get involved in the matter? Please feel free to use a recent example?

Probes:

What is involved in your personal role regarding making decisions about public policy matters when they come up?

What about the following:

- The board of directors?
- Volunteers?
- Clients?
- Donors?
- Other members?
- Does your organization have committees that deal with policy issues?

Q. What is the role of associations or other coalitions in your decisions about getting involved in public policy matters?

Probes:

Is your organization a member of any associations or other organizations? Does membership:

- Help you to get more involved?
- Substitute for your direct involvement?

Q. What would aid your management decisions related to matters of public policy? What would help you in your position, and what would help your organization?

Probes:

- Education and training?
- More funding?
- Changes in the laws and regulations?
- More interest from staff or board?
- Technology?

Q. What would you like to receive from the associations your organization is a member of in terms of support or assistance?

Thank you for taking the time to do this interview, we will send you a copy of the final report.

QUESTIONS ABOUT REVENUE SOURCES

Segue to impact of different sources of revenue

Q. How does funding affect your public policy work? Do different sources of funding affect your work in different ways?

Q. How does each of the following groups influence your organization's decisions and actions about public policy work?

- Foundations
- Government funders
- Individual donors
- Volunteers
- Corporations
- Associations and coalitions your organization is a part of

Probes:

What do you think would happen if you got involved on a issue that ran contrary to the interest or attitudes of one or more of these groups? Please give an example?

Are there any public policy related limitations associated with the funding your organization receives? If so, how do these limitations affect your work?

Thank you for taking the time to do this interview. We will send you a copy of the final report.

Appendix E
Focus Group Protocols

Discussion Group Questions For Executive Directors

Opening Question

Tell us who you are including your name, your organization and staff position there. Share with us one thing you enjoy doing when you are not working in your nonprofit organization.

Introductory question

Our study is trying to understand what influences nonprofits as they make decisions and take actions related to participation in public policymaking. One of our goals is to identify ways of helping nonprofit staff and volunteers make informed decisions about participation.

What comes to mind when you think of public policy work or public policy participation?

(If they report out with words like lobbying, advocacy, organizing, etc., then ask)

- What do these words mean? For example when advocacy or lobbying is going on what activities are undertaken? Feel free to give an example from your organization.

Let's take a couple examples:

- If I send out a newsletter to people my organization serves about new legislation, am I lobbying, advocating, or educating?

- If I prepare a paper that analyzes a new city policy on public housing and hold a discussion at the board meeting about the merits of the policy, am I advocating, lobbying, or educating?

- If I convene a meeting of people my organization serves with the mayor to discuss the city budget, contracts that my organization has with the city and to give her/him a tour of the neighborhood, am I educating, lobbying, or advocating?

Transition questions

Think back to when you started in your position. What was your perception of the public policy role of your organization. How has it changed since then?

What is the benefit to your organization of being involved?

- Mission
- Ethics – is it appropriate or inappropriate for 501(c)(3)s to get involved?
- Resources for services
- Politics/Public Relations
- Other?

How would you describe your organization's relationship with government? What I mean by this is what do you want from government? What does government want from you? What is the state of the relationship? It may be government at the local, state or national level. Feel free to share a brief story or illustrative example if it helps.

Key Questions

What influences your public policy participation? (Get a few answers...)

Let's use this sheet as a guide to discuss issues that have been brought up in similar discussions and rank them. (Pass out ranking sheet.)

(Discussion and ranking)

(Introduce SNAP data on barriers and motivators.)

What does this data suggest if anything?

If your organization were to "move up a level," so to speak, in its public policy work, what would that look like? What would be the difference from today? If you are already where you want to be, then tell us why.

What needs to be done or has to change to get to the next level? Specifically, what barriers or obstacles are present?

Internal factors:
Time
Staff capacity
Staff/Volunteer expertise
Available money
Technology
Board of Directors

External

Legal rules

Legal advisers

Government influence (politics – grants and contracts)

Foundation influence
- (If you could say one thing to a foundation president about what they could do to play a supportive role in your public policy work, what would that be?)

Associations and Coalitions

Media/community perceptions

(Ask participants what they would want to see different about foundations or government.)

As we said before, one of the goals of the study is to find out what would aid nonprofits as they consider public policy participation and what would help their work. We'd like to know from you what has helped you get engaged and stay engaged in public policy work and what might help you in the future?

(Use examples from previous discussion to start the discussion.)

Ending questions

All things considered…

Reflecting upon our conversation here what is the single number 1 most important issue within your organization and number 1 issue outside your organization that should be changed in order to help and improve your public policy work? When I mean inside, I am referring to things inside your organization such as staff expertise, technology, time, your board of directors. Outside your organization refers to things like what your funders think, the legal rules for policy participation, etc. Let's take a moment to think about these issues before we go around the room.

(Go around the room to get comment from all participants.)

What have we missed today? Is there anything that we should have talked about but didn't?

Discussion Group Questions for Board Members

Opening question

Tell us your name, your board affiliation and how long you have been on the board, your profession and business/nonprofit you work for.

Introductory questions

Our study aims to develop a better understanding of the reasons nonprofits are involved or not involved in the public policy process. An important goal of the discussion groups we are conducting is to find out what would aid nonprofit leaders, including board members such as you, in their management and governance decisions in relation to public policy.

What comes to mind when you think of public policy work or public policy participation?

(If they report out with words like lobbying, advocacy, organizing, etc., then ask)

- What do these words mean? For example, when advocacy or lobbying is going on what activities are undertaken? Feel free to give an example from your organization.

Transition questions

What is the benefit to your organization of being involved?

- Mission
- Ethics – is it appropriate or inappropriate for 501(c)(3)s to get involved?
- Resources for services
- Politics/Public Relations
- Other?

How would you describe your organization's relationship with government? What I mean by this is what do you want from government? What does government want from you? What is the state of the relationship? It may be government at the local, state or national level. Feel free to share a brief story or illustrative example if it helps.

Key Questions

As a board member, what is your role in your organization's public policy work?

What are appropriate responsibilities of board members in public policy?

When your organization makes decisions about involvement in public policy matters, what considerations or factors do you as board members need to think about that are distinctive from staff or other volunteers?

If your organization were to "move up a level," so to speak, in its public policy work, what would that look like? What would be the difference from today? If you are already where you want to be, then tell us why.

What needs to be done or has to change to get to the next higher level? If there are any barriers or obstacles, please tell us about them. (After discussion introduce data on barriers)

Internal factors:
Executive Director
Time
Staff capacity

Staff/Volunteer expertise
Available money
Technology
Board of Directors

External

Legal rules

Government influence (politics – grants and contracts)

Foundation influence
- (If you could say one thing to a foundation president about what they could do to play a supportive role in your public policy work, what would that be?)

Associations and Coalitions

Media/community perceptions

As we said before, one of the goals of the study is to find out what would aid nonprofits as they consider public policy participation and what would help their work.

What has helped you as a board member to get engaged and stay engaged in public policy work and what might help you in the future?

(Use examples from previous discussion to start the discussion.)

Ending questions

All things considered…

Reflecting upon our conversation here, what is the most important condition that should be changed or important new information, skills or resources you could have that would help your public policy work?
(Go around the room to get comment from all participants.)

What have we missed today? Is there anything that we should have talked about but didn't?

Appendix F
List of Tax-Exempt Organization Categories

501(c)(1): Corporations Organized Under Act of Congress (including Federal Credit Unions)

501(c)(2): Title Holding Corporation For Exempt Organization

501(c)(3): Religious, Educational, Charitable, Scientific, Literary, Testing for Public Safety, to Foster National or International Amateur Sports Competition, or Prevention of Cruelty to Children or Animals Organizations

501(c)(4): Civic Leagues, Social Welfare Organizations, and Local Associations of Employees

501(c)(5): Labor, Agricultural, and Horticultural Organizations

501(c)(6): Business Leagues, Chambers of Commerce, Real Estate Boards, etc.

501(c)(7): Social and Recreation Clubs

501(c)(8): Fraternal Beneficiary Societies and Associations

501(c)(9): Voluntary Employees' Beneficiary Associations (providing for the payment of benefits to their members and their members' dependents or designated beneficiaries)

501(c)(10): Domestic Fraternal Societies and Associations

501(c)(11): Teachers' Retirement Fund Associations

501(c)(12): Benevolent Life Insurance Associations, Mutual Ditch or Irrigation Companies, Mutual or Cooperative Telephone Companies, etc.

501(c)(13): Cemetery Companies

501(c)(14): State Chartered Credit Unions, Mutual Reserve Funds

501(c)(15): Mutual Insurance Companies or Associations

501(c)(16): Cooperative Organizations to Finance Crop Operations

501(c)(17): Supplemental Unemployment Benefit Trusts

501(c)(18): Employee-Funded Pension Trust (created before June 25, 1959)

501(c)(19): Post or Organization of Past or Present Members of the Armed Forces

501(c)(20): Group Legal Services Plan Organizations

501(c)(21): Black Lung Benefit Trusts

501(c)(22): Withdrawal Liability Payment Fund

501(c)(23): Veterans Organization (created before 1880)

501(c)(25): Title Holding Corporations or Trusts with Multiple Parents

501(c)(26): State-Sponsored High-Risk Health Coverage Organizations
501(c)(27): State-Sponsored Workers Compensation Reinsurance Organization
501(d): Religious and Apostolic Associations
501(e): Cooperative Hospital Service Organizations
501(f): Cooperative Service Organization of Operating Educational Organizations
501(k): Child-Care Organization
501(n): Charitable Risk Pools
521(a): Farmers' Cooperative Associations
527: Political Committees

About the Authors

Gary Bass is the founder and executive director of OMB Watch, an organization addressing government accountability and citizen participation. Since founding the advocacy organization in 1983, Dr. Bass has testified before Congress, appeared on national television, addressed groups across the country, and written extensively on issues dealing with government secrecy, fiscal policy, and regulatory protections. He has led a variety of national campaigns, including those to protect the advocacy rights of nonprofit organizations. Prior to OMB Watch, Dr. Bass work for the U.S. Council for the International Year of the Disabled, and the Human Services Information Center. He is adjunct faculty at Georgetown University's Public Policy Institute where he teaches about advocacy and social change. Dr. Bass serves on numerous nonprofit boards and advisory committees. He received his doctorate from the University of Michigan.

Kay Guinane is Director, Nonprofit Speech Rights at OMB Watch, where she is responsible for monitoring and analyzing federal legislative and regulatory actions that affect nonprofit advocacy rights and advocacy efforts to protect them. She is a co-author of numerous reports on advocacy rights and issues. Prior to coming to OMB Watch, Ms. Guinane acted as legal counsel to a wide variety of nonprofit organizations, both as an advocate on issues and an advisor on tax and nonprofit law. Ms. Guinane graduated from the State University of New York at Buffalo School of Law in 1976, where she received a B.A. in Political Science (with honors) in 1972. She is a member of the bar in Kentucky, Maryland and the District of Columbia.

David Arons serves the nonprofit sector as an attorney, advocate and volunteer. He is formerly Co-Director of the Center for Lobbying in the Public Interest, in Washington, D.C. and was a lobbyist at Independent Sector. Mr. Arons taught courses in nonprofit advocacy at Johns Hopkins University and Georgetown University's Executive Nonprofit Management Program. He is the co-author of *A Voice for Nonprofits* (Brookings Institution Press, 2003) with Jeffrey Berry and is the Editor of *Power in Policy: A Funder's Guide to Advocacy and Civic Participation,* (Fieldstone Alliance, 2007). Mr. Arons received his J.D. from William Mitchell College of Law, M.A. in Urban and Environmental Policy from Tufts University and B.S. in Political Science from James Madison University.

Matt Carter served as Public Affairs Liaison and Policy Analyst at OMB Watch from 1998 until 2005 when he took over administration of NPAction.org. He moved to Cleveland, Ohio, in 2005, where he works as both the Outreach Coordinator and Technology Director of Adoption Network Cleveland.

Susan Rees has been a researcher, consultant and advocate in Washington, DC, for over 25 years. She is the author of Effective Nonprofit Advocacy published by the Aspen Institute's Nonprofit Sector Research Fund. She has been director of policy and research for the McAuley Institute, a national affordable housing nonprofit, and was executive director of the Coalition on Human Needs from 1983-92. She has a master's degree in urban and regional planning from the University of Illinois in Urbana and a bachelor's in journalism from Marquette University.